ON THE EDGE

Evocative, beautiful, rending ... this is a book about learning to listen to the voice of the ocean, and how to bear what you hear. It invites you to a transformation of consciousness - not as an abstract, intellectual exercise, but as a discovery in practice of what it means to share the life of earth. Jan Morgan and Graeme Garrett have written humbly and honestly; a deeply necessary book for our time.

Sarah Bachelard,
Founding Director of Benedictus Contemplative Church, Canberra and a teacher in the World Community for Christian Meditation.
Author of *Resurrection and Moral Imagination.*

This is a wonderful witness to the depth and beauty of life. While the dying of the oceans and the disappearance of biodiversity can spiral us into despair and hopelessness, this book will pick us up and restores our confidence in the depth and beauty of life. Somehow after reading it one feels more confident to get up in the morning, raise the arms, turn your face to the sun and enjoy the deep tranquillity of the ocean. Worth reading. It will change you!

Professor Thorwald Lorenzen,
School of Theology Charles Sturt University
Author of *Towards a Culture of Freedom*

ON THE EDGE
A-Way with the Ocean

Jan Morgan & Graeme Garrett

Published by Acorn Press
An imprint of Bible Society AustraliaACN 148 058 306
Charity licence 19 000 528
GPO Box 4161
Sydney NSW 2001
Australia
www.acornpress.net.au | www.biblesociety.org.au

© Jan Morgan and Graeme Garrett, 2024. All rights reserved.

ISBN 978-0-647-53339-0

First published by Morning Star Publishing in 2018,
ISBN 978-0-648-23245-2

Jan Morgan and Graeme Garrett assert their rights under section 193 of the *Copyright Act 1968* (Cth) to be identified as the author of this work.

Apart from any fair dealing for the purposes of private study, research, criticism or review, no part of this work may be reproduced by electronic or other means without the permission of the publisher.

The Idea of Order at Key West by Wallace Stevens printed with permission of Faber and Faber Ltd.

Photos of Tathra Beach copyright © Gilbert Zangger

 A catalogue record for this work is available from the National Library of Australia

Design and typesetting: John Healy

The ocean is life itself, without which everything dies. Ah! how I want life itself, without which everything dies!
I do not have enough. I gaze at the sea. All this fills me, I who am bounded.
But here, and wherever I look, and here on the other side,
There is more, and still more, and there too, and always, and the same, and much more!
Always, dear heart!

Paul Claudel

If there is a divine beauty, we cannot be its spectators, but only its witnesses. And the witnesses of such beauty speak in proportion to their wound and their sense of being torn apart.

Jean-Louis Chrétien

Contents

Acknowledgements 9

1. The Visible Voice / Away with the Ocean 11
    Learning a practice of attention (1) 31

2. Call of Beauty / Sea of Plastic 33
    Learning a practice of attention (2) 63

3. Living Together / Tearing Apart 65
    Learning a practice of attention (3) 107

4. Look! Hear! / A Wicked Problem 109
    Learning a practice of attention (4) 139

5. Heartbreak / Coalophobia 141
    Learning a practice of attention (5) 169

6. Adoration 171

Concluding unapologetic postscript - A way with the ocean 201

Appendix 1 217

Appendix 2 219

Appendix 3 223

Select Bibliography 225

Acknowledgements

Many conversations have shaped and re-shaped our response to the ocean. Some of the major participants, including the ocean itself, appear in the pages of this book. Our appreciation of their differing contributions to human life (our own included), and the life of Earth as a whole, will, we hope, be clear to the reader. Moreover, we are especially grateful to friends who, with care and critical insight, read earlier drafts and talked with us about them: Thorwald and Jill Lorenzen, Sarah Bachelard, Neil Millar, John and Wendy Langmore, Jill Manton, Noelene Kelly and Pat Long. We treasure their generous gifts of wisdom and encouragement. Our heartfelt thanks also to Morning Star Publishing. Without John Healy's early encouragement, this work may never have seen the light of day. Amanda McKenna has been a brilliant editorial guide along the tricky path between manuscript and printed text. The beautiful photographs of Tathra beach are the work and gift of local photographer Gilbert Zangger. Finally, we want to celebrate Lona Berlowitz and Caro Fraser and the team at Tathra Beach Café. In that lovely place, we spent many hours wrangling with ideas, thoughts and feelings, and the words that give them voice.

On the 18th March 2018 wild fire swept through the town of Tathra. Along with hundreds of others, we fled the advancing flames with hardly more than we stood up in. Many houses were lost or damaged. Large tracts of beautiful bushland destroyed. No human lives were lost, though many animals died or were injured. This book was going to press as these events took place. We want to acknowledge and honour the courage, resilience and solidarity of so many who stuck together through tragedy and trauma, and are now rebuilding their town, their homes, their lives.

*Conscious of the uncertainty of the future
in the wild hope
they too may find
in the world
beauty and abundance
diversity and wilderness
love and joy
we dedicate this book to our grandchildren*

Tom, Molly, Sasha, Harry, Max

Yusuf, Luqman, Jasper, Jono, Lily, Chris, Imran, Zahra, Annabelle

1. The Visible Voice / Away with the Ocean

All journeys have secret destinations of which the traveller is unaware.

Martin Buber

Do things speak?

That dark-furred wallaby upright and motionless in the grass outside the window, joey at her side, for example. Or the stately spotted gums standing silently together on the hillside behind us. And what of the grey-white sky so low to the ground today the hem of its skirts trail through the streets of town. Or the white-capped waves rolling endlessly towards the shore of Tathra Beach. Do they speak?

In a brilliant short story, Ursula Le Guin imagines some indeterminate time in the future when any university worth its salt will have a well-established department of 'therolinguistics' whose research task is to locate, translate and interpret, among other species, the language and literature of 'pelican', 'ant' and 'dolphin'. Just down the corridor the 'phytolinguists' are working away on the vegetative communication of plants. Over a cup of coffee in the common room, they look back on the beginnings of their discipline in the 21st century with a wry smile and say, 'Do you realize that they couldn't even read Eggplant?' The 'geolinguists' go deeper. Reading below the transient lyrics of the lichens, they listen for the 'wholly atemporal, cold, volcanic poetry of the rocks: each one a word spoken, how long ago, by the earth itself, in the immense solitude, the immenser community, of space.'[1]

But for most of our lives the question didn't arise for us. And it wasn't that it was just waiting there and we hadn't quite got around to thinking about it. It went deeper than that. The question didn't arise because the cultural framework in which we grew up—that well sealed 'bell jar' of mid 20th century western technological consumerism—didn't have a way of formulating it, nor was much interested in doing so.[2]

---

[1] Ursula K. Le Guin, *The Compass Rose* (London: Panther Books, 1983), pp. 11-19, at p. 19. Thero- is a prefix meaning 'pertaining to an animal'; phyto- 'pertaining to a plant'. Le Guin is an American writer best known for her *Earthsea* fantasy fiction.

[2] A bell jar is a large (usually) glass jar similar in shape to a bell. Such jars are often used

As for fantasy fiction, if you write as well as Ursula Le Guin you can make any wild dream seem plausible.

Cracks in the bell jar

Maybe all is not quite as hermetically sealed as it seems.

Child's play?

Late afternoon. Gold, touching the warm mounds of pale sand, the vast blue, every ripple and cresting wave a siren call. Silken sheets of myriad colours at the water's edge appear then disappear with each hiss of the retreating wave. Seagulls strut by on red stick legs. Tiny shells and seaweed crunch deliciously under the skin of shoeless feet. A world glowing from within. Like most Australian children, I longed in summer to be at the beach.[3] Decades later, memories of an enchanted timeless world linger on; sun-bright, brown bodies playing in the sand, salty lips, sunburn, freedom, grapes, buns sticky with soft white icing as thick as your finger, and later, the sun sliding lower and lower, the sky a glory of pinks, reds and gold. Desperate plea bargains struck with parents—not yet! But it is the utter joy of being *in* these 'mountainous atmospheres of sky and sea',[4] of being among voices—yes at times of the test cricket commentator—but always of the waves and wind. A world alive. Vibrating.

When the day came to pack up our little grey Vauxhall car, and 'turn toward the town', my heart became heavy. We drove away, and as we neared the city of Geelong, the flat industrial ugliness felt an assault. My eyes could not bear to look out the window, and I hid my face, crouching, in those pre-seatbelt days, behind the back of the front passenger seat, head down, pressed against my bent knees, trying to 'not

---

in school laboratories to form a vacuum and demonstrate how sound (e.g., an electric bell inside the jar) is dampened and then extinguished as the vacuum increases. The class can see the bell vibrating but cannot hear anything.

[3] These memories belong specifically to Jan. Writing a book jointly is a challenge. For the most part, we use the pronouns 'we' and 'us' as authentically representing our voices. Occasionally, as here, 'I' and 'me' are required to make sense of things.

[4] The reference here is to the poem by Wallace Stevens, *The Idea of Order at Key West*. Similar allusions to this work will recur throughout the book. The full text of the poem is set out and discussed in the Postscript.

see' this awfulness, trying to 'not hear' the noisy engine, trying to hold in my memory the bliss in which I had bathed, trying to make-believe that this drab other world did not exist. Why, why do we have to go home?

Mere nostalgia?

Black water rising

20th April, 2010. An oil rig in the Gulf of Mexico erupts spectacularly in a ball of flame. Exploratory drilling was underway 1.6 kilometres below the surface of the water when methane gas rose at high pressure into the rig, ignited and exploded, engulfing the platform in fire. Eleven people died and seventeen others working on the rig were injured. Two days later, the rig—ironically named 'Deepwater Horizon'—sank, and we saw on our TV screens black oil beginning to spread out in all directions from the site.

One month later, despite all efforts, the oil slick, now clearly visible from a NASA satellite, covered 180,000 square kilometres of ocean, (three times the size of Tasmania). Along with millions, we watched with mounting horror as day by day attempts to staunch the flow failed, and failed again. The well, owned by BP and part of the Macondo Prospect, lay 66 kilometres off the coast of Louisiana. It took almost three gruelling months before it was officially declared sealed. But by that time, the wound deep in the ocean floor had bled an estimated 4.9 million barrels.[5]

The damage is impossible to measure. Heartbreaking photographs of oil sodden pelicans and seals are still vivid in our imaginations. Each pelican and each seal is part of, and dependent on, an intricate web of life. Tides, winds, waves and currents carry the deadly molecules, as they carry nutrients, dispersing them across the surface of the sea and down into the deep. The Gulf is home to over eight thousand species of fish, birds, molluscs, crustaceans, polychaetes (annelid marine worms), sea turtles and marine mammals, to name a few. Their habitats—the ocean, the shoreline, marshes and estuaries—were all savagely affected.

An oil dispersant named Corexit exacerbated the damage. Only used as a surface applicant prior to this, 6.96 million litres were released

---

[5] BP argued in court for a much lower figure of 2.5 million barrels over an 87 day period.

experimentally under water. The effect was that oil that would naturally rise to the surface remained in suspension in fine droplets between the ocean floor and the surface, a deadly oil/dispersant mixture that significantly increased the toxicity to ecosystems. Permeating the food chain through the zooplankton, it was later found in pelican eggs and in migratory birds in Minnesota, over 1800 kilometres away.

Clean-up operations began, as did court proceedings. Three years later, clean-up crews had recovered 2.1 million kilograms of oily material from along the coastline. Tar balls washed up on the shores of the Mississippi. Oily sheen trails, and fouled wetlands, trees and grasses dead from oil exposure, lead to erosion of coastal islands. 50% of shrimp were found to be lacking eyes and eye sockets. A similar increase in deformities and lesions occurred in fish populations. Dead baby dolphins washed up at six times the normal rate.

Parents of a third of the children living less than 15 kilometres from the coast in Louisiana and Florida reported unexplained symptoms such as bleeding from the nose and ears, and unusually early onset of menses. A huge range of physical and mental health problems in adults is still being monitored.

BP has paid fines and claims, and estimates its total costs at $61.6 billion.[6] Under water oil drilling continues.

Money talks.

And we can't even read pelican?

Augustine at Tathra

In the late summer of 2012, we rented a house at Tathra Beach on the NSW south coast, 18 kilometres east of the town of Bega. A welcome four weeks break from the uproar of Melbourne city life. With open-plan interior and wide glass windows opening to the outside world, the house nestled into a hill high above the beach. Each day we woke to the rustle of the gum trees with their abundant bird life, and a glimpse of the ocean with its constant water music.

---

[6] Though named the worst environmental disaster in US history, we are aware that other problems now are far greater. For example, the vast wastelands of relatively invisible oxygen-starved zones called 'blobs'.

1. The Visible Voice / Away with the Ocean

We had an array of books, an odd mixture of things thrown in as we packed the car for our journey from Melbourne. Something to suit any mood that might take our fancy. One was a slim paperback by a contemporary French philosopher, Jean-Louis Chrétien, with the title, *The Call and the Response*. As philosophy goes it looked manageable, not much over one hundred pages. And there was a certain intrigue in the title. What call? Whose response?

We began reading it aloud, sometimes on the deck, sometimes on the beach, sometimes in a coffee shop. Chrétien is interested in tracing the origins of speech, a difficult assignment since, as he points out, when we start speaking, we always find ourselves already in the midst of the world of speech. 'We take our turn,' he says, 'only by taking speech up where it left off.'[7] My 'response' presupposes a previous 'call', by which you invite me to speak; but your call in turn is a response to an earlier call, itself another response, and so on. Our lives are caught up in and expressed through a great 'chorus' of voices with whom we share the world in a network of speech.

The book is a masterly demonstration of the thesis. Starting with Plato's meditation on the Greek word *kalein* (to call) in the *Cratylus*, Chrétien himself proceeds to 'call' all sorts of witnesses onto the stage. And they make their 'responses', speaking back and forth to each other and to us, the readers. Some we knew, by name anyway (Plato, Aristotle, Heidegger). Others we'd never heard of ('Mechtild of Magdeburg' and somebody called 'Isaac of Stella'!). With great skill, Chrétien shows how these voices, disparate across space and time, interact with each other, one evoking ('calling') comment from another ('response'), a third then adding to the second and revisiting the first. The chain is unending until you come to the primal call (the 'real' origin of speech) and the primal response. 'The first vocation is the vocation to be, the first answer, to be there.'[8]

At first we assumed that by these 'many voices', Chrétien meant many *human* voices. And he did. There they were on the page. But we soon

---
[7] Jean-Louis Chrétien, *The Call and the Response*, trans. Anne A. Davenport (New York: Fordham University Press, 2004), p. 4.
[8] Chrétien, *The Call and the Response*, p. 18.

found out that he had no intention of restricting the chorus in that way. Suddenly a new voice entered the conversation. Chrétien quoted a passage from Augustine's *Confessions* just at the moment when he (Augustine) turns away from analysing the soul (a central interest of the text) towards the external world, to the world of nature, to earth and sky and sea. The words almost leapt from the page.

> But what are you my God? I put my question to the earth. It answered, 'I am not God', and all things on earth declared the same. I asked the sea and the chasms of the deep and the living things that creep in them, but they answered, 'We are not your God. Seek what is above us.' I spoke to the winds that blow, and the whole air and all that lives in it replied, 'Anaximenes is wrong. I am not God.' I asked the sky, the sun, the moon, and the stars, but they all told me, 'Neither are we the God you seek.' I spoke to all these things that are about me, all that can be admitted by the door of the senses, and I said, 'Since you are not my God, tell me about him. Tell me something of my God.' Clear and loud they answered, 'God is he who made us.' I asked these questions simply by gazing at these things, and their beauty was the answer they gave.'[9]

How were we to hear this astonishing utterance? We fled straight to our default. Earth, sea, sky, wind, animals and so on, don't actually 'say' anything. Augustine is taking anthropomorphic licence. What he is *really* doing is reflecting rationally on the relationship between the world and God ('he made us'). This 'dialogue' with the world is just a picturesque way of making a theological point. Isn't it?

Chrétien rejects that suggestion outright. He thinks it fails to hear what Augustine is trying to say, and makes him say something he is not, or not only.

We read those words on the beach that day. This wasn't the seminar room or library. No walls here to cage the imagination. Augustine, it

---

[9] Augustine, *Confessions*, trans. R. S. Pine-Coffin (Harmondsworth, Middlesex: Penguin, 1961), X, 27, 231. Augustine (354-430 CE) was an early Christian theologian and philosopher, bishop of Hippo in North Africa. In this passage, he clearly uses the male pronoun for God. We employ inclusive language wherever possible in this book, but quotations from the works of others are left as given. Anaximenes was a pre-Socratic philosopher (c.585-c.528 BCE) who held to a doctrine of material monism.

seems was talking with the very things that now enveloped us, sky, earth, sea.

But if that's *not* figurative, what is it?

Country

In Tathra we are in Yuin country. For Yuin people the land speaks … all the time. They have lived in this place for sixty thousand years, some two thousand generations before we, white settlers, invaded and named it New South Wales in 1788!

An Aboriginal Yuin elder, Max Dulumunmun Harrison (Uncle Max), has undertaken the daunting and astonishingly generous task of trying to communicate to whitefellas his people's traditional connection to 'Country', connection to earth and sea, to sky and river, to rock and tree. 'I am trying to raise awareness of Aboriginal spirituality,' he writes, 'and to explain how we connect to the land. I am trying to capture in words the beauty of the land I see around me'.[10]

The land. For us land is wealth and security, something people own. Early white settlers saw 'resources' here. A weathered cliff below which swirled deep water. Boats could be launched bound for Sydney town. Seals and whales were abundant. Loggers felled trees. Farms began to produce milk and cheese.

These days the wharf at Tathra is heritage listed, and home to a fine 'locavore' eating place, a favourite site for fishing, and seasonal whale watching. Houses, shops, schools, roads, farms, forests have boundaries. Fences mark the limits and 'no trespassing' signs announce their occupation. Someone, somewhere owns the place and has a deed of possession to prove it. Even the sea has its boundaries. Invisible though they may be to the naked eye, they are there, gazetted by whiteman's law

---

[10] Max Dulumunmun Harrison, *My People's Dreaming* (Sydney: HarperCollins*Publishers*, 2009), p. 7. The English word 'Uncle' in the Indigenous context means elder, teacher, relative, respected man or guardian. This book came into being (at least on a surface reading) through a photographer, Peter McConchie, a man with a passionate commitment to healing cultural divisions, and learning deeper connections with the natural world. His exquisite photographs of Yuin country are woven into the verbal text. He reports a conversation in which he describes to Uncle Max how he (McConchie) came to find him. He received this reply. 'You think so. I have been singing someone up for years for this.' See p. 159.

and precisely mapped; fishing zones, national and state borders, marine parks. For Uncle Max the reverse is the truth.

> We belong to the land because Mother Earth feeds us and births everything. Non-indigenous people think they own the land and they look on it as wealth. They start to rape the land and therefore uplift their own spirits, but the old Koori, he sings the land down and tries to hold the sacredness in the land.[11]

For whitefellas to begin to hear something of this singing, Uncle Max recommends going to the sea. 'Stand in there for a while and she can tell you something. She will give you good insight. You just go and stand and let her wash up on you, with your eyes closed. And you'll get those vibrations,'[12] the vibrations of a sacred chorus.

When we wish to get our bearings in Tathra, we fold open our trusty map flat, or as flat as possible, on our knees. Cleared land is coloured yellow, forested areas green, lakes and rivers blue. Highways (black), roads (red) and tracks (grey) crisscross the page. Towns are marked as dots and named. Distances between indicated with exact numbers. The ocean appears as a dark blue border at the edge.

But Uncle Max's 'Country' cannot be laid out on a flat homogenous page. 'Country' is alive with the 'Dreaming' and shaped by powerful sacred story pathways 'going wherever [they] will go'.

> Our Dreaming starts up near Braidwood and Majors Creek, my great-grandmother and grandmother's country. As the Shoalhaven River winds around and bends, it brings with it all the different stories from the different parts of the river. The river leads us to the sea, and shows us that we are freshwater and saltwater water people. If we didn't follow the stories that the Shoalhaven River brings us we would not be able to find our way down to the sea and to our homeland.[13]

What is this mysterious English word 'Dreaming'? It disturbs our 'settled' categories. Where is it located? In the land? The sea? The mind?

---

11 Harrison, *My People's Dreaming*, p. 96.
12 Max Dulumunmun Harrison, *Mind Moon Circle*, Sydney Zen Centre, Spring 2008, p. 6.
13 Harrison, *My People's Dreaming*, p. 13. Yuin land follows the coast all the way from Wollongong to the Snowy River in Victoria.

The past? The future? In specific things? Everywhere? The Dreaming brings stories, stories are to be followed, to help 'find our way'. But how does a river carry stories 'as it winds around and bends'? And how does all this make a homeland, and form an identity known through kinship with water; 'we are freshwater and saltwater water people'?

'Tathra' is an Indigenous word, embedded in Indigenous Country. It means 'beautiful place', which it certainly is. We come to see it. To see the ocean. To see the sky. To see the wide, white sand. We are the onlookers. Tathra is the looked upon. For Uncle Max, again, this is almost back to front. To see, for him, is to be in a conversation, to encounter and to be encountered.

> Seeing is so important ... really seeing what the land is telling you. Seeing what the land is offering you to take.
>
> When I take people [whitefellas] out into the land I say: 'Let's watch the land talk to us.' And you'll see some jaws drop. But that's what it's doin' – it's talking to us without a voice. Our land does that all the time; our water does that, our wind. Grandmother Moon, Grandfather Sun do it all the time. They show us things, what's happening. They are talking to us constantly. And what do we do? We ignore them.[14]

Talking Country? What do we do?

The visible voice[15]

When Uncle Max says, 'let's *watch* the land talk to us', is he playing with an empty paradox, or is it possible he is giving expression to a 'rigorously phenomenological property of human sight'?[16] When Augustine says of the sky, the sea and the stars, 'Clear and loud they answered, "God is he who made us"', is that just a figure of speech in which inanimate things are personified, or does it bear a deeper significance? The conclusion of the passage from the *Confessions* quoted above divulges, or at least hints at, such a deeper meaning. 'I asked these questions simply by gazing at these things, and their beauty was the answer they gave.' Here is a seeing

---

14 Harrison, *My People's Dreaming*, p. 7.
15 This is the title of the second chapter in Chrétien's *The Call and the Response*, pp. 33-43, and is foundational for this whole exploration.
16 Chrétien, *The Call and the Response*, p. 33.

that asks questions by its very way of looking. And here the things looked upon 'answer', with 'their beauty'. Uncle Max appears to be saying something similar. 'I am trying to capture in words the beauty of the land I see around me'. Beauty that 'talks'. This all sounds and feels very odd. And yet the French philosopher, in line as it were with both Uncle Max and Augustine, concludes 'if beauty is the very voice of things, the face-to-face encounter through which beauty grips us is not in essence a speechless contemplation but a *dialogue*.'[17] And that means the beauty of things becomes properly visible, that is we see them truly, if and only if they speak to us, and we question them. And that implies the world is not 'an inaudible visible', but rather 'a visible voice'.[18]

Everything is a voice, everything is a fragrance.

Everything, infinitely, says something to someone.[19]

How are we to understand this? Augustine himself gives a clue. A few pages before the passage cited, he argues that everyone whose senses are not impaired is aware of the universe around them. But the universe 'does not give the same message to us all.'[20] Not because it sometimes speaks and sometimes remains silent, and not because it speaks one language to this person and another to that; but because it depends on *how* we approach it. To look at the world merely as a complex arrangement of stuff, some animate some inanimate, or with an attitude of mastery through technical reason, is completely different from approaching the world as a visible voice, with eyes that really listen. 'To the man who merely looks', says Augustine, 'it [i.e., the universe] says nothing, while to another it gives an answer.'[21]

That hit a nerve. Have we lived all this time on Earth as those who 'merely look'? Or have we at times been 'spoken to' unawares? And suppose we were to try to 'do an Augustine', out there with the sky and the earth and the sea, how would we go about it? You can't just call out to 'the chasms of the deep', not in a public spot like this, anyway. So how?

---

[17] Chrétien, *The Call and the Response*, p. 35. Italics added.
[18] Chrétien, *The Call and the Response*, p. 33.
[19] Chrétien, *The Call and the Response*, p. 43, quoting Victor Hugo.
[20] Augustine, *Confessions*, X, 6, 212.
[21] Augustine, *Confessions*, X, 6, 213.

Chrétien approaches an answer to this question diagonally, as it were, starting with ourselves. Genuine attention in the human world, that is, any real listening to another person—especially if what is coming to speech is confused, broken, mixed up, or hard to get at—demands an effort to attend to what is 'unheard of'; that is, to the *new* which is struggling to find words. If we are not prepared to stay open to this 'unheard of', if we are not prepared to be caught off guard, disoriented, challenged, we will simply miss what is coming to speech. 'For the [one] who is on his guard, and sticks to the commands set out in his programme of possibilities, will never see anything happen but what he has already seen and will never hear anything but what has already been said.'[22] Listening for the unheard of and looking for the unseen in what another person says means 'following a patient, laborious path, sometimes getting lost and needing to start all over again, with all that is improvisational and, as it were, caressing in the act of *attention*, towards the singularity of the event that calls for ... speech.' Thus, Chrétien concludes in a dramatic image, 'every act of speech is a hand-to-hand combat with silence, with what cannot be said and yet will be said.'[23]

Does such a hand-to-hand combat with 'what cannot be said and yet will be said' apply somehow to Uncle Max's watching that allows the land to talk? Is it apposite to Augustine's attentive gaze towards the earth, the sky, the sea, that they spoke to him as they did? Slowly we began to notice 'calls' and 'responses' swirling between childhood memories, oil spill catastrophes, French philosophers, and Indigenous elders, and somehow this seemed to shift the weight of plausibilities. If we just stick to the options set out in our given 'bell jar' of possibilities, it is likely we 'will never see anything happen but what [we have] already seen and will never hear anything but what has already been said'. So what if we don't understand? Isn't that the point? What if this 'call' (if that is what it is) is not to elicit a 'response' of *understanding*, but of *doing, being* and *becoming*? What if hand-to-hand combat with silence is what is called for here, not mind to mind discussion of ideas? What have we got to

---

[22] Jean-Louis Chrétien, *The Ark of Speech*, trans. Andrew Brown (London: Routledge, 2004), p. 14.
[23] Chrétien, *The Ark of Speech*, p. 14. Italics added.

lose? The prospect of attending to the world this way seemed enticing. Why not a dialogue with beauty? There's plenty of it here in Tathra. Who knows where it might take us?

Sea see/hearing

We had no idea how one might go about such a dialogue. Here we were at Tathra Beach. There was no doubt it was beautiful. But what next? Uncle Max's advice seemed simple: 'You just go and stand and let her [the ocean] wash up on you, with your eyes closed. And you'll get those vibrations.' With no better suggestion to hand, we decided to give it a shot. The next day, we walked north along the beach away from the café with its salty windows and the surf club building crouched beside it; away from the sun bathers, swimmers, surfboard riders and life-savers; north to where the beach curves away into the distance and the sand empties of people and the surf runs in serried ranks toward the shore, undisturbed by human intrusion. It seemed better to try this alone. Departing somewhat from Uncle Max's instructions, we sat well back from the water's edge, high on a grassy dune. And, remembering Augustine's experience, we kept our eyes open; 'I asked these questions simply by *gazing* at these things.' The ocean spread out before us, a blue mirror. It was afternoon. The sun behind us cast the shadow of our hunched figures across the lumpy sand. For half an hour we sat, watching and listening with as much sensual openness as we could muster.

Later we talked about the experience. It felt 'significant', we agreed. But just what the significance consisted in we couldn't say. All we had were halting descriptions and a few fuzzy metaphors. The ocean was like a 'mother'; the source of life on earth. Who wouldn't want to attend to such a mother's voice? The blue expanse seemed to an unfocussed gaze like a 'wall of water' rising up toward the horizon. That felt slightly threatening, as if it might collapse downward and flood the sands on which we were sitting. The gift dimension Uncle Max alluded to ('just go and stand there ... you'll get those vibrations') was tangible. The ocean was all beauty and movement, dancing light streaming from every rise and fall of its surface. We only had to open our eyes, our ears, our mouths to feel its generosity. There was sadness too. What took you so long? How old are you that it is only now you take time to come?

Not much to go on. But a start. We set ourselves to attend in silence to the 'visible voice' of the sea—if there was one—for half an hour each day. No easy task, it turned out. Chrétien was right, listening for the unheard of and looking for the unseen in this strange situation meant 'following a patient, laborious path, sometimes getting lost and needing to start all over again'. Yet the experience of setting ourselves to look and listen, to attend the ocean in this way, continued to entice. We kept it up intermittently over a period of years, more intensively during the three to four month periods we were able to be in Tathra, less regularly when back in Melbourne. Learning from ancient meditative traditions, a practice gradually took shape which for want of a better name we called 'sea see/hearing' (we pronounced it 'sea se(h)earing'!) Details of the practice will be introduced and explained throughout the chapters that follow.[24] But for the moment it suffices to say that we would walk silently for about half an hour along the beach until we reached our selected spot. There we would stand for the agreed time facing the ocean, following as best we could the disciplines of attending that we were discovering as we went along. When the time was up, with a gesture of respect toward the sea, we turned and walked back.

From the beginning we kept a journal of our experiences. Upon arriving back home, we sat down immediately and in turn spoke about what had happened for us that day in the sea see/hearing practice, the other person writing down verbatim what was said. We then reversed roles. Making such a record was a slow, reflective process, full of stops and starts. And naturally took time. But what came out of it was surprising. In offering to each other an hospitable silence into which we could speak without fear of censorship or the need to 'tidy things up', we discovered that what at first glance seemed an unremarkable session of quiet attention to the ocean, in fact held intimations, or even quite detailed illuminations, of the world around us and of our place within it. It may seem grandiose to speak of 'revelation' in this context. But the exercise of journaling at times

---

[24] Suggestions for the practice are progressively introduced in the pages interleaving the chapters. Appendix 2 gathers this practical material together in one place.

brought us close to the feeling that we were being offered gifts that were so far beyond the range of our own capacities for apprehending things that some such description was not unfitting. Of course, there is plenty in our reports that is ordinary, unremarkable and even boring! But this much does seem true. Such intentional deep listening to the other not only provided ongoing encouragement and support for the journey we were undertaking, but enabled powerful material that we might easily overlook or naturally repress to be brought to consciousness, and thus become available for reflection, comparison and, ultimately, integration into ongoing life and thought.

By the end of four years we had one hundred and fifty pages of journal. This became the primary data, the seed-bed from which this book has grown, and from which the extracts quoted are taken. Reflecting upon it drew us into a wide and rich conversation, into streams of thought and practice, which we found (to our surprise) we shared with many others. We began to grasp that we, along with these others, were on a journey; a journey into the unknown, outwardly in relation to the ocean and inwardly in relation to the self. Almost inevitably this invited comparison with what has classically been known as a pilgrimage. By changing her habitual way of life, the patterns that assure her of her identity and hold her there, the pilgrim hopes for something new, a breaking of old structures and an expanding of the self's horizons. Transformation is the objective. We were not travelling to Mecca or Jerusalem, nor walking the way of the Camino de Santiago, but we were certainly moving in foreign worlds, listening for the unheard of, looking for the unseen. Although we did not initially seek nor especially want it, we quickly found that sea see/hearing threatened to crack open the 'bell jar' of many of our habitual assumptions about the world and about ourselves within it. At times this brought with it delight, surprise and discovery; at times resistance, horror and sadness. What follows is the story of that conflicted journey.

The structure of the chapters reflects these conflicts. Meditations on aspects of the generosity and magnificence of the ocean clash with stories of disfigurement, threat and damage. We have not attempted to smooth the transitions, but to echo our lived experience of such confrontations as jagged and painful. The stories often depend on an engagement with science. We are not scientists, but in the course of our journey we have become aware of how critical the work and witness of science is. The volume of material, however, is sometimes overwhelming, difficult to access and continually changing. We recognise how superficial our grasp is. The stories are fragmentary, but there seems nothing for it but to do what we can and accept the limitations. Without the astonishing and sometimes disturbing testimony of scientists, things may manifest themselves, but we will not see; they may speak, but we will not hear.

The Visible Voice / **Away with the Ocean**

Over forty years ago, in 1976, the now world famous oceanographer and marine biologist, Sylvia Earle, visited Melbourne for a conference about ocean exploration. She recalls standing on the shore of Port Phillip Bay with a young reporter who thrust a microphone under her chin and fired a series of questions.

> 'Suppose the oceans dried up tomorrow. Why should I care? I don't swim. I hate boats. I get seasick! I don't even like to eat fish. Why should I object if some of them—or all of them—go extinct? Who needs the ocean?'

> Groaning silently [Earle says] I thought, *Good grief! Can she be serious? Suppose the oceans dried up tomorrow! What a concept! Who needs the ocean? Who doesn't need the ocean!* I glanced at the rippled edge of the vast, sparkling blueness that dominates the planet, embraces islands and continents, shapes the character of climate and weather, and from the sunlit surface to the greatest, darkest depths seven miles down is home to most of life on earth. Then I said, with a sweep of my arms:

> 'Right, dry up the oceans. Think of all the good stuff lost at sea that you could just scoop up. The trouble is, there wouldn't be anybody around to do that. Without the ocean, there would be no life – no people, anyway.'

> 'Well, how so?' she prodded. 'People don't *drink* saltwater.' 'Okay,'

I began. 'Get rid of the ocean, and Earth would be a lot like Mars. Cold, barren, inhospitable. Ask those who are trying to figure out how astronauts can live there. Or, how about the moon. There's a place with no bothersome ocean. And no life. Or Venus. Yes, the beautiful—and lifeless—hot planet with no ocean. It doesn't matter where on Earth you live, everyone is utterly dependent on the existence of that lovely, living saltwater soup. There's plenty of water in the universe without life, but nowhere is there life without water.'

I paused, looked back at the incoming waves, then added ... 'The *living* ocean drives planetary chemistry, governs climate and weather, and otherwise provides the cornerstone of the life-support system for all creatures on our planet, from the deep-sea starfish to desert sagebrush. *That's* why the ocean matters. If the sea is sick, we'll feel it. If it dies, we die. Our future and the state of the oceans are one.'[25]

'No blue, no green.'[26]

In the intervening period, one thing has become very clear. The ocean is sick. And we humans are the primary drivers of its illness. In those forty years we have taken and consumed vast quantities of fish, depleting, in some cases to the point of extinction or near extinction, certain species on a global scale (e.g., the blue fin tuna). Almost half the coral reefs, nurseries of so much marine life, have disappeared. The Great Barrier Reef is now suffering severe damage from coral bleaching. Huge amounts of rubbish and toxic chemicals are dumped daily into the ocean. Pesticides, herbicides and fertilizer-runoff spill from our agriculture and wind up in the waves. Dredging, drilling, mining—with their inevitable accidents—go on with ever increasing intensity and in ever more risky locations. But the greatest threat is coming from the

---

[25] Sylvia Alice Earle, *Sea Change: A Message of the Oceans* (New York: Fawcett Books, 1995), pp. xi-xii. Italics in text. Sylvia Earle is one of the scientific experts called to testify before the U.S. House of Representatives Committee on Transportation and Infrastructure in its inquiry into the Deepwater Horizon Oil Spill (see pp. 13-14 above) on May 19, 2010. A full transcript of her testimony can be found in Sylvia A. Earle, *The World is Blue: How Our Fate and the Ocean's are One* (Washington, D. C.: National Geographic Society, [2009] 2010), pp. 271-285.

[26] Sylvia A. Earle, *Blue Hope: Exploring and Caring for Earth's Magnificent Ocean* (Washington, D. C.: National Geographic Society, 2014), pp. 21-41.

gigantic flow-on effects from the emission of greenhouse gases into the atmosphere. Climate change is both warming and acidifying the ocean.

We are changing the physics, chemistry, biology and thermodynamics of the sea in ways that have never been possible before in the long history of human interaction with the ocean. A thousand years ago it didn't matter much what we did or thought. The oceans, the lands, the atmosphere were so vast and resilient our human economies and industries were of little consequence. But in the last one hundred years, and especially the last fifty, our numbers have expanded exponentially and our technologies have reached a level of sophistication such that humans now represent a new planetary force; a force which is having accelerating and often deeply damaging effects on the biosphere.[27] Alanna Mitchell writes:

> What we do and how we think does matter now ... because finally the actions and belief systems of humans are damaging the oceans. Our actions are dangerous to us and to millions of other living things. We are altering not just bits of the sea with dreadful oil spills or eroding shores or vast extinctions of fish, but the whole, interconnected global system that is the ocean, the main medium of life on earth.[28]

In her brilliant and challenging book, *This Changes Everything*, Naomi Klein goes so far as to name this situation a 'war'. Our human economic system and the planetary system are now locked in a fateful struggle with each other, which means in effect that our economies are in a fateful struggle with the life-support system which sustains our life.

> What the climate needs to avoid collapse is a contraction in humanity's use of resources; what our economic model demands to avoid collapse is unfettered expansion. Only one of these sets of rules can be changed, and it's not the laws of nature.[29]

---

[27] These changes in Earth's geology and ecosystems are so extensive that the term 'Anthropocene' is now being used in an attempt to describe a whole new geological era. A Working Party brought this recommendation to the International Geological Congress in 2016.
[28] Alanna Mitchell, *Sea Sick: The Global Ocean in Crisis* (Millers Point, NSW: Murdoch Books Australia, 2010), p. 26.
[29] Naomi Klein, *This Changes Everything: Capitalism vs. The Climate* (London: Penguin Random House UK, 2015), p. 21.

But it's a hard lesson to learn. In December 2015, Greg Hunt, Australia's environment minister at the time, along with hundreds of other world leaders, went to Paris to what was vaunted as a 'make or break' conference on climate change. Before the talks began, Hunt expressed his hope that the world would reach a strong and binding agreement, adding that this was 'a deeply personal goal and commitment, as well as a national objective.' He and his colleagues were successful it seems. After lengthy and sometimes heated discussion, the final text of the conference, agreed to by all the major political leaders of the world, pledged to 'holding the increase in the global average temperature to well below 2°C above pre-industrial levels and to pursue efforts to limit the temperature increase to 1.5°C above pre-industrial levels, recognising that this would significantly reduce the risks and impacts of climate change.'[30] As a political achievement, gaining such a significant agreement amongst such a large and diverse group of stakeholders was no doubt an unusual thing, and rightly to be lauded. But what does it actually mean?

Say we really are going to hold the temperature rise of the planet to 2°C. What actions need to be taken? The science is clear. In an article published in *Nature* in 2015, Christophe McGlade and Paul Ekins of University College London, argue that to have even a 50% chance of keeping global warming to this target 'cumulative carbon emissions between 2010 and 2050 need to be limited to around 1,100 gigatonnes of carbon dioxide (Gt CO_2).' However, the greenhouse gas emissions contained in present estimates of global fossil fuel reserves are, they state, around three times higher than this. And 'so the unabated use of all current fossil fuel reserves is incompatible with a warming limit of 2°C.' In order to have any chance to meet the agreed target globally, 'a third of oil reserves, half of gas reserves and over 80% of current coal reserves should remain unused from 2010 to 2050.'[31] This means drilling for oil and gas, say, in the Arctic, or any increase in unconventional oil production elsewhere is incommensurate with efforts to reach the stated

---

[30] See Bill McKibben's masterly response to the Paris agreement, "This is not ideology," *The Monthly*, Issue 119, February 2016, pp. 9-10.
[31] Christophe McGlade & Paul Ekins, "The geographical distribution of fossil fuels unused when limiting global warming to 2°C," *Nature* 517, (Jan 2015), p. 187.

goal. For Australia to play its part, this would mean leaving around 90% of our coal reserves in the ground.

But what about trying to meet that 1.5°C target? In that case, says Bill McKibben bluntly, we'd have to stop mining coal tomorrow.

> This is not ideology. This is not propaganda. This is math, chemistry and physics. No one has challenged the numbers, because the numbers line up with science the world over. And the science lines up with ... the relentless rise in temperatures. The steady melt of glaciers. The rapid acidification of the planet's oceans. The rise in extreme weather ... .[32]

However, a matter of days after the Paris agreement, the Queensland Land Court threw out an appeal from environmentalists to stop the huge Adani Carmichael coal mine from going ahead in the Galilee Basin. The mine, Australia's biggest mining project to date, will consist of six open-cut pits and up to five underground mines, and is intended to supply Indian power stations with enough coal to generate electricity for up to one hundred million people. At the same time, in order to facilitate export of the coal, environment minister Greg Hunt gave the go-ahead for the expansion of the Abbot Point Coal Terminal near Bowen, which involves dredging 1.1 million cubic meters of seabed near the Great Barrier Reef Marine Park, to make it one of the largest coal ports in the world.[33]

Controversy still goes on. And it is not yet clear that the Carmichael mine will go ahead. But the point here is the *disconnect* between Paris and the Galilee Basin. You can't have both the Paris climate agreement and the Carmichael coalmine. To have any chance of keeping an increase of temperature to 2°C, much less 1.5°C, Australia can't responsibly develop massive new coal reserves. This is the Klein dilemma, 'only one of these sets of rules can be changed, and it's not the laws of nature.'

Since first writing this chapter, Donald Trump has been elected President of the United States and the whole politics of global climate change has shifted dramatically. In March 2017, Trump signed an

---

32 McKibben, "This is not ideology," p. 9.
33 See the following sites: www.abc.net.au/news/2015-12-15/adani-court-rejects-bid-to-stop-adani-coal-mine; and www.abc.net.au/news/2015-12-22/massive-abbot-point-coal-project. Accessed 6 April 2016.

executive order dismantling a range of Obama-era climate change regulations designed to help the US meet its commitments to the Paris accord.[34] 'I am taking historic steps to lift restrictions on American energy, to reverse government intrusion, and to cancel job-killing regulations,' Trump said, speaking at the Environmental Protection Agency headquarters on a stage lined with coal miners.[35]

We are all caught in it. The Klein dilemma is now the global background to any trip we make to the beach. It is the global background of our sea see/hearing practice at Tathra. It is not a dilemma for politicians and economists alone, though clearly they have special public leadership responsibilities in the matter. But politics and economics are just other names for the way we live our lives together. If we are to be honest with ourselves, the Klein dilemma is our dilemma, which means we need to bring it from the background into the foreground. Our squirming under the rigours of this demand is clear in our journals.

> The walk in along the beach is terrific. The wind is strong. The sun is out and the light and the water mingle with their usual magic. My heart lifts. When I get to the point of sea see/hearing I feel today is a day to give thanks. Heartfelt. ... But something almost physical prevents me from acting on that intention. I feel myself sucked back into all the problems of ecological damage I've been reading about in Sylvia Earle. And I do not want to go there! John Howard's infamous remark, 'I'm not going to adopt a black armband view of history'—meaning I am not responsible and I am not going to apologise for what other people have done to the Indigenous Peoples of this land over the last 200 years—springs unbidden into my mind. I don't want a black armband view of sea see/hearing. All this damage to the sea isn't my doing! ... But even as I think this, I know it's a cop-out. The same way Howard's stance was a cop-out. And I remember the judgement I passed on him at the time! [G, 6/3/15][36]

---

[34] The main target of the so-called 'Energy Independence' order is Obama's Clean Power Plan which required states to slash carbon emissions from electricity power plants. But the order also reverses a ban on coal leases on federal lands and undoes rules to curb methane emissions from oil and gas production.

[35] www.abc.net.au/news/2017-03-29/trump-signs-executive-order. Accessed 29 March 2017.

[36] For an introduction to this and following journal quotations, see above, pp. 21-22. The journal is a record of our individual responses to sea see/hearing. In extracts cited we indicate the date and the voice at the end. J=Jan. G=Graeme.

Learning a practice of attention (1)

Trying seriously to engage with the visible voice of the other-than-human world requires learning new ways of attending to that world. Through trial and error, and with the guidance of a number of Indigenous traditions, we slowly developed what we call 'a practice of attention' that seemed to facilitate our aim and help hold us steady in its pursuit. An outline of elements of the practice is set out in these shaded pages that follow each chapter (except the last). Nothing is prescriptive. Different traditions offer different practices. We offer our experience only as an example of one way.

* * * * * *

Place

Place is significant. To attend to the visible voice of things requires that we be in a place where that voice has a chance to unconceal itself. This means finding a place where you feel a sense of being in the presence of nature, but not crowded by other people. It might be (as for us) by the ocean. But it could be on a cliff top, in the mountains, in the bush, or forest, or desert, or grassland, by a river, a pond, or wetlands. Somewhere that calls to you. Somewhere you can go easily and regularly.

For city dwellers the choice is a bit harder. Search for a place that is as near to a 'natural' wild order, or as intact an ecosystem, as you can find; a tract of remnant bush in parkland, at the edge of a re-vegetated creek, by a lovely tree, or even in the presence of a single pot plant.

Standing

We found standing was best. But, if this proves too demanding, of course sitting is a sensible alternative.

Set your feet comfortably and firmly on the ground, legs slightly apart, balancing the weight of your body evenly. Stand straight and push upwards gently from the top of your head. Some traditions liken this stance to that of a tree, planted in the earth and stretching its trunk and branches upwards toward the sky. Patient, alive, interactive.

Relax the muscles of your body, almost as if you intend to 'let the flesh fall off your bones' (as a Taoist teacher puts it!). In particular, relax the muscles of your stomach and jaw. Unlock your knees. Tension in the body has a distracting effect.

Place the tip of your tongue behind your front teeth.

Looking

Keep your eyes open. Soften your gaze; an angle down of about 45 degrees is comfortable to begin with.

With increasing experience, we learned that our looking can take a variety of different forms; sometimes focussing on particular features; a wave, a colour, a bird, sometimes embracing the whole scene.

Centering

Empty your mind of the buzzing busyness of the day. If distracting thoughts intrude, gently let them pass by as clouds across the sky, and return to the practice.

Timing

Keep up the practice for 30 minutes or so. (At first 5 minutes may seem very long. Give your body time to learn new patterns!)

2. Call of Beauty / Sea of Plastic

When we walk on the earth with reverence, beauty will decide to trust us.

John O'Donohue

The sea is beautiful. Everybody knows that. One of the basic reasons Australians flock to the beach is that we find there a beauty that seems somehow primal and life-enhancing. Beyond the contours of our city streetscapes, the uproar of our business, and the common place of our talk, something arresting confronts us on the shore. To stand by the sea with the sun's light spearing the waves, salt spray shimmering above deep blue, the roar of the surf in our ears, is to feel instinctively—and probably say so out loud—'isn't it beautiful?' Having said it, we may feel slightly ridiculous. It's so obvious. Why say it? Except faced with this spectacle, it is hard not to say something. Though we've seen it all before, this splendour 'strikes' us afresh, like a physical blow. Somehow it doesn't seem right, or even possible, just to stand there and stare. The sea calls for something. It requires a reaction. And yet it's difficult to find words. 'Surf's up.' 'Great day.' 'Stunning colours.' 'This is the life.' Such utterances strive to give voice in response to the call. And they succeed in their way. But in the end, for all its banality, 'isn't it beautiful?' is difficult to avoid. It comes out as a question. And that's not insignificant. To say 'it is beautiful' is not quite the same as saying 'isn't it beautiful?' It's not that we think anyone might disagree. If they did we wouldn't believe it; or would immediately recognize intended irony. The question seeks affirmation, not because we are unsure of our ground, but because we are bedazzled by what our senses deliver to us. The splendour takes us by surprise. Can I *believe* this radiance? Do *you* feel it too?

In the journal we kept of our efforts at sea see/hearing, one thing stands out. Whatever the day, sunny or overcast; whatever the water, wild or still; whatever the beach, populated or empty; our reports always (or almost always) contain the words, 'it is so beautiful', 'the sea is very beautiful', or the like. Careful attending to the sea seems to confirm what common experience intuits. Beauty and the sea, the sea and beauty belong together. But what does that mean? Can we get any further than the involuntary utterance of a truism? What is beauty? And what is the beauty of the sea?

The feeling that the sea calls to us, that it pulls or draws us to come to it, is taken for granted in Tathra. The town is full of people who are there exactly for that reason, we among them. What we did not understand, however, is that this common experience has behind it a long and deep history of meditation on the experience of beauty. In the western tradition the sense of call has in fact defined the essential nature of beauty itself. Chrétien, as we have seen, traces this line of thinking back to the dialogue of Plato known as the *Cratylus*, which deals with the origins of words and the power of words to name things. In the dialogue, Plato notes that the Greek word *kalon*, meaning 'the beautiful', is linked to the word *kalein*, which means 'to call'. *Kalein* in Greek has the same double meaning as in English. It means to call out, to summon, to demand attention; and it means to bestow a name, to name something. That which calls, *to kaloun*, produces, or names, *ta kala*, beautiful things. And beauty itself, *kalon*, continues to call through and in *ta kala*, beautiful things. The essence of beauty so understood is *call*; its manifestation is a summons. In a passage that became a guiding light for us, Chrétien writes:

> To think beauty from the starting point of the call implies that the address sent to us by beauty is not a contingent feature, added over and above its essence, but actually defines it as such. The in-itself of beauty is to be for-the-other, aimed at gathering the other back to itself. What is beautiful is what calls out by manifesting itself and manifests itself by calling out. To draw us to itself as such, to put us in motion towards it, to move us, to come and find us where we are so that we will seek it—such is beauty's call and such our vocation.[1]

This feels right. The sea draws us to itself. And its beauty is what calls to us. The two are not separable. We feel the attraction of the sea *in* its beauty and we feel the beauty of the sea *in* its attraction. The 'in-

---

[1] Jean-Louis Chrétien, *The Call and the Response*, trans. Anne A. Davenport (New York: Fordham University Press, 2004) p. 9.

itself' of beauty is a power that reaches out for us and 'gathers' us back to itself. We are moved by it. That is, we are set 'in motion' in the simple physical sense of placing our bodies in the vicinity of the sea, on the shore or in the water. We *go* to the sea. But we are also 'moved' in the other sense, of being 'stirred up'. Our emotions are engaged. We feel longing, or wonder, or exhilaration in the presence of the splendour that meets us in the ocean.

But how does this all take place? What are the elements at work in a beauty that 'calls out by manifesting itself and manifests itself by calling out'? Our experience of sea see/hearing reveals that this 'manifest call' is both simple and complex. It is simple in that the apprehension of the beauty of the sea is a single unified experience. We stand by the shore. We see, hear, taste, smell and feel the scene as one whole: 'Ah! the sea!' And we are moved inwardly. 'Isn't it beautiful?' A child can experience it. On the other hand, if we reflect on that one, simple, whole experience, it quickly becomes obvious that it is made up of many interacting parts that have their own particular calls, which demand their own particular responses. The sky today is a stunning blue that is almost tangible. It grabs our attention. Tomorrow the surf is wild, full of sound and movement that clamours at us to take note. The day after waves are huge and seem perfectly formed as they run toward the shore. It is hard not to be captivated by them. Colour, sound, shape, each of these in turn is beautiful, and each has its own 'manifestation' and 'call'.

Colour

Colour is central. We exult daily in the exquisite colours the ocean displays. And squirm daily with our inability to do them justice.

> The colours of the sea are so powerful I almost feel physically overwhelmed. I look at the water between the peaks of the breaking waves. It is a colour that always stirs my heart to the depths, the palest, silky blue that mirrors the sky blue. At this time of day it takes on an incredible iridescent sheen, like the inside of mother-of-pearl shell. I am close to the water's edge. My feet are touching the rim of this colour in the film of water left as a wave retreats. I revel in it. I can't get enough. What is it about this colour? I have loved it for as long

as I can remember. Just then a wave reaches to where I am standing and washes around my feet, swirling water across my ankles. It is the gentlest of warm caresses. [J, 16/4/14]

Colour is unmistakeably a part of the 'call' that beauty makes to us. And there is no question that it is, or can be, 'moving'. At times colour is so insistent that it feels like a physical force which assaults ('overwhelms') us from without. The blue of the sea and the blue of the sky are dancing before and around us. Other. Over against. Sheer given-ness. But the assault from without meets a desire from within. The colour enters us, gathering us back to itself. It 'stirs my heart to the depths'. 'I revel in it'. This 'mother-of-pearl' calls up memories, taking us back to childhood, and even beyond. And it is delivered bodily. To be sure the eyes are primary. We *see* the colours. But the waves wash around our feet, and we *feel* the colours like a 'caress'. The colours of the water approach us in the touch of the water.

Then there is what we might call vibrancy.

The sea today is (yes, the cliché) 'stunningly beautiful'; something that 'stops me in my tracks' suddenly, irresistibly. I feel speechless. The blue of the sea is exhilarating. There seems to be a dozen shades of it shifting and melding into one another out to the horizon; a vast blue field which meets at the horizon a second even vaster field—the blue sky. Two blue worlds completely fill my vision. There is no room for anything else. But it doesn't feel crammed or cramped. This colour blue is running in excess of itself, juggling more than it can hold, spilling over. The waves are huge. Their white crowns shimmer in the sunlight. The white contrast magnifies the brilliance of the blue. [G, 6/5/14]

The sea is more than blue and white, of course. In the journal over 20 different colours in the sea are named from time to time. But blue seems to be the signature colour of the sea at Tathra. It 'fills my vision'. Moreover, there is something about *this* blue day that is especially beautiful ('stunning'). Two blue worlds seem to be at their brilliant best. It feels as if this manifestation of the sea and sky sets some sort of 'bench mark', as it were, for marine beauty. That is not to suggest that every day and every mood of the ocean doesn't have its own special loveliness. But there is something about *this* sense of excess, of 'juggling more than it can hold, spilling over', that comes with the perception of colours in the sea at their peak. This beauty seems to call us (or move us) beyond the immediate perceptions that crowd in on us. It first fills us so it seems 'there is no room for anything else'. But then it pushes us further, 'spilling over' into another space, which reflecting back, sets a 'bench mark' of perfection for what this colour means, or can mean in the scheme of things.

Sound

But the colour of the sea is not silent. If we were to block our ears while standing on the beach, what we would know of the sea would be radically altered. A soundless sea is almost no sea at all. And vice versa. With eyes closed we can still hear the sea. But that is not the beauty of the ocean. The voice of the sea is a 'visible voice' and the sight of the sea is an 'audible eye' (Chrétien).

> The beach is windswept and wild. Heavy waves heave and twist in the wind, tumbling in a profusion of foam and spray. Between waves, the water moves incessantly, laced with white and green. Low grey clouds threaten rain. A hail of perceptions clamours for attention. Wind against my face. A taste of salt. The touch of sand. Light over the surface of the waves. But above all is the thunder of falling water. A mountainous roar of sound. It is all around, coming from behind as well as in front. I am mesmerized by the huge volumes of water driving towards me. The world is singing. ... I realize suddenly that sound I am hearing today on this beach is a sound that has been around for 4 billion years. A sound almost as old as Earth itself. A sound that preceded any ears to hear it. And such ears as might develop the potential to hear would come from the sea itself. The sea is the *ur*-womb of the ear. The sea ultimately gives birth to its own hearers and seers. An eerie feeling creeps over me. [G, 25/3/12]

The sound of the sea in full voice is 'mesmerizing'. If we listen closely and carefully and for long enough it becomes spellbinding, absorbing the mind to the exclusion of other things. The sound has a certain uniformity about it that is recognizable instantly wherever it is heard in the world. Words to describe it are few and blunt: roar, thunder, trampling, churning. And yet it is a highly complex and delicately changing sound. Percussive moments—the crash of a falling wave—play over an underlying 'basso continuo' of moving water surging over the surface of other water, and of air 'water-walled' (Stevens) plunging and surfacing and plunging again. Sound rises and falls in regular intervals as waves run up the beach and expire. If this is the 'voice' of the sea, it is voice set to music. The sea is song.

And there is something about the song that fascinates. Simple tunes remembered from childhood days can evoke strong emotional reactions in us and call immediately to mind long past situations and people. So too with the sea. The sound of the surf 'calls' and in calling 'calls up' the past. We remember other times and other places by the sea, a childhood love of rock pools, say, or shells and spider crabs. But sea music has much deeper roots than these. We know—feel bodily—that this sound is truly ancient. Not merely that our distant ancestors heard what we now hear, but that before there were human ancestors, indeed before there were beings equipped with hearing of any kind, this music played and played. The sea is the '*ur*-womb of the ear'; the origin of life. To listen to this sound is to listen to the sound of our beginnings. This is 'Mother's lullaby', the music of life's nursery.

And it is felt within. The sound of the sea calls up in us a kind of echo, a recollection of an ancient belonging that seems to precede and anticipate our present experience. It is as though the sound 'aimed at gathering [us] back to itself'. In the journal that follows, this being 'gathered back' finds expression through the ancient chant of *om* that roots in Hindu meditative practice.[2]

> I stand for the whole time. It is familiar and comfortable. I chant *om* slowly and softly from the outset and keep it going until the end. ... Listening to the sound of the sea and blending my voice with its steady rhythms seems to 'tune' my voice to the sea, and 'tune out' extraneous noise. I love the bodily sense of it; the joining of my fleshly voice with the voices of the world, the ocean, the wind, the birds. I feel re-placed,

---

[2] The Hindu practice of intoning *om* as a way of aligning the self, body and soul, to the impenetrable source of being and its manifestation in the processes of everyday life, is well known. We tried to learn something of this practice in our attending to the sea. A more detailed introduction to the chant is given on pp. 118-119.

by which I mean, put in my place. And I don't altogether mind the element of reprimand that comes with the phrase. I need to be de-centred—'unselfed' as Iris Murdoch called it—away from myself in the first instance, but away also from the dominant place and dominant voice of the human world. This is a bigger world, a prior world, a depreciated world. I need to move aside, give it space. The alien sound of *om* and its strange repetitive utterance helps break the spell of the self over itself. It lets in the other, the not self, the not human, the sea. I feel the sea sound and stir within, not alien but kin. [J, 11/3/13]

The chant of *om* allows us to participate bodily in the 'chorus' (Chrétien) of beings; 'joining ... my fleshly voice with the voices of the world, the ocean, the wind, the birds'. And like any good chorus there is a blending of inner and outer. The music of the choir and instruments around us becomes the music of the soul, 'not alien but kin'. No doubt this is part of the 'moving' quality of beauty mentioned earlier. To enter into the sound of the sea is inevitably to find ourselves 'put in our place'. And that place is certainly not centre stage. This chorus of nature is very large and very old; 'a bigger world, a prior world, a depreciated world'. Joining it, or even coming close, turns us outward not inward; to the other not to the self. Sea see/hearing and 'unselfing' are two sides of one coin.

Shape

The call of beauty in colour and sound in the sea is not shapeless. It comes formed and then reformed, moving and changing constantly in time and space. The wave is its most exquisite expression. Wave theory in physics, both at the macro-level in fluid dynamics and at the micro-level in quantum mechanics, is an elegant mathematical science. The great 20th century physicist Werner Heisenberg called it 'beautiful'; and he knew he had good reason for it. Wave manifestation in the sea, though the equations (for us) are well out of reach, is as breathtaking as any quantum calculation, and quite as complex in its order.

> The sun is warm on my back, the sea a beautiful blue. It is calm at the Surf Club end of the beach, but here the breakers are rolling splendidly. I am fascinated just watching each wave rise, crest, break, spill and foam; and then watch it all over again, and again, and again. ... I watch

myself watching this beautiful display and realize that I am waiting for the thrill of the 'perfect wave'. It comes. A huge breaker rises up without any sand in the curve, a pure, smooth, glassy, deep, clear, greenish-blue mountain that breaks with a spectacular 'boom' and spills foam and froth of the brightest blue-white you could imagine, then runs, pushing its white breast before it, until with a liquid sigh it washes up on the beach and melts into the sand. ... Involuntarily, I let out an audible 'oohh ...!', a wordless affirmation of wonder and joy. [J, 6/5/14]

The wave process is endless, as ancient as its sound. Its familiarity tends to blind us to its wonder. To watch a 'perfect wave' from its moment of rising to its arrival on the beach is to behold one of the true splendours of nature. We name, that is 'call' (*kalein*) it, a breaker. The word fits. A wave does break to pieces. The smooth heap of moving water reaches a tipping point where its shape can no longer hold the volume of water that makes it. It collapses into turbulence and tumbles over itself, shattered. But this is only half the story. The wave is not only breaking, it is also continuously *making* itself in new forms. So we might just as well call these rolling giants 'makers' as 'breakers'. Surf is not some broken object, like a wine glass splintered on a concrete floor. It is a whole dynamic unity, more complex and intricate than the water that went before, but not without form and certainly not without beauty. The breaker/maker exudes a 'blessed rage for order' (Stevens), spilling its energies into ecstatic patterns of wondrous delicacy and detail. If we were able to see such a wave once only in our life we would be astonished that such a glory had come our way, and would remember it as we remember our children's faces. But we can see it three hundred times an hour, and wonder ebbs away.

The sublime

The sea is beautiful. But it is certainly not benign. Thus far we have emphasised the wondrous aspects of the sea's manifestations; colour, sound and form. Fair enough. These are the first things to impress themselves. But there is another side—perhaps it would be more accurate to say another *dimension*—to the sea and its magnificence. For the most part, and probably as a consequence of attending the sea from the safety of the shore, this other dimension is experienced by us somewhat indirectly, at the edge of perception more than its focus.

> The surf is stupendous. Tiers of great waves 4 or 5 deep, snow-topped, trample toward the beach. The wind is gusting off-shore. Spray streams from the watery peaks. From side on, the waves look like lions' heads with manes of white billowing in the air. Overhead, great dobs of cloud echo the white water in a welter of shapes and sizes, dazzling against the magnificence of the sky. Sunlight spills across everything. I let this great beauty wash through me. I am *in* it, not just observing it. A shiver runs down my back. Ambivalent feelings of wonder and danger jostle within. Everything is benign and in order. But in truth, I am standing in the presence of a pent-up energy which, unleashed, might tear the land in pieces. [J, 16/6/13]

The sea may be 'mother' and its music a 'lullaby'. But, like time itself, and just as relentlessly, the sea is an immensity that devours its children with sublime indifference.

This unsettling awareness was brought home to us with stark and horrifying force. A few days after we arrived in Tathra to continue our pilgrimage in April 2014, a group of swimmers, affectionately known as 'the Pod', made (what we later learned to be) their ritual daily swim from the Surf Club to the wharf, a distance of about a kilometre, where their custom was to share a cup of coffee before setting off for the tasks of the day. This particular morning one of their number, a middle aged woman, for reasons unknown, turned away from the group at one point and began swimming back toward the beach. A moment later she disappeared. An extensive search revealed that she had been taken by a shark. The body was never recovered. The shock and grief in the little town of Tathra was terrible. This beautiful beach took on a radically different ambience.

> I feel horror, stress and fear about what happened here last Thursday. And shudder as my imagination involuntarily conjures up the wrenching lunge of a great shark from below. I think of all the words I have used so easily of the sea: serene, beautiful, peaceful, gentle, choppy. The shark attack brings a new sense of the alien medium

which is this water; a medium which harbours beings for whom I am prospective prey. A meal, nothing more. [G, 6/4/14]

A few days later the Surf Club, of which the victim was a member, held a memorial service for her on the beach, exactly at the time and place from which 'the Pod' had taken to the water that fateful morning. The community turned out in force. All the speakers at the service were one in saying how much she respected the sea, loved the sea, delighted in the sea. The sea was her home in life and in death, they said. It was deeply moving.

A paradox. The service is held on the very beach where this woman had been so awfully killed. But today the sea is at its beautiful best. Perfectly formed and regularly breaking waves provide a musical accompaniment to the proceedings that would rival Bach on the organ. And yet this same water, these very same waves, a few days ago were the theatre of human horror. ... The capacity of the sea to close over us and then proceed as if nothing has happened is a blunt reminder that the sea is alien. I know almost nothing about it. Nothing of its history, physical structure, life forms, secret changes. I am on the fringe—literally on the edge—of a mountainous mystery. ... I feel two things strongly: the impenetrable otherness of the sea; and my pathetic attempts to attend to it. [G, 14/4/14]

People have always been aware of the contrast and connection between the beautiful which induces delight; and the uncanny, which calls forth fear and terror in our human interaction with nature. The latter—long named 'the sublime' by philosophers—has, like its counterpoint beauty, generated much erudite debate over the years.[3] In popular parlance, the word sublime has now lost most of its earlier connection with the uncanny or horrifying, while retaining a sense of the exulted, the glorious and the great. This latter aspect is certainly emphasised by Kant. 'Sublime is the name given to that which is absolutely great', he writes.[4]

---

[3] A fascinating introduction to the whole subject of the sublime can be found in Timothy M. Costelloe, *The Sublime: From Antiquity to the Present* (Cambridge: Cambridge University Press, 2012).

[4] Immanuel Kant, *The Critique of Judgement*, trans. James Creed Meredith (Oxford: Oxford University Press, 1911), §25, p. 248. (This work was first published in 1790). Kant (1724

For him, the sublime is strictly speaking a limit concept; that which is great without comparison (i.e., 'absolutely great') refers to the infinite or to God. But in the finite world of perception, including the world of nature, we meet with encounters that can be called, in a derivative fashion, sublime. 'The astonishment amounting almost to terror, the awe and thrill of devout feeling, that takes hold of one when gazing upon the prospect of mountains ascending to heaven, deep ravines and torrents raging there, deep shadowed solitudes that invite brooding melancholy, and the like'; these are portals of the sublime for Kant. Nature in its extremes, in 'its wildest and most irregular disorder and desolation', rather than in its serene perfection, is what arouses in us the sense and idea of the sublime.[5] Hence, Kant makes his famous distinction between the beautiful and the sublime; the distinction between form and formlessness, limit and limitlessness, part and totality.

> The beautiful in nature is a question of the form of object, and this consists in limitation, whereas the sublime is to be found in an object even devoid of form, so far as it immediately involves, or else by its presence provokes a representation of limitlessness, yet with a superadded thought of its totality.[6]

In connection with the ocean in particular, Kant argues that if we would feel what is sublime we must contemplate the sea not in terms of any finite 'ends' that we might imagine for it, for example, the sea as home for aquatic creatures, or as reservoir 'from which are drawn the vapours that fill the air with clouds', or as a highway for international commerce. Instead, we must

> be able to see sublimity in the ocean, regarding it, as the poets do, according to what the impression upon the eye reveals, as, let us say, in its calm a clear mirror of water bounded only by the heavens, or, be it disturbed, as threatening to overwhelm and engulf everything.[7]

−1804) was a German philosopher central to the development of modern western thinking.
[5] Kant, *The Critique of Judgement*, §23, p. 246.
[6] Kant, *The Critique of Judgement*, §23, p. 244.
[7] Kant, *The Critique of Judgement*, §29, p. 270.

Again, the qualities of boundlessness and lurking danger define the sublime. In his early and influential essay on the sublime, Edmund Burke argues that the sublime and the beautiful are mutually exclusive, as light is exclusive of darkness, as terror of delight.[8] But Kant opts for a more incremental and interconnected interpretation. He uses the term 'splendid' to describe objects which produce in us feeling for *both* the beautiful and the sublime. Our journal seems to be Kantian more than Burkean in this regard. The paradox of the memorial service was exactly this, that both things—beauty and horror—were present simultaneously. And one of the remarkable features of the service was how 'the Pod' insisted upon reclaiming the ocean as beautiful, life-giving, welcoming, loved despite what had happened. The daily swim resumed almost immediately. It was astonishing and moving to see that group of grieving people walk together into the sea, then plunge under and start to swim.

Burke and Kant agree that the mind is 'set in motion' by the experience of both the beautiful and the sublime. In the case of beauty the motion is unilateral, toward delight and 'restful contemplation'.[9] But in that of the sublime, it is distinctly vibratory, 'repulsion and attraction' are produced by the same object.[10] For Burke 'terror is in all cases whatsoever, either more openly or latently, the ruling principle of the sublime.'[11] But the terror is qualified by pleasure and attraction; 'a sort of delightful horror, a sort of tranquillity tinged with terror.' For Kant the emphasis is more the other way around; the 'awe and thrill' of 'devout experience' produces in us 'astonishment' which (also) 'amounts almost to terror.'[12]

---

[8] Edmund Burke, *A Philosophical Enquiry into the Origin of Our Ideas of the Sublime and Beautiful*, (1756). An extract from this work is reprinted in James Bradley, *The Penguin Book of the Sea* (Camberwell, Victoria: Penguin Group (Australia), 2010), pp. 41-42.
[9] Kant, *The Critique of Judgement*, §27, p. 258.
[10] Kant, *The Critique of Judgement*, §27, p. 258.
[11] Bradley, *The Penguin Book of the Sea*, p. 42. Compare also Pascal's famous remark about the boundlessness of space. 'The eternal silence of these infinite spaces terrifies me.'
[12] This ambivalence of feeling in association with the sublime is again emphasised in Rudolf Otto's famous analysis of the experience of the Holy. For Otto this experience is characterised by a sense of a *mysterium tremendum et fascinans* – a mystery at once tremendous (fearful) and fascinating. See Rudolf Otto, *The Idea of the Holy*, trans. John W. Harvey (Harmondsworth, Middlesex: Penguin, 1959).

For the project of sea see/hearing, beauty and the sublime are inextricably intertwined. On the whole, for us, beauty predominates. Doubtless this is a consequence of the relative safety of our position of observation. We are not swimming for that distant wharf. And although the word 'sublime' does not appear much in the journal (a function perhaps of our acceptance of its common connotations), its referent, that sense of threat or terror, does; and especially when our attention to the sea takes on its broadest aspects—far horizons, dark depths, massive power, enormous size and the like. The 'limitlessness' which Kant talks about *is* characteristic of the experience. Even in the case of the shark attack, which is a very particular ('limited') event, a large part of the terror induced has to do with a sense of unknown ('limitless') threats that lurk in the vastness of the sea. We were impressed that there was no call for the capture and killing of the shark that attacked at Tathra. In other cases around Australia such demands are sometimes made and carried out. It is not just revenge. The demand has to do with an urgent need to bring order and control back into life. The action of killing the killer helps us feel we can set some limits to the sense of a 'formless terror' that such events unleash in our imaginations. The sublime is re-caged.

The beauty of the sea cannot be deeply entered without at the same time encountering the sublimity of the sea. And the feelings that accompany both—delight, wonder, admiration, pleasure, exultation in the case of beauty—astonishment, respect, fear, terror in the case of the sublime, may be distinguishable, but they are hardly separable. Attempts to find some composite description; 'delightful terror' (Edmund Burke), 'agreeable horror' (Moses Mendelssohn) seem somewhat forced, but they do alert us to an aspect of the beautiful that is widespread, and especially intense when our encounters are with nature untamed; nature in its 'inhuman' (Stevens) grandeur.

The beauty of the sea is one beauty. Isn't *it* beautiful? But the manifestation of that beauty is complex. It calls to us through many channels; colour, sound, shape and immensity being four of the most obvious. Each of these has its own beauty, different from the beauty of the others, yet intrinsically connected to them. We can think separately of 'blue' and 'roar' and 'crest' and 'magnitude' and meditate on the different ways these forms affect us, as we have done. But it is important to remember that such analysis is an accessory after the fact. In the first instance we undergo one experience, one unified perception of the sea. A blue wave crests and breaks against the horizon that shimmers at the edge of the world. We see it, we hear it, we feel it as a unity. But can we say more specifically what this *one* perception of the sea entails? Before we attempt an answer some further analytical work is needed.

Beauty and truth

Carl Friedrich von Weizsäcker, the great German physicist/philosopher, argues that 'Beauty is a form of the truth'; and 'the sense of the beautiful is a genuine perception, that is, a particular capacity for perceiving reality.'[13] We encounter 'truth', or aspects of what is 'real', in a variety of ways. Scientific enquiry, for example, yields insight into the way the world functions physically. The oceanographer describes the chemical composition of sea water or the equations that govern wave formation. Practical engagement with the sea gives rise to a different sort of truth. The fisherman or woman knows the local currents, intuits the likely movements of fish, and senses immediately the vagaries of wind and water. But, if von Weizsäcker is correct, perceiving the beauty of the ocean is also a way of perceiving reality, of coming to know aspects of the truth about the world. What might these be? Can we uncover more explicitly what 'form of truth' comes to us in the beauty of the ocean? We begin our search for an answer by looking first at the most basic element of the experiences described above, our direct sense perceptions.

Von Weizsäcker makes a simple threefold analysis of perception, to which he later adds a fourth. (i) First there are the pure *sensations* presented to our minds by our sense organs. I *see* blue. I *hear* a roar. I *taste* salt.[14] (ii) Then there are *judgements* that seem implicit in the sensations. Standing on the shore, I *think* 'this is the ocean at Tathra'.

---

[13] Carl Friedrich von Weizsäcker, *Zeit und Wissen* (München: Carl Hanser Verlag, 1992), p. 411. This citation comes from an important essay entitled "Das Schöne" (Beauty or The Beautiful), pp. 409-420. We are indebted to this essay for much of what follows in this section. All translations from the German are ours.

[14] No doubt these sensations are themselves complex phenomena involving the intricate physical operation of eyes, ears, nose, etc., but that lies beyond our scope and competence here.

(iii) In addition, accompanying these sensations and judgments certain *affects* or feelings inevitably arise. I *feel* 'almost physically overwhelmed', 'exhilarated'. Von Weizsäcker insists that these are not three distinct operations. They belong together intrinsically. I *hear* a roar; I *think* 'the thunder of falling water'; I *feel* 'in tune' with the voice of the sea. I *see* a group on the beach; I *think* the memorial service for a woman taken by a shark; I *feel* 'sadness, horror, stress and fear'. The differentiation of sensation, judgment and feeling is a subsequent analysis of an experience that is originally undifferentiated. Without the advantage of such philosophical rumination, we simply say: 'I see the astonishing beauty of the Tathra Ocean.' 'I hear the ancient sound of the surf.' 'I feel a part of a common human grief and fear.' And no one is in any doubt about what we mean.

(iv) Feeling is not the final component of the act of perception, according to von Weizsäcker. 'Perception and *action* cannot be separated', he argues.[15] The vision of overwhelming beauty makes me feel, 'I can't get enough'. And so I *decide* to continue with this practice of sea see/hearing. The mesmerizing sound of the surf lifts me out of myself. I *determine*, 'I need to be decentred ... away from myself'. The grief and terror of the shark attack jolts me. I am *pressed* to re-think my whole attitude to the sea. That perception can, to a certain extent, be uncoupled from action is a capacity that differentiates human behaviour from that of other animals. It allows us, at least to a certain degree, to replace reaction by action; 'must' by 'will'. This introduces the importance of memory into the perceptual process. Recollections of childhood, a store of concepts, ideas, words, cultural images and assumptions, and so on, offer a range of options from which we can choose to act and think in relation to our sensual encounter with the sea.

This ability leads von Weizsäcker to introduce the important idea of *Mitwahnehmung*, or co-perception, into his discussion of beauty. 'Rooted in this highly differentiated kind of experience [i.e., the fourfold complex of perception]' he writes, 'is a phenomenon which I like to call the co-perception (*Mitwahrnehmung*) of a higher level (*Stufe*), and the

---

[15] von Weizsäcker, *Zeit und Wissen*, p. 412. Italics added.

sense of the beautiful is, if I am not mistaken, just such a co-perception.'[16] In perceiving beautiful things—this colour, that wave form, these sounds—we perceive simultaneously, von Weizsäcker insists, something that exceeds the particular beauties before us and unites them as being examples that warrant the same description: 'this is beautiful'. He calls this co-perception 'the sense of the beautiful'. In every particular sense perception, judgment, and feeling there lies embedded another, higher, more general 'co-perception' that is the condition which makes the particular perception, judgment and feeling possible in the first place.

'What is it about this colour' that 'I can't get enough'? Something presses for recognition in and with the perception of *this* 'silky blue'. The colour is 'spilling over', pushing us beyond immediate impressions. With the perception of this blue comes a co-perception of a 'bench mark' blue, a sense of completion or perfection of colour that seems to reflect back into our experience and invite a comparison with and judgement of the colour we are now looking at. And what is it about the sound of breaking waves that seems to bring with it a sense that this is 'an ancient sound', a 'deep sound', a sound that reaches out to us from the origins of things? To be sure we are hearing this particular sound at this particular moment, but it seems to include a co-reference to a reality that exceeds the moment. And the perception of the grieving crowd on the beach. It harbours not only the awareness of a particular tragedy, but also a wider sense—a co-perception—of what we might call the mystery and mayhem of life. On this beach on this day in the midst of mourning this tragedy, we sense also the contingency of existence at large; our life is given, not owned. And we feel the weight of chance; things happen to us that make us feel both the preciousness and the precariousness of life. We know 'being alive' takes place just once, just now. Perceptions of colour, sound, shape and the sublime bring with them co-perceptions (however hazy) of perfection, completion, depth, contingency, and the like. This is what Chrétien means when he argues that the call of beauty in beautiful things draws us back to itself. 'The in-itself of beauty is to be for-the-other, aimed at gathering the other [i.e., us] back to itself.'[17]

---

[16] von Weizsäcker, *Zeit und Wissen*, p. 413.
[17] See footnote 1.

We may choose to disregard such co-perceptions or dismiss them as fanciful meanderings. But it is hard to deny their presence in and with the original experience.

'The harmony without which we cannot live'

We began this chapter with the common experience of encountering the sea as beautiful. Initially this experience is single and whole. It takes in the sea not just in particular aspects—water, waves, colours, shadows, sand—but in its most inclusive and general sense. It apprehends the sea in the broad context of sun, sky, land, air, clouds, light and so on. 'Isn't it beautiful?' refers to this scene as a whole and to the whole of the scene. It tries to absorb everything that manifests itself to us in the full blaze of the day. But *what* is given in this global manifestation of beauty? Ronald Hepburn, the British philosopher, speaks of 'metaphysical imagination' in relation to such broad, inclusive apprehensions of the world. The language is somewhat daunting, but what he is pointing to is really an aspect of that simple and spontaneous response to the sea. 'Isn't it beautiful?' What Hepburn means by metaphysical imagination is simply 'an element of interpretation that helps determine the *overall experience* of a scene in nature.' It is metaphysical not in the sense that we speculate about the ultimate nature of reality, but in the sense that we look beyond immediate physical perceptions of a scene toward an appreciation of its unity. Our attention is directed 'to the *whole of experience* and not only to what is experienced at the present moment.'[18]

This has strong resonances with von Weizsäcker's concept of *Mitwahrnehmung* (co-perception). Something is given with the multiple phenomena that clamour for our attention in the details of a scene in nature that transcends particular sense impressions and lends them unity, coherence and depth. For both Hepburn and von Weizsäcker this 'given' comes embedded in the experience itself and is in no way a mere add on. The *imagination* in Hepburn's 'metaphysical imagination' is not a fanciful makeover of an experience that is basically something other. It is the bringing to awareness of what is perhaps hidden or veiled

---

[18] Ronald Hepburn, "Landscape and Metaphysical Imagination," *Environmental Values* 5 (1996), p. 192, cited in Emily Brady, "The Environmental Sublime," in Costelloe, *The Sublime: From Antiquity to the Present*, p. 176. Italics added.

(Heidegger) in the phenomena themselves.[19] But this veiled thing, 'is no less an element of the concrete present landscape experience: it is fused with the sensory components, *not a meditation aroused by these*.'[20]

What, then, is 'fused with the sensory components' in our encounter with the beauty of the sea? Hepburn and von Weizsäcker are right. It is not so easy to say. Yet in our experience their claim is correct. There is a 'something' that is present in our experience, even if veiled and hard to get at.

> The things I can say about the sea are all so obvious. The colours are beautiful. The water is lively. Waves break. Sea sounds emerge from the process effortlessly. And so on. ... But all this is not really what it is about today. At this moment I have a sense of peacefulness, of being-where-I-belong, and being welcome here. It's not an ecstatic experience in some eerie way. It feels very ordinary. What is it? ... I think I have a sense of being 'fed' or 'nourished'. Something is being provided for me, without my request or effort. Something I need. What? I'm not sure. The nearest I can get is to say 'the truth'. That sounds pompous. But I don't know how else to express it. I feel some deep truth of being, including my life, is here. It's being held out to me. But I don't quite know how to take it. It seems real and living. But out of reach. I remember Chrétien's reference to Merleau-Ponty. The call of the sensible, he says, is 'the *logos* that pronounces itself in every sensible thing.'[21] But what is that? [G, 25/4/14]

If some *logos*, some word or truth, is pronounced here, what is it? Chrétien says beauty is a call that *recalls* us to ourselves, to our origins. 'The event of the beautiful lies in the fact that the origin calls out audibly

---

[19] 'There is essentially nothing "behind" the phenomena of phenomenology, yet what is to become a phenomenon may well be in retreat. Phenomenology is needed precisely because phenomena, most often and initially, are *not* given. Veiled-being (*Verdecktheit*) is the complementary concept of "phenomenon."' Martin Heidegger, *Sein und Zeit*, 36, cited in Chrétien, *The Call and the Response*, p. 87.

[20] Hepburn, "Landscape and Metaphysical Imagination," p. 192, in Costelloe, *The Sublime: From Antiquity to the Present*, p. 176. Italics added.

[21] Maurice Merleau-Ponty, *Le Visible et l'invisible* (Paris: Gallimard, 1964), p. 261, cited in Chrétien, *The Call and the Response*, p. 15.

in the visible, calling us back to the origin.'[22] That seems true to the extract from the journal just quoted. But both remain vague, without any clear delineation. What 'origin', what 'truth', are we talking about?

Hepburn takes us a further step. Functioning in a non-fanciful mode in response to natural objects and phenomena ('It feels very ordinary'), Hepburn argues, the metaphysical imagination 'interprets nature as revealing ... insights about things such as the meaning of life, the human condition, or our place in the cosmos.'[23] Once again, this is broad brush stuff, but it points us in the right direction. The power of beauty to attract us, to draw us into itself, involves all kinds of elements to do with the love of colour, sound and wonderful shapes. Beauty also grips us with a sense of awe and, on occasion, even terror. But ultimately, in and through all these particularities, beauty attracts us, holds our attention; beauty calls us, because it concerns the 'meaning of our lives'. Of course, this can sound like yet another case of crass anthropocentrism. Beauty is great because it is all about *us*. There is no escaping such possible distortion. Self-centredness is a constant bias in all human efforts to relate to others, to the world, and to beauty. However, the experience of beauty as Hepburn, von Weizsäcker and Chrétien envisage it is anything but narcissistic. Beauty calls us to ourselves and to our origins precisely by calling us *out* of ourselves—'unselfing' us—by calling us 'to our place in the cosmos', *not* the cosmos to its place in us. The truly beautiful in this sense is 'out of reach'; it beckons and calls us, but from beyond ourselves, and it most certainly does not bend to us.

> What we conquer is the small,
> and the success makes us small.
> The eternal and the immense
> will not be bent by us.[24]

Just this is the difference between the beautiful and the pretty.

Von Weizsäcker, as we have seen, claims that beauty is a form of the truth, and 'the sense of the beautiful ... a particular capacity for perceiving

---

[22] Chrétien, *The Call and the Response*, p. 9.
[23] Hepburn, "Landscape and Metaphysical Imagination," p. 192 in Costelloe, *The Sublime: From Antiquity to the Present*, p. 176.
[24] Rainer Maria Rilke, *Der Schauende*, our translation.

reality.'[25] This is a modified form of Platonism. Beauty is a form given to the human mind not created by it. But—and this is the modification—its perception and interpretation is historically and culturally shaped. How beauty is interpreted in 21st century settler Australian society differs markedly from the way beauty is perceived and received in Yuin history and culture. That said and agreed, what can we say about the perception of 'reality' that is given in the 'whole experience' of attending to the ocean in our time and place? What does 'Isn't it beautiful?' finally mean? A lovely wave? No. A stirring sound? No. A threatening danger? No. What we finally sense looking at the ocean in its full glory on a sunlit day at Tathra is, albeit inchoately, the manifestation of what was classically called the 'Harmony of Nature', or what von Weizsäcker calls, 'the ecological balance' (*das ökologische Gleichgewicht*[26]).

For something like 4 billion years, the ocean has been evolving in intricate interaction with land and air, day and night, heat and cold, depth and surface, gravitational pull and wind disturbance. Across this enormous interval of time, the great hydrological cycle of evaporation, cloud formation, precipitation and inundation has scoured the land and drained all manner of chemical and biochemical materials through the rivers back into the sea, gradually building and changing its chemical composition. The steady rotation of the earth on its axis, bringing constantly changing periods of light and dark, has driven great currents of air and water to circulate around the planet, regulating temperatures, distributing moisture, generating nutrients. The long slow process of the formation and evolution of life, beginning with the tiniest of single cell creatures and leading to the brilliant abundance of a million different life forms, arises in and continues to depend on the fecundity of the seas, which in turn depends on all the other great interlocking natural cycles. All this, and everything else that belongs to the web of being that makes up planet Earth, is implicit in the spectacle that the sea presents to our senses. This is what its beauty *is*. This is, finally, what we 'see' and 'hear' when we see and hear the sea.

---

[25] von Weizsäcker, *Zeit und Wissen*, p. 411.
[26] von Weizsäcker, *Zeit und Wissen*, p. 417.

And clearly it is fundamental to our existence. Human beings are latecomers in this massive, evolving planetary interaction and balance of things. We depend absolutely for our lives on the air, water, light, plants and animals, which make up the habitat that produces and sustains everything. Thus, when we 'perceive this balance as beautiful', von Weizsäcker says, '*we perceive the harmony without which we cannot live*.'[27] That is why, ultimately, this beauty holds such a fascination, such a 'pull' on us. And that is why, amongst other things, this beauty, the beauty of the sea, gives us a measure which transcends what we might regard as our immediate (economic) interests by which to judge our human actions in the world and, indeed, to evaluate what are, in the final analysis, our *real* interests as individuals and as a species. Von Weizsäcker concludes, speaking in a somewhat sombre mode, 'a humanity which disregards and destroys the balance [i.e., the beauty] of the landscape, presuming it to be economically inconsequential, is a humanity gone mad.'[28] To disfigure this beauty means not only to deface what is exquisite to behold; it means to undermine our own foundations in the world. This is the origin from which the call of beauty proceeds. And this is the end to which the call of beauty invites.

Call of Beauty / **Plastic Ocean**

It is cold and dark. Late winter in Melbourne. We are driving across the city. A lecture is to be held in a church somewhere out in the eastern suburbs. To do with plastics and the ocean, we're told. Traffic is heavy. The going is slow. We are among those few hardy souls who still linger in the vanishing world of pre-GPS navigation systems. An ancient Melways street directory lies open on the dashboard. The passenger light inside the car is dim. Peering at the page, Jan says she thinks she can find the way. But at some point we make a false turn. Now we are on a divided highway heading in the wrong direction. It seems forever before a break in the median strip shows up and we manage an illegal U-turn. By the

---

[27] von Weizsäcker, *Zeit und Wissen*, p. 417. Italics added.
[28] von Weizsäcker, *Zeit und Wissen*, p. 417.

time we pull up at our destination it's way past the hour. The church is packed. A man who seems to be in the know ushers us to a seat at the very back. We slip in muttering apologies to those around. Up front in the distance, a young woman is standing at a lectern. She is speaking quietly, but it is immediately clear she has the full attention of her audience. On a screen to her left is a picture of a large dark brown bird with wings raised. It has a pinkish bill and strange white coloured legs. As the talk proceeds, we learn it is a Flesh-footed Shearwater (*Puffinus carneipes*). Its home is on Lord Howe Island, 600 kilometres east of Port Macquarie off the coast of NSW.

The speaker is Dr Jennifer Lavers from Monash University. She has been studying sea birds in Southern Australia for years, and particularly the shearwaters. The colony on Lord Howe is the largest in the world, she says, but it has been in serious decline for more than two decades. 'Bycatch' (so-called) of the birds on long line fishing trawls and loss of habitat have contributed to the decline. However, she is concerned most about plastic debris that the shearwaters ingest, mistaking it for food. An image goes up on the screen. It shows the skeletal remains of a juvenile shearwater. Ragged remnants of dark decaying feathers cluster around a delicate ribcage picked clean of flesh and bleached white in the sun. In the centre of this little temple of curved bones, where once the digestive tract of the animal worked its magic, lies a heap of plastic rubble—blue, red, yellow, white, green. Here you can make out the lid of a small bottle. There what looks like the cap of a biro. The rest ... well, just bits and pieces. The speaker holds up an array of snap-lock plastic bags. Even at this distance there is no mistaking it. Each bag holds a cluster of plastic trinkets, which is the detritus found in the belly of a dead shearwater bird. Numbered. Weighed. Dated. One bag, the remnants of a chick which weighed 445gm when it died, amounts to 276 separate pieces of plastic, weighing 64.1gm or 14.4% of the bird's body mass. 'That's the equivalent of you or me eating 10 kilograms of plastic rubbish,' Lavers says softly.[29]

---

[29] For a detailed report and analysis of this data see, Jennifer L. Lavers *et al*, "Plastic ingestion by Flesh-footed Shearwaters (*Puffinus carneipes*): Implications for fledgling body condition and the accumulation of plastic-derived chemicals," *Environmental Pollution* 187 (2014), pp. 124-129. Available at www.elsevier.com/locate/envpol. Lavers now works

Once ingested, the plastic debris contributes to a wide range of impacts on the birds. It 'can block or rupture the digestive tract and leak contaminants into the bird's blood stream resulting in ulcerations, liver damage, infertility, and in many cases, death.'[30] In 2005, Lavers found that 79% of fledgling shearwaters on Lord Howe Island had significant—meaning detrimental levels of—plastic debris in their guts. By 2014, that number had reached almost 100%. 'It's just so heartbreaking to go back year after year,' she says, 'and see the problem get worse and worse.' And the fate of the shearwaters is a significant marker. As it goes with the shearwaters, so it goes with virtually every other sea bird of Australia.

At the end of the talk, Jennifer Lavers makes an appeal. 'Each of us can do something about this starting now,' she says. 'Cut down, or cut out, your use of plastic bags. Balloons are a disaster. They're brightly coloured. They attract attention. And they completely clog the digestive systems of animals that eat them. And they take years to break down. Be careful how you dispose of plastic toothbrushes. You'd be amazed how many end up in the digestive tracts of large birds, like the Albatross. Bottle tops are lethal. And if you fish, don't leave plastic lures or broken fishing line behind in the sea. They always go somewhere. And it's often onto or into the bodies of fish or seals or dolphins or birds. The ocean is drowning in plastic. Don't make it worse.'

Jennifer Lavers' view that seabirds are 'the sentinels of marine health' is undisputed in the community of those who have studied the problem. There is now no place in the oceans, however remote geographically (the Antarctic) or however deep beneath the surface (the Mariana Trench), where humanly generated pollutants are not found, and found to be increasing. Our generation's global signature, says Sylvia Earle, 'is written in hard trash, heavy metals, chemical wastes and spills, agricultural runoff, industrial and domestic wastes, oil spills, radioactive materials, even noise and electromagnetic fields.'[31] Jennifer Lavers is right again, that amongst this avalanche of rubbish, plastic is far and away the most

---

for the University of Tasmania.
30 Jennifer Lavers, "Seabirds as sentinels of marine health," www.jenniferlavers.org/research/, p. 2.
31 Sylvia Earle, *Sea Change: A Message of the Oceans* (New York: Fawcett Books, 1995), p. 227.

abundant, dangerous and persistent debris in the marine environment. And it is growing at an exponential rate.

Plastics, we can't live without them. (Though once—not so long ago we're told—we did!) Think of the day's routine. The alarm clock that (maddeningly) just went off by the bed is plastic, as is the shade on the bedside lamp, and the switch that controls it. In the bathroom the toothbrush is plastic, and the cup it sits in. The tube that contains the toothpaste is plastic, and beside it is a razor made of plastic sitting there in its plastic holder. The soap container is light blue, and plastic. The toilet seat and the reservoir above it are all plastic; so is the shower curtain, and the hooks that hold it to the rail. A plastic waste basket sits in the corner, a plastic bag as its liner. The comb and hair dryer by the basin are largely plastic, as is the mirror frame. In the kitchen, the jug standing ready for that first desperately needed cup of coffee is moulded plastic, red in this instance. And those lovely fair trade coffee grounds are right next to it in an airtight plastic jar. The microwave above the toaster presents as a solid black and white plastic box. The cupboards surrounding it are covered with a veneer of white plastic; really fresh looking, easy to clean. In the fridge the cholesterol-reducing margarine is snug in its plastic tub. Last night's left over chicken sits in a plastic snap-top box. The mineral water, 'with a twist of lemon', resting in the base of the door comes in a sexily-shaped plastic bottle with a yellow plastic lid. In the pantry a dozen packets of goodies, from muesli to cous cous are sealed in plastic wrapping. Beneath them is the 60 meter roll of cling-wrap plastic filament. Plastic bags ('biodegradable') from last week's shopping sit in another plastic bag awaiting disposal. The dishes from last night's dinner have dripped dried nicely in their plastic drainer. And we haven't even picked up the iphone, turned on the computer, or got to the car.

Plastics are an integral and vital part of the global economy, combining unrivalled functional properties with low cost. According to a recent study by the World Economic Forum (WEF),

> Plastics production has surged over the past 50 years, from 15 million tonnes in 1964 to 311 million tonnes in 2014, and is expected to double again over the next 20 years, as plastics come to serve increasingly many applications.

The difficulty is that safe disposal and recycling of plastic has not kept pace with the burgeoning production. The WEF estimates that 95% of plastic packaging material, valued at somewhere between $80 and $120 billion annually, is lost to the economy after a short one term usage. The recycling rate for plastics in general is even lower than that for plastic packaging (which is about 14%) and both are well below global recycling rates for paper (58%) and iron and steel (70-90%). As a result,

> Each year, at least 8 million tonnes of plastics leak into the ocean—which is equivalent to dumping the contents of one garbage truck into the ocean every minute. If no action is taken, this is expected to increase to two per minute by 2030 and four per minute by 2050.[32]

Because of the complexity of the problem, it is difficult to get exact figures, but the best research currently available estimates that there are somewhere between 150 and 250 million tonnes of plastic garbage in the ocean today. That means in 'a business-as-usual scenario, the ocean is expected to contain 1 tonne of plastic for every 3 tonnes of fish by 2025, and by 2050, more plastics than fish (by weight).'[33]

This has implications not only for the state of the oceans, but also for the state of the atmosphere. Given the present low level of recycling, 90% of plastics produced today derive from 'virgin fossil feedstocks'. This represents about 6% of current global oil consumption, which in turn is equivalent to the oil consumption of the world's aviation industry. 'If the current strong growth of plastic usage continues as expected, the plastic sector will account for 20% of total oil consumption and 15% of the global annual carbon budget by 2050.'[34] This is the budget that must be met in order to achieve the accepted goal of the Paris agreement to keep global temperature rise below 2°C by the turn of the century.

Once present in the ocean, plastic items are dispersed by ocean currents and wind patterns resulting in their ubiquitous global

---

[32] *The New Plastics Economy: Rethinking the future of plastics*, World Economic Forum, 2016 at www3.weforum.org/docs/WEF_The_New_Plastics_Economy.pdf, p. 7.
[33] *The New Plastics Economy*, p. 7. See also Jennifer L. Lavers *et al*, "Plastic Ingestion by fish in the Southern Hemisphere: A baseline study and review of methods," Article in press, *Marine Pollution Bulletin* (2016), available at www.elsevier.com/locate/marpolbul, p. 1.
[34] *The New Plastics Economy*, p. 15.

distribution. Some of this is visible—we see it washed up on any beach around the country that we choose to visit—but most of it is not, anyway not from the shore. In 2005, the United Nations Environmental Programme estimated that over 13,000 pieces of litter float on every square kilometre of ocean.[35] That concentration has increased in the intervening years. In addition to this general distribution, there are regions where rubbish is known to concentrate. The North Pacific Gyre (or Great Pacific Garbage Patch) is a vast convergence of marine trash containing levels of floating micro debris representing near to a million items per square kilometre. The patch swirls in the currents of the North Pacific Ocean, located near Hawaii, roughly between 135° to 155°W and 35° to 42°N, and extends over an indeterminate area—as big as Texas?, as big as France?—with estimates varying according to the degree of plastic concentration used to define it. However, this is merely one of five such huge trash vortices. Others are located in each of the major ocean basins.[36] Sylvia Earle comments:

> The sunlit surface of the sea is the place where most of Earth's oxygen is generated, where the great majority of carbon dioxide is extracted from the atmosphere, where food is generated to power the great ocean food webs. Does it matter that this critical part of Earth's life-support system is awash in plastic minestrone?[37]

As well as debris that floats on or near the surface, plastic trash spreads throughout the whole water column and litters the ocean floor. All of it is potentially dangerous, even lethal, to sea life of every kind, seabirds as we have seen, but also whales, whale sharks, seals, dolphins, turtles and dugongs. Indeed, writes Jennifer Lavers, 'negative encounters between wildlife and marine plastic pollution have increased from 267 species in 1997 to 693 species in 2015, demonstrating an increase of nearly 75%

---

[35] *Marine Litter: an analytical overview*, United Nations Environmental Programme, 2005 at www.unep.org/regionalseas/marinelitter/punlications/docs/overview.pdf, p. 4. Also the later publication, *Marine Litter: A Global Challenge*, UNEP 2009 at www.unep.org/Regionalseas/marinelitter/publications/docs/Marine_Litter_A_Global_Challenge.pdf.
[36] Sylvia Earle, *The World is Blue: How Our Fate and the Ocean's Are One*, (Washington, D. C.: National Geographic, 2010), pp. 101-102.
[37] Earle, *The World is Blue*, p. 112.

2. Call of Beauty / Sea of Plastic

in less than two decades.'[38] As with the shearwaters, so with fish and marine mammals. The plastic is indigestible. When swallowed it blocks the digestive tract and inhibits or shuts down food assimilation. Sylvia Earle reports that 'a whale, washed ashore in California in 2007, died of "unknown causes" but had 181 kilograms (400 pounds) of plastic in its stomach.'[39] The total death toll from such pollution is unknown, but it is measured in the hundreds of thousands annually.

And plastics are highly durable. They can retain their original form in the ocean for tens or even hundreds of years. Eden is a town situated about 30 minutes drive south from Tathra; a popular tourist, fishing and boating centre in this lovely part of the world. We heard there was an ocean research institute there and we are keen to visit it. Still without that GPS, we lose our way several times before finally locating a modest building down near the marina. This is home to the Sapphire Coast Marine Discovery Centre. It turns out to be mainly an educational centre for primary and secondary school students, but has a modest research lab for visiting scientists. 'More a base to work from', our guide tells us. We get the impression that the ocean research being done here is driven by Universities or Government Departments. The latter are mainly concerned with fishing. One to three nautical miles out from the coast line is, apparently, under State jurisdiction. From 3 to 100 nautical miles is Commonwealth responsibility. Our guide says management of fisheries and fishing in this area is about as good as can be. The biggest problem is illegal fishing, which is almost impossible to police. And the problem gets worse the further north you go.

After this introduction we are left to our own devices. The Centre has some fascinating displays; photographs, artefacts, exhibits of marine life both living and dead, local history and information. One in particular catches our attention. It is a time line tracing the durability of common items of rubbish found in the oceans around Tathra.

---

[38] Lavers, "Plastic ingestion by fish in the Southern Hemisphere," p. 1.
[39] Earle, *The World is Blue*, p. 105.

apple core – 1 month

newspapers – 2½ months

paper towels – 3 months

cardboard box – 4 months

milk carton – 5 months

woollen glove – 1 year

plywood – 2 years

cigarette butt – 10 years

plastic bags – 20 years

foam cup – 50 years

styrofoam buoy – 100 years

fishing float – 130 years

plastic straws – 150 years

plastic cutlery – 160 years

aluminium can – 200 years

plastic containers – 230 years

plastic bottle lids – 250 years

disposable nappies – 450 years

plastic bottles – 500 years

microfilament fishing line – 600 years

Plastic heads the rubbish endurance test by orders of magnitude. It lasts and lasts. And even when it does break down, it does not go away. Plastic disintegrates into smaller and smaller particles while retaining its basic chemical properties. As a result, it gets dispersed more finely and more widely than in its macro forms. Then it becomes available for ingestion by smaller and smaller animals, including oysters, shellfish and even plankton. Thus plastic and all the chemicals that are used in its manufacture enter the food chain from the very base, and rise from there. And it is a cumulative phenomenon. What is dumped in the ocean stays in the ocean and continues to circulate in water and in living marine bodies for time periods measured not in years but in centuries. There appears to be no limit, writes Sylvia Earle,

> to how far down the food chain the accumulation of plastics and their toxic chemical baggage can go, reaching even the microbial swarms that dominate life in the sea. ... The consequences to ocean chemistry are simply unknown, but they need to be understood and factored in to the growing numbers of issues directly affecting the ocean's health, and thus our own.[40]

That this effort 'to understand' is beginning to be taken seriously at the highest levels is encouraging. The WEF report on *The New Plastics Economy* (2016) is a leading case in point. 'The plastic ocean'[41] is a clear and present threat to that beautiful marine 'harmony without which we cannot live.' Plastics are not about to go away. But we can take steps the WEF argues: (a) to begin removing as much rubbish from the sea as is possible; (b) stop dumping further plastic into the sea by drastic recycling or sequestering waste at its source (i.e., on land); (c) invest in research to develop genuinely bio-benign plastics that are still recyclable; (d) avoid colours and shapes that are typically ingested or otherwise harmful to marine life for plastic applications that are of high risk of leakage; (e) reduce the complex of additives to plastics such as stabilizers, pigments and dyes that have toxic consequences when leeched.[42]

And for every one of us, Jennifer Lavers' plea: 'The ocean is drowning in plastic. Don't make it worse.'

---

[40] Earle, *The World is Blue*, p. 114.
[41] The terrible phrase 'plastic ocean' was coined by Charles Moore in his TED Talk of 2009. This powerful speech can be accessed on youtube.
[42] See especially, *The New Plastics Economy*, pp. 16-20.

Learning a practice of attention (2)

Augustine engaged in a deliberate dialogue with the earth, the sea, the sky, the animals. He put questions to them. His questions were theological. 'Who is my God?' and the like. This is a legitimate approach, of course. A practice like this can be understood as a form of prayer. But we live in a pluralist context, Christian, or even theistic, assumptions are not mandated. What is required is a heart and mind open to the possibility that we live in a communicative world. We can follow Augustine's inquiring lead, without sharing his particular convictions, or using his particular questions. Certain Native American traditions offer some deceptively simple alternative questions, which we found to be extraordinarily fruitful.[1]

* * * * * *

Questions

Are you willing to communicate with me?

Asking the question reminds us of our place in the scheme of things. In this encounter we (as humans) are not in a position of control or mastery. We come late on the scene, and need to wait our turn to enter the 'chorus'. Courtesy is an expression of respect in inter-human communication. No less is needed here. After putting the question wait for an answer. If it seems to be 'yes', then move on to the other questions. If 'no', then simply continue the practice. It may be that you are not ready.

Is there a message?

Wait. Frequently we find that particular thoughts come forcibly into our minds in the course of the practice. Sometimes they are brief, 'keep on!' But at other times such 'messages' can be detailed

---
[1] See Appendix 1, 'Stone Circles – Medicine Wheels'.

and surprising. See, for example, the journal entries discussed in chapter 5.

Is there a lesson?

Wait. This way of attending the world yields not only engagement with the world, it also leads to insight, often critical insight, into our own self-understanding. Sea see/hearing is an 'unselfing' journey.

Is there an offering?

Wait. Having received gifts, make an offering of thanksgiving. Attending the visible voice of the world also calls us to account, facing us with obligations and specific challenges. This opens the moral dimension of the practice.

3. Living Together / Tearing Apart

At times I feel as if I am spread over the landscape, and am myself living in every tree, in the splashing of the waves, in the clouds and the animals that come and go, in the procession of the seasons.

C. J. Jung

Hand to hand combat

> The colours of the sea are striking. Blue, grey, green. Above, the clouds are heaped in heavy dollops. I feel bathed and cleansed in the presence of the continually breaking water. Its running sound washes through me. ... I sense the great cosmic rhythms: waves, breathing, labour pains, death agonies, sun setting, sun rising, moon pulling up tides, wind swirling the earth, everything in motion. Always. What is the sea saying? What is the sea's view of itself (herself?)? I am reduced to silence. I try to imagine myself as a home for all the creatures of the sea. And then I think about all the plastics and garbage in the sea, especially the tiny particles that get into the base of the food chain. It's the old duality again, beauty and ugliness, life and death. But overall I am grateful. I am blessed today; blessed by the sea. [J, 6/6/13]

What kind of talk is this? The boundary between the self-watching and the sea-being-watched seems to blur here. The sea plays with me. I am 'washed', literally by waves around my feet, but inwardly too, a sort of 'cleansing' and renewal of resolve. And I play with the sea. 'I try to imagine myself as a home for all the creatures of the sea.' I wonder 'what the sea is saying'. The vastness of the natural order, those 'cosmic rhythms'—sun setting, sun rising, labour pains, death agonies—threaten to swamp me. And 'I am reduced to silence'. On the other hand, they also lift me out of myself. I feel exhilarated, expanded inwardly. 'I am blessed today, blessed by the sea.' And running through the whole interplay is an uneasy foreboding. A balance is shifting. All those tiny plastic particles at the 'base of the food chain.'

This kind of imaginative conversation between the sea and us is a constant feature of our journal, as constant as the awareness of beauty, but just as constant is a struggle to know how to deal with it. Chrétien speaks of the 'hand to hand combat' that accompanies every effort to attend 'what cannot be said and yet will be said.'[1] This is one place where we felt the heat of that combat sharply. To ask, 'what is the sea's view of itself (herself?)', or 'what is the sea saying', is decidedly odd. Surely the sea has no view of itself; and no intentionality (or ability!) to speak of it. The sea is not 'she'. The sea is a vast agglomeration of salt water. To indulge in such language is to play games with *ourselves*, isn't it? Sea see/hearing begins to look like an echo chamber in which we speak and then, hearing our own voice projected, imagine that we are somehow in a real conversation with 'the-more-than-human-world', the sea in this instance. What is the point?

> An inner sense of fretfulness matches the sea's fretting movements. This morning's work fills my mind. I can't let it go. But the sea is here in front of me. As it was yesterday and will be tomorrow. I sense its (her?) patience, imperturbability, constancy. ... As soon as I say this, that other part of me breaks into the conversation with mocking disbelief. 'What else are you going to attribute to the sea?—sympathy? love perhaps? or how about a sense of humour?' A familiar feeling of futility. ... I am conditioned to a view of the world that does not—most definitely does *not*—include the sea (or the trees, or the rocks, not even the birds and lizards) as a 'thou', a present other. ... Crudely put, matter is mindless; hearing and speaking belong exclusively to the realm of mind or soul. To speak to the sea or strain to hear its voice seems daft; poetic licence at best, derangement at worst. ... Out of the blue (!) the white caps of waves appear to me like teeth in a smile. All sorts of smiles. Here a huge grin. There a laugh. At the water's edge, a half hidden smirk. ... Is this just crackers? [G, 20/3/13 & 12/3/13]

This 'feeling of futility', or worse, feeling of *stupidity* ('is this just crackers?') was especially common in the early months of our pilgrimage. It remains today a persistent companion on the way. We always try to find places that are empty of people to engage in our sea

---

[1] See pp. 21-22 above.

see/hearing practice. The manifest reason is that isolation minimizes potential disruptions and nurtures concentration, which is true. Behind that lurks a well-justified self-consciousness. Who in our day and age stands on the edge of the ocean and stares out to sea for half an hour on end? And then does it again? and again? It looks silly. It feels silly. It's embarrassing. If you're going to do it, do it privately!

What is happening here? We spoke in chapter 1 of the 'bell jar of mid-twentieth century western technological consumerism'.[2] And here is the point of combat. The kind of attention to the world that is entailed in the sea see/hearing practice runs us full tilt into the walls of that jar. 'I am conditioned to a view of the world that does not—most definitely does *not*—include the sea (or the trees, or the rocks, not even the birds and lizards) as a 'thou', a present other.' The *view of the world* that conditions our, and large sections of our culture's, way of approaching things assumes deep down a radical differentiation and separation of the realm of matter from the realm of mind; the differentiation and separation of Descartes' 'extended being' (*res extensa*) from his 'thinking being' (*res cogitans*). Such a dualist view makes 'speaking oceans' necessarily 'seem daft; poetic licence at best, derangement at worst.'

In our culture the question is unavoidable. Coleridge called it 'humanizing' of the natural world. 'Art,' he said, 'is ... the power of humanizing nature, of infusing the thoughts and passions of man into everything which is the object of his contemplation.'[3] The fear is that, in sea see/hearing, we are indulging ourselves in 'art' of this kind. Is the effort to attend to the sea really bringing us closer to what we say is the subject (object?) of our interest? Or is it a roundabout way to talk about ourselves, to explore our own emotions, ideas, ambitions, with the sea as our backdrop?

> Today's colours are my favourites. The water is a beautiful milky pale green and the foam a brilliant white, sparkling in the sun. I remember that the colour of my 'birth position' on the Medicine Wheel is white,

---

[2] See . p. 11.
[3] Quoted by Ronald Hepburn in, "Contemporary aesthetics and the neglect of natural beauty," in Bernard Williams and Alan Montefiore (eds), *British Analytical Philosophy* (London: Routledge and Kegan Paul, 1966), p. 296.

and suddenly realize that I am in the presence of masses of whiteness: the dancing riot of continually breaking waves, the lacy foam between them, the misty spray in the air all around. And today I saw the great egret flying, a languid, liquid, graceful form, wings white and huge and luminous against a blue sky. I ask the sea the three Medicine Wheel questions. 'Is there a message?' Reply: 'Love me.' 'Is there a lesson?' 'Stop examining the foundations.' 'Is there an offering?' 'Keep on in hard times.'[4] [J, 10/6/14]

Reading this sort of stuff a scientist, or indeed anyone living in our contemporary technological culture, is likely to raise her eyebrows. The job of science is precisely to undercut this sort of sentimental fantasy. If you want to know something about the sea, something true to the sea itself, that is, you have resolutely to strip away all sentimentality ('my favourite colours'), personal entanglement ('love me'), projection ('is there a message?') and the like, and focus humbly on what is actually given, what is there before you and what is there *other* than you in the object of your concern. In the early stages of the development of modern scientific/technical understandings, David Hume expressed this disciplined, deliberately un-anthropomorphic, attitude of serious science and philosophy with great precision and power.

> There is an universal tendency amongst mankind to conceive all beings like themselves, and to transfer to every object those qualities with which they are familiarly acquainted, and of which they are intimately conscious. We find human faces in the moon, armies in the clouds, and by a natural propensity, if not corrected by experience and reflection, ascribe malice and good will to everything that hurts or pleases us. Hence the frequency and beauty of the *prosopopaeia* [personification] in poetry, where trees, mountains, and streams are personified, and the inanimate parts of nature acquire sentiment and passion. And though these poetical figures and expressions gain not on the belief, they may serve, at least, to prove a certain tendency in the imagination, without which they could neither be beautiful nor natural. Nor is a river-god or hamadryad always taken for a mere poetical or imaginary personage; but may sometimes enter into the real creed of the ignorant vulgar;

---

[4] For details about the Medicine Wheel and its practice, see Appendix 1.

while each grove or field is represented as possessed of a particular *genius* or invisible power, which inhabits or protects it.⁵

The same tendency to humanize the unknown, Hume continues, distorts philosophy and theology in attempting to speak about the transcendent realm of God or the gods. We 'transfer' human passions, powers and infirmities to the deity or deities thus making them over in our own image. The basic motivation for this kind of transference in our dealings with nature and divinity, he argues, is ignorance and fear. 'No wonder, then, that mankind, being placed in such absolute ignorance of causes, and being at the same time so anxious concerning their futures, should immediately acknowledge a dependence on invisible powers possessed of sentiment and intelligence.'⁶

In other and earlier times, lacking any real sense of how the world actually operates, people imagined the world to be like themselves. If the world is thought to resemble us we feel reassured, we know better where we stand and feel more confident about how to act. But those times are well and truly gone. Descartes, Kepler, Galileo, Newton have spoken. And we have heard. Hume is prepared to allow some leeway for poetry as expressive of our human appreciation of nature, provided that it 'gain not on the belief', i.e., that it not be mistaken for the truth of things as they really are. Yes, it's nice to have an Augustine express his appreciation of the natural world in the form of an elegant dialogue, but let's recognize it for what it is: *prosopopaeia*. Anything that strays beyond the boundaries of this clear-eyed understanding of reality is an absurdity, 'the creed of the ignorant vulgar', to be corrected by 'experience and reflection'. Nature is not human, and to ascribe to it human characteristics is to distort it and thus to undermine any genuine, that is accurate, attempt to know it as it really is. In other words, anthropomorphism is *disrespectful* of the natural world (to say nothing of God).

---

5 David Hume, *A Natural History of Religion*, 1757 §3, quoted in Graham Harvey, *Animism: Respecting the Living World* (London: Hurst & Company, 2005), p. 4. David Hume (1711-1776) was a Scottish philosopher, historian and economist. He is best known today for his critical defence of empiricism, scepticism and naturalism.
6 Hume, *A Natural History of Religion*, 1757 §3.

How should we respond to this? In our pilgrimage we frequently, perhaps always, bring our inner life, our thoughts, emotions and worries, with us to the experience of attending the sea. And we are not alone in this. One does not have to be a Wordsworthian Romantic or Augustinian believer to feel the tug of comradeship, or a sense of belonging, or a feeling of being at home in and with the natural world around us. Most of us have known it, or something like it, at one time or another, even if we have to reach back to childhood to find it. Can we, then, justly distinguish between the kind of humanizing subjectivism which fails to respect the *otherness* of the object of appreciation by overwhelming it with inappropriate anthropomorphic features, from a different kind, which honours the truth of the other for what it is, 'yet *at the same time* mix[es] our affective life and our images of self with the image of nature in ways that minister innocently to the deepening and diversifying of feeling'?[7]

In chapter 1 we noted that the voice of Uncle Max might just represent a crack in the bell jar of modernity. Does it?

Indigenous voices

As we have said, Tathra is Yuin country. The Yuin people have related to this land and water for thousands of years. The richness and complexity of their relating is held in stories. Uncle Max invites us (whitefellas) to listen, not just to our own stories—stories told by the likes of Hume and Descartes and Newton—but also to their stories. Well, we can try.

> Grandmother Moon, she comes up and shines down her light upon us. She pulls the tides of the sea. She has that much strength she can pull water up into the sky and hold it, until it's time to water her garden, Mother Earth. Mother Earth, Father Sky, Grandmother Moon and Grandfather Sun have the major roles to play in all life. Water is connected to Mother Earth and to Father Sky. Water is also connected to Grandmother Moon, as she can lift the water and drop it down through Father Sky. Mother Earth then takes the water and she

---

[7] Ronald Hepburn, "Nature Humanised: Nature Respected," *Environmental Values* 7 (1998), p. 268. Italics in the text. This is a fascinating essay and we have drawn heavily on it in this section of the chapter.

distributes it through rivers, streams and lakes. Father Sky holds many stories; through time he has led the way for us to navigate over water and land. He's there for us, he helps us find our way.[8]

This is a story of harmony, everything moving together in a matrix of mutual flourishing. Earth here is 'Mother Earth', fire is 'Grandfather Sun', air is 'Father Sky'. Like members of the family, they are gendered and named. Water is linked with everything (or everyone), Mother Earth and Father Sky, and Grandmother Moon and Grandfather Sun. Water is pulled up, held, dropped down to nourish Mother Earth and distributed by her through rivers, streams and lakes. The powerful presences in this story relate to humans in personal ways; 'he's there for us', 'has led the way for us', 'helps us'. Moreover, these living realities communicate with us. The land talks. '[T]hat's what it's doin'—it's talking to us without a voice. Our land does that all the time; our water does that, our wind. Grandmother Moon, Grandfather Sun do it all the time. They show us things, what's happening.'[9]

At first glance, Uncle Max seems to embody everything that David Hume regards as absurd, 'the ignorant vulgar', in our relating to the natural world. Like Hume, he is deeply concerned with *disrespect*, but for diametrically opposite reasons. For Hume, the disrespect consists in projecting our human qualities onto nature, thereby disregarding its true otherness. Only by rigorous disinterested investigation, by scientific interrogation, can we learn what the world about us really is, and respect it as such. For Uncle Max, the disrespect, by contrast, is precisely failing to acknowledge our *kinship* with the-other-than-human-world; of thinking and acting as if human beings are really somehow 'other' than this world; as if we are somehow placed over against, and even in charge of this world. As if we can use—and abuse—this world as we see fit. That, for Uncle Max, is anything but respect.

We'll come back to whitefella's way of knowing the world in due course. For the moment let's stick with Uncle Max. When he speaks of the Earth being 'Mother' and of the Sky being 'Father', he is not speaking in some

---

[8] Max Dulumunmun Harrison, *My People's Dreaming: an Aboriginal Elder speaks on life, land, spirit and forgiveness* (Sydney: HarperCollinsPublishers, 2013), p. 10.
[9] Harrison, *My People's Dreaming*, p. 7.

vague sentimental *prosopopaeiaic* way of the land and the atmosphere. He is not even speaking poetically, if by that we mean metaphorically or figuratively. He means that his actual biological line, his mother and father, and their parents, and theirs, and so on, come from these great and prior Ancestors, the Mother Earth, Father Sky, Grandfather Sun. These are his origins. These his providers. These his life.

> Mother Earth births everything for us. Father Sky carries the water and oxygen for us to breathe. Grandfather Sun warms the planet, warms our bodies, gives us light so we can see, raises food that the Mother births ... all of our plants and trees.[10]

As a result, Uncle Max understands himself as belonging to the world, not owning it. The land is not possession and private wealth. It is life and spirit. Land is *country*, not real estate. This is hard for Humeans to grasp. We own land. And we are rapidly expanding our ownership to the seas. Speaking with the Yuin people of this area, it quickly becomes plain that for them the sea cannot be parcelled-up in this way. Country is known and loved as a vital reality. All things are connected and all things interdependent. Everything shares a common blood, a sacred place, a living story. In this vibrant whole, we and all things, live, move and have our being.

Uncle Max tells a wonderful story of how he was taught this by his grandfather.

> What you call fire I call Grandfather Sun. When I was around nine years old, climbing a tree, my grandfather said to me, 'Dulumunmun, did you get permission from that tree to climb it?'
>
> 'No,' I replied.
>
> 'Dulumunmun, you should get permission,' he said.
>
> 'But this tree is dead,' I said.
>
> He yelled at me to get down, then he never said a word until it was time to eat. Then Grandfather said to me, 'You go and get some of the dead tree for the fire.' So I went and got all these dead sticks and limbs

---

[10] Harrison, *My People's Dreaming*, p. 9.

to make the fire.

After the billy was boiled and the damper cooked and we had finished our lunch, Grandfather said to me, 'Dulumunmun, pick up those hot coals.'

I looked at him and said, 'I can't pick them up.'

'Why? They're dead, aren't they?' he asked.

'No, they're alive.' And then I shut up. That's when he told me about Grandfather Sun.

'These coals are still a part of Grandfather Sun, and you thought that tree was dead. That tree is part of Grandfather Sun, that bit of black charcoal is holding Grandfather Sun.'[11]

Dulumunmun (Uncle Max) is related to all things in Yuin Country. Trees, sticks, flowers, coals, rocks, rivers, animals, winds, grasses, ancestors and living people; indeed the kinship connections reach out to Sun and Sky, to Moon and Ocean. 'Everyday when Grandfather Sun comes up all these little plants and flowers open up to greet him and welcome him. *And that's what we do too, greet Grandfather and pay our respects.*'[12] Invisible threads bind all people and all inanimate and animate things of country into a living whole. In the words of Deborah Bird Rose who has lived for decades with Indigenous peoples of the Northern Territory:

> People talk about country in the same way that they would talk about a person: they speak to country, sing to country, visit country, worry about country, grieve for country and long for country. People say that country knows, hears, smells, takes notice, takes care, is sorry or happy. Country is a living entity with a yesterday, today and tomorrow, with consciousness, action, and a will toward life. Because of this richness of meaning, country is home and peace; nourishment for body, mind and spirit; and heart's ease.[13]

---

[11] Harrison, *My People's Dreaming*, p. 43.
[12] Harrison, *My People's Dreaming*, p. 43. Italics added.
[13] Deborah Bird Rose with Sharon D'Amico, Nancy Daiyi, Kathy Deveraux, Margaret Daiyi, Linda Ford and April Bright, *Country of the Heart: An Indigenous Australian Homeland* (Canberra: Aboriginal Studies Press, 2002), p. 14.

Such an understanding naturally makes Uncle Max and his people guardians and defenders of country; carers for its physical well-being and for the Law and knowledge that are intrinsic to it. Trying to translate this vision of things into our conceptual framework is difficult, perhaps impossible, but at very least it seems to entail a radical relational ontology and ethics. To *be* is to be in living relationship with all one's environment. To live *responsibly* is to live in a relationship of care and of being cared for in the vital web of connections in which human lives are enmeshed.

We feel hesitant to draw confident conclusions from these stories. We are such outsiders. The differences between western scientific world views and Indigenous ecologies are stark. Science (at least in its classical form) tells a story of a world of objects separate from us and at our disposal. In exquisite detail it analyses their physical features at both the micro- and macroscopic levels, and investigates the universal regularities that govern their movements and interactions regardless of particular contexts. And it calls these 'natural laws'. By contrast, Indigenous ecologies are synthetic and local, embedded in a matrix of living beings and life-systems that inter-connect with one another in a particular place and time. And they call this 'country'. 'Country is a zone of connectivities organizing itself towards mutually flourishing inter-dependencies,' says Rose.[14]

For Yuin people the ocean is *Gadu*[15], part of country; part of that 'zone of connectivities' which contributes to 'mutual flourishing'. The question of whether, in our particular time and place, we are engaging with an ailing, perhaps dying, rather than a flourishing system, is an urgent one as we have noted. For the moment it is enough to acknowledge that *Gadu* is sacred to the Yuin because, amongst other things (like food), it is the source of all waters that bring life to Mother Earth.

Attending the sea, addressing the sea, listening to the sea, caring for the sea, worrying about the sea in such a life-world makes eminent sense. This is respect for the world in which we live.

---

[14] Deborah Bird Rose, *Wild Dog Dreaming: Love and Extinction* (London: University of Virginia Press, 2011), p. 91.
[15] Harrison, *My People's Dreaming*, p. 15.

Lebenswelt – between David Hume and Uncle Max

We seem stranded somewhere between David Hume and Uncle Max; on the edge. We are not Yuin people, obviously, and we are ill-equipped to enter their world. But neither (it seems) are we out-and-out Humean 'objective observers' of the world. Much contemporary science has abandoned rigid subject/object dualisms, but Hume's influence remains tacitly powerful. Both views seem to hold important wisdom for human interaction with the oceans in our times, but what? And how might we appropriate it better?

Hume has a point. Whether there is 'an universal tendency' among human beings in their encounters with nature to see the human where in fact it does not exist, we can leave open. But there certainly is in *us*. In sea see/hearing we 'humanize' in our imagination what is not human in reality. In such moments, attending the ocean *feels* like engagement, not a stand-off; interaction not objective observation. Is this subjective fantasy? Has it to do exclusively with the moods of the self and not the meanings of the world? What happens if we refuse the either/or, Hume *or* Uncle Max?

Well, we would certainly not be alone. Early in the 20th century the philosopher, Edmund Husserl, a German Jew, grew increasingly uneasy with the dominance of the analytic, objectifying, controlling way of understanding and relating to the world. Hume's way. Not that he was opposed to science. Husserl was well aware of the enormous contribution scientific approaches to nature have made to human health and well-being. His point was only that the brilliant success of science threatens to swamp another, and in his view more primordial, way for humans to be in and know the reality around them. Husserl called this reality *Die Lebenswelt*, literally 'the life-world'.[16] Both terms are significant. The 'world', the totality of inter-connected entities (earth, air, water, light, plants, animals, etc.) which encompass us (and every sentient being) is

---

[16] This section is indebted to the fine discussion of phenomenology given in David Abram's superb exposition of the place of humans and other-than-humans in the threatened world today, *The Spell of the Sensuous: Perception and Language in a More-Than-Human World* (New York: Random House, 1997), pp. 31-72. Husserl's ground-breaking text was, *Cartesian Meditations: An Introduction to Phenomenology*, trans. Dorion Cairns (The Hague: Martinus Nijhoff, 1960). The book was first completed in 1929.

the context from which we spring, the stuff from which we are made, the environment in which we flourish, and the soil—the *humus*—into which we die. The world is our home, our place of being in the most basic sense, our life-support system. In short, the world is our 'life-world'; and the *life*-world of every other creature who shares the planet with us. For Husserl, science with its sophisticated research methods and astonishing consequent knowledge, is rooted in and accountable to this same life-world with which we engage in ordinary existence. The world we perceive through our eyes, ears, nose, mouth and skin. The world we enjoy and feed upon. The world we love and fear. The world we live *bodily*. The world called Tathra Beach.

Husserl was interested in attending carefully to this *Lebenswelt* as it presents itself to our immediate experience, prior to any systematic conceptual appropriation or manipulation. In doing so, he inaugurated the philosophical movement known as phenomenology. In contrast to the mainstream sciences, Husserl did not seek to explain or analyse things in terms of their component parts and the rules that govern their interactions. He tried to describe as carefully as possible the way the world and the things that belong to it *manifest* themselves to our direct sense-experience. How does a wave look? What is this experience of the colour blue? What is it like to hear the sound of surf rolling? Attending to these *phenomena* and the way they present themselves to our awareness, to feel their rhythms, forms, textures and sounds, to note the aspects they manifest in their approach to us and the aspects they conceal, is to return to a fundamental mode of being-in-the-world which precedes and grounds all other ways of knowing and responding. The French phenomenologist Maurice Merleau-Ponty writes:

> To return to things themselves is to return to that world which precedes knowledge, of which knowledge always *speaks*, and in relation to which every scientific schematization is an abstract and derivative sign-language, as is geography in relation to the countryside in which we have learnt beforehand what a forest, a prairie or a river is.[17]

---

[17] Maurice Merleau-Ponty followed and developed the thought of Husserl. The citation is from his book, *Phenomenology of Perception*, trans. Colin Smith (London: Routledge & Kegan Paul, 1962), p. ix, quoted in Abram, *The Spell of the Sensuous*, p. 36.

3. Living Together / Tearing Apart

At this basic level of experience, we are never just spectators of the world around us. Our everyday, spontaneous experience of sunlight, clouds, grass, trees, possums and magpies, to say nothing of other people, is necessarily informed, that is given shape and colour and weight, by our moods and dispositions, and by perspectives that come from our personal stories.

> I feel a kind of peacefulness, which I take over from the sea, which is very gentle. The waves are geometrical and regular, waiting to break close to the shore. I feel content standing on my little mound of sand, simply being here. The sun is warm on my back. I revel in glorious colour. The scene before me resolves into horizontal strips: bands of deep blue, aqua and sapphire in the surface of the sea, broad white lines of foam on the ridge of rolling waves, a strip of yellow sand. All bounded by the wide dome of a blue-white sky. This is Fred Williams. I am grateful for the eyes with which he sees the ocean. Art is to the eye what poetry is to the ear. And both to the understanding. I think about words and where they come from; think of my struggle to find 'the words to say it' in response to the sea. Mary Oliver is amazing. It is not that she uses special terms. Most of her lines consist of words any child knows. Yet the way she combines them gives voice with tenderness and exquisite accuracy to water in a pond, the flight of an egret, or grass dying in a field. She 'hears' the world of the pond and speaks its life; as Fred Williams 'sees' the sea by re-forming its shape and colours on canvas. As I look at the paintings, I say 'yes! that is what it *is*'. He 'sees' this world. I am trying to find a way to see and hear the sea; and to find a 'voice' to speak it. I feel lost. I can keep going only in community (communion?) with others (Oliver, Williams, Claudel, etc.). [J, 22/6/13]

Trying to find a way to hear and see the ocean is bound up with being *bodily* immersed in colour, shape, movement and sound, framed by 'the wide dome of a blue-white sky'. We are inside this scene looking through it, not outside looking at it. Yes, the waves are 'geometrical and regular'. They could well be scientifically described.[18] But prior to this, the phenomena appear as a living whole, infused with emotion. 'Peace'

---

[18] For an interesting description of the formation, propagation and dynamics of sea waves, see Sebastian Junger, 'The Perfect Storm' in James Bradley (ed), *The Penguin Book of the*

and 'content' are coming from the ocean itself. The interaction of inner and outer is fluid—who is giver and who receiver here?—and presents itself as integral to the experience, not imported or imposed upon it from outside. Today the affective atmosphere is contentment. Tomorrow is may be agitation. The sea as it appears now, in this lived moment, manifests itself precisely *in* the changing emotion-charged interaction.

Western culture since the time of Kepler and Galileo has tended to interpret such responses as 'purely subjective', to do with the observing self, not the observed world. Husserl encourages us not to submit to this ruling too quickly. The *Lebenswelt* is not solipsistic, locked up in the consciousness of the individual perceiver. It may be hard to find the 'voice' to speak the sea in a way that feels 'true' to the practice of sea see/hearing, but this difficulty is not to do with the problems of articulating private feelings. The *Lebenswelt* is a *shared* world. Fred Williams and Mary Oliver are co-attenders to water, sand, sky and bird. Our felt experience of the sea is tested and refined, re-framed and revealed in conversation with them and others. Eye and ear are in fact enabled to see and to hear (to 'see/hear') 'only in community (communion?) with others'. Oliver 'hears' in such a way that she can speak 'the world of the pond'. Williams 'sees' on the canvas in such a way that we cannot help but say, 'yes! that is what it *is*'. Feelings are ours, to be sure, but they are not ours alone. They are open to the critique of the experience of others in engagement with the sea.

More than this; 'The world and I reciprocate one another,' says David Abram.[19] Felt interaction, not disinterested observation, is at the core of it. The sea has certain ways 'of invading us' in sea see/hearing, and we have certain ways 'of meeting that invasion.'[20] The journal entry below was cited in the previous chapter, but holds further insights about the nature of reciprocity between self and world.

> The blue of the sea is wonderful. There seems to be a dozen shades of it, shifting and melding into one another out to the horizon; a vast blue field, which meets at the horizon a second even vaster field—the blue

---

Ocean (Camberwell, Victoria: Penguin, Hamish Hamilton, 2010), pp. 307-312.
19 *The Spell of the Sensuous*, p. 33.
20 'Invasion' is a term used by Merleau-Ponty, see *The Spell of the Sensuous*, p. 54.

sky. The two blue worlds completely fill my vision. There is no room for anything else. But it doesn't feel crammed or cramped. This colour blue is in excess of itself, juggling more than it can hold, spilling over. The waves are large, their white crowns shimmering in the sunlight. The contrast with the blue magnifies the brilliance of both colours. [G, 6/5/14]

This is awkwardly expressed, but it grapples with a genuine, if somewhat confused, experience. It is as though the world of sea and sky presents (in Merleau-Ponty's phrase) 'a kind of muddled problem for my body to solve'. The problem of 'blue'. Shifting shades of blue mix and dissolve into each other. There is no escape from them either below or above. An invasion takes place. 'Blue worlds' flood into me until 'there is no room for anything else.' And yet this fullness seems not to be my issue alone. I intuit that the blue of the world is in 'excess of itself'. It struggles to contain its own plenitude, like a juggler with too many skittles in the air. Speaking of the colour blue, Merleau-Ponty describes with astonishing subtlety the mutuality of the encounter between this sensible thing, blue, and the sensing body seeing blue:

> I must find the attitude which will provide it with the means of becoming determinate, of showing up as blue; I must find the reply to a question which is obscurely expressed. And yet I do so only when I am invited by it; my attitude is never sufficient to make me really see blue or really touch a hard surface. The sensible gives back to me what I lent to it, but this is only what I took from it in the first place. As I contemplate the blue of the sky ... I abandon myself to it and plunge into this mystery, it 'thinks itself within me,' I am the sky itself as it is drawn together and unified, and as it begins to exist for itself; my consciousness is saturated with this limitless blue.[21]

In Humean culture, the 'thing' perceived (in this instance the blue of the sea/sky) is considered given, a 'fact'. For the purposes of scientific

---

21 *Phenomenology of Perception*, p. 214 cited in Abram, *The Spell of the Sensuous*, p. 54. A brief and informative discussion of the *physics* of the blue colour found in both sky and sea can be found in Mark W. Denny, *Air and Water: the Biology and Physics of Life's Media* (Princeton: Princeton University Press, 1993), pp. 234-235. A very different reading of 'blue' in comparison with that of Merleau-Ponty!

investigation what is required is a dispassionate approach. However, there is another, more primordial dimension. For Merleau-Ponty the sensible 'thing' is also apprehended in *active* mode. I contemplate the blue of the sky. But the sky 'thinks itself within me'. The sky 'exists for itself', but precisely in that, it invites or lures me to 'abandon myself to it'. A mutual invasion gets underway. I 'plunge into this mystery' until finally 'I am the sky itself'. This shifting, animate, active *reciprocity* between the sea and our attending the sea, between inner and outer, seems to describe something true of the essence of the sea see/hearing experience.

James Turrell's astonishing exhibition at the National Gallery of Australia, Canberra, in early 2015 was all about the sensual experience of light. To stand in his 'colour room' and feel the pressure and texture of slowly changing hues, from white, to orange, to red, to blue, is to 'plunge into the mystery' of colour with the entire body, not just the eyes. My awareness is saturated with 'limitless blue'. The colour 'thinks itself within me'. Turrell's art is an arresting demonstration of Merleau-Ponty's colour phenomenology; Merleau-Ponty's phenomenology a brilliant exegesis of Turrell's art. 'Light is not so much something that reveals, as it is itself revelation.' (James Turrell)

Sea see/hearing is a journey toward the heart of the *Lebenswelt*.

Science and sin

If Uncle Max's stress on kinship with country threatens to put a crack in the bell jar of modernity by challenging its tendency to disconnect mind from matter, subject from object, then the Deepwater Horizon disaster, with its image of dark water rising, perhaps augers an even deeper fracture.

Remember Sylvia Earle's encounter with the brash young reporter on the shore of Port Phillip Bay; 'Suppose the oceans dried up tomorrow. Why should I care? I don't swim. I hate boats. I get seasick! I don't even like to eat fish. Why should I object if some of them—or all of them—go extinct? Who needs the ocean?' The oceanographer groaned inwardly, 'Good grief! Can she be serious?'[22]

---

[22] See chapter 1, pp. 25-26.

The journalist probably wasn't all that serious. She was after a provocative story. Earle's groan was not so much about a well-tried professional gambit. It was about the stark human reality that lies behind it. Our propensity to see and to treat the world exclusively from the point of view of our own interests and desires. Why should I care? *I don't swim*. Why should I object if fish go extinct? *I don't even like to eat fish*.

This isn't just a gambit and it's not just an individual life-style choice. This is a corner stone, or at least an indication of a corner stone, of our whole culture's identity. This is our stubborn anthropocentric way of dealing with the world, the other-than-human-world, as if it were nothing but our pantry, mine and latrine. It is this disposition and all that flows from it that concerns Naomi Klein from an economic perspective when she writes,

> What the climate needs to avoid collapse is a contraction in humanity's use of resources; what our economic model demands to avoid collapse is unfettered expansion. Only one of these sets of rules can be changed, and it's not the laws of nature.[23]

And it is this disposition that Daphne Sheldrake fears from a scientific point of view:

> With amazing arrogance we presume omnipotence and an understanding of the complexities of Nature, and with amazing impertinence, we firmly believe that we can better it. ... We have forgotten that we, ourselves, are just a part of nature, an animal which seems to have taken the wrong turning, bent on total destruction.[24]

Of course, a tendency to see everything from the point of view of our own interests and to desire 'unfettered expansion' of our influence in the world is no modern novelty. Martin Luther classically described 'sin' as *incurvatus in se*, the turning or curving inward of the human being upon itself; a turning *in* which involves a turning *away* from God and from fellow human beings. The curved-in self, Luther argues, 'seeks itself and

---

[23] Naomi Klein, *This Changes Everything: Capitalism vs. the Climate* (London: Penguin Random House UK, 2015), p. 21.
[24] Quoted by Sylvia A. Earle, *Sea Change: A Message of the Oceans* (New York: Fawcett Books, 1995), p. 226.

its own interests in everything: it brings it about that man [sic] is finally and ultimately concerned only for himself.'[25] Luther was addressing the radical distortion that this attitude introduces into personal, social and religious life. The legitimate interests of others (including God) are discounted or displaced altogether in a rush for the overriding interests of the self. Our modern situation gives this ancient analysis a new and more sinister twist. The *incurvatus* that marks our time has blown out beyond self and society. It has become planetary. Human activity is now impacting destructively on Earth itself. The assumption that the Earth exists for human convenience and its bounty for human consumption pervades. We live and breathe it daily. Given our numbers and our technology, this means humans are in fact living at the expense of almost every other species on Earth, and finally of Earth itself.

When we were growing up, it was evangelistic preachers who spoke about 'sin' in these terms and called for 'repentance' and a changing of our ways. It is something of a surprise to find that now it is scientists who are sounding a warning about the dire consequences of our *incurvatus* and calling for a radical change from the course we are embarked upon! The language may be different. 'Arrogance', 'impertinence', 'omnipotence' replace the religious word 'sin'. 'Bent on total destruction' and 'the wrong turning' replace 'repentance', but the dynamics of the discourse is eerily similar.

'Who needs the ocean?' Sylvia Earle, one of the world's leading oceanographers, has dedicated much of her life to trying to catch the attention of those of us who lack the technical and scientific background to follow first-hand the conversations and concerns of the experts. She believes that it is vital for the future of the planet that we, the public, become at least minimally informed about what contemporary science reveals of what the ocean means for human life, and what human life means for the ocean. 'It doesn't matter where on Earth you live, everyone is utterly dependent on the existence of that lovely, living saltwater soup.

---

[25] *Luther: Lectures on Romans*, trans. Wilhelm Pauck, The Library of Christian Classics, Vol. XV (London: SCM Press, 1961), p. 225. Martin Luther (1483–1556) was a German priest, monk and theologian. He was a seminal figure in the Protestant Reformation.

There's plenty of water in the universe without life, but nowhere is there life without water.'[26]

As non-scientists we are at a radical disadvantage. The literature generated from scientific ways of approaching, exploring and describing the ocean, especially in the last four decades, is immense. Biology, physics, chemistry, geology, physiology, thermodynamics, hydraulics, wave mechanics, cartography, palaeontology and probability theory have all contributed to an explosion in detailed understanding of the sea, the creatures that live in it, the forces that shape and move it, the interactions it has with light, land and air, and our human impact upon it. This is a great gift in our time. No previous generation has had anything like such detailed and documented insight, but it is also a great barrier. The knowledge is there, but gaining access to it is daunting, even for experts.

In what follows, we try to pay attention not only to the sea itself and what it 'says' directly to our attending, but also to Sylvia Earle and her ilk, and what they, the scientists, have to say on behalf of the sea. We are beginners in both spheres of attention; sea see/hearing and ocean science. And we have no doubt made mistakes in our stumbling efforts to attend. However, we hope it might be (for us at least) the start of an *instructed* attention to what, in our times, is the authentic 'visible voice' of the ocean.

Space

From our foothold on the shore at Tathra, we can see some 10 kilometres out to the horizon in front of us, and maybe 25 or 30 kilometres from the limits of sight to the north to its corresponding reach in the south. This is hardly more than a key-hole vista, of course, yet it portends an immensity that feels as if it leads on to infinity.

> The beach is shrouded in a deep white mist, low to the ground. Visibility is reduced to 50 or 60 metres at most. The few people (and dogs) on the shore move in and out of the fog like ghosts. Out to sea, the great grey dome of the sky and the great grey orb of the sea melt into each other. ... I feel very much on the edge. The edge of the sea. The edge of the land. The edge of my own understanding. The mist thins. Slowly

---

[26] Earle, *Sea Change*, p. xii.

I can see further and further until the horizon drifts into focus. It is as if the sea lifts her veil ever so slightly to allow me to see that what I can see is just a tiny fraction of vast areas of space and depth and time. Then as quietly as it lifted, the veil falls again. The fog envelops me as if to underline the lesson. Remember you are only on the edge of this. Don't think you are more than that. [G, 11/3/16]

What is this vastness actually? 'No word can shrink it down to fit the mind,' says the poet.[27] But what does the scientist say? The beach on which we stand is washed by the Pacific Ocean, the oldest, largest and deepest expanse of water on the planet. Seen from an orbiting space craft 250 kilometres up, Australia appears as a modest patch of greenish-yellow adrift in a massive arc of shimmering James Turrell blue. The Pacific covers in excess of 150 million square kilometres of Earth's surface at an average depth of 4,200 metres. At the deepest point, the so-called Challenger Deep in the Mariana Trench east of the Philippines,[28] it drops to 10,994 metres below sea level and the pressure rises to a crushing 1125 kg/cm^2 (about 8 tons per square inch). Huge though it is, the Pacific accounts for less than half the total ocean area, which exceeds 361 million square kilometres, or 70.8% of Earth's surface. This works out to a staggering 1.37 billion cubic kilometres[29] of water. 'If the water in the earth's oceans were formed into a separate planet, it would be roughly one tenth the diameter of the earth, about half the diameter of the moon.' Oceans contain virtually all of Earth's free water. Some 2.5% is locked away, frozen as ice in glaciers and the polar icecaps, or sequestered in groundwater. The water present in lakes, streams and rivers 'amounts to less than 0.01% of the water available to living things.'[30] 'The sea lifts her veil ever so slightly to allow me to see that …' size matters. On this measure alone, Ocean dominates Earth.

---

[27] The words come from the poem, "Facing the Pacific at Night" by Kevin Hart, in Bradley (ed) *The Penguin Book of the Ocean*, p. 297.
[28] 11° 21' North latitude, 142° 12' East longitude.
[29] Taking one billion to be 10^9 or 1,000,000,000.
[30] Quotations from Denny, *Air and Water*, p. 5. We have drawn these data from this source along with additional information from Sylvia A. Earle, *Blue Hope: Exploring and Caring for Earth's Magnificent Ocean* (Washington D.C.: National Geographic, 2014), pp. 40-41; and *The World is Blue: How Our Fate and the Ocean's are One* (Washington D.C.: National Geographic, 2010), pp. 15ff.

3. Living Together / Tearing Apart

Life

What is this water in front of me? Instinctively my mind goes down the scientific path. Water is H_2O. And what is that? Atoms of hydrogen and oxygen. And what are they? Entities composed of elementary particles, neutrons, protons, electrons. And what are they? Vaguely my mind jumps to quantum waves. But I really have no idea what that means. I am stumped. I don't know enough. I try another tack. Water is the source and support of life. My body is 60% water. Blood, spinal fluid, tears, saliva, etc. are water based. So, one of the things I am attending here is life and its source. Von Weizsäcker claims that meditation is attention to what is an intrinsic *Mitwahrnemung* (co-perception) within immediate perception. Looked at this way, the co-perception, which I can't access without the perception it accompanies, that is, the perception of water (the ocean) in front of me, is of *life*. Life is what draws me, or lures me, in the practice of sea see/hearing. Or at least this seems to be a part of it. [G, 25/3/15]

Ocean dominates *life*. The term 'biosphere' was coined by an Austrian Geologist, Edward Seuss, in 1875, to describe 'a specific, life-saturated envelope of the Earth's crust', i.e., that narrow band between the lithosphere (the hard rock rim of the planet) and the lower reaches of the atmosphere in which living things exist and interact.[31] It encompasses the two great media of life, water and air. The biosphere is tiny, around 14 to 20 kilometres thick. Its bottom is the depth of the deepest ocean (11 kilometres at Challenger), but its top is more difficult to determine. On land, the biosphere extends a few metres down into the soil where roots, worms and microbes live, but what are the upper limits of life in air? A Mountain Ash (*Eucalyptus regnans*) can grow to a height in excess of 100 metres. On rare occasions birds and insects have been known to soar to heights of 10 kilometres or more. A few plants (mosses and lichens) can survive at altitudes in excess of 6 kilometres, but most of the space available to support the processes of life in air lies below the 2 kilometre mark.

---

[31] Cited in Mary E. White, *Earth Alive!: from Microbes to a Living Planet* (Dural, NSW: Rosenberg Publishing, 2003), p. 1.

As air-breathing, sun-loving creatures, we tend to focus on the brightly illuminated sections of the Earth that are easily accessible to us, the land and the forms of life that inhabit it.

> I am conscious of the sun on my back ... and say out loud a word of gratitude to the sun for warmth and light; and for the blessing of sunlight that means the plants, grasses and trees can grow. [J, 7/5/14]

Well and true, but the fact is 'all of life on Earth lives in the dark at least half of the time, and much of it lives in the dark all of the time—in the depths of the sea.'[32] Beyond a depth of 200 metres sunlight fades for the human eye, and at 1000 metres we approach the aptly named 'aphotic' zone, a world of perpetual midnight, almost completely unknown to scientists and divers.[33] More so to the rest of us. Thus we easily overlook the fact that more than 95% of the biosphere, the space where living things can thrive on this planet, is the ocean.[34] All sea water contains life. The marine biosphere includes every drop of water in the ocean, all 1.37×10^9 cubic kilometres of it; a complex, thriving, inter-dependent society of large, medium, small and microscopic creatures living together 'in ways that make Earth hospitable for life as we know it.'[35]

That's hard to take in. The magnitude and diversity of life in the ocean boggles the imagination, even of experts. New forms and species of life—plant, animal, microbial—are being discovered and documented daily. To date less than 5% of the ocean has been seriously explored; below 300 metres that figure drops dramatically. 'It is now estimated that the ocean holds at least ten million species', says Earle, and 'some believe the number may be closer to a hundred million'. And this is not including the microbes that outstrip all other forms of life in 'numbers and sheer

---

[32] Earle, *Sea Change*, p. 111.
[33] This, again, is a *human* perspective. The world of the deep may be dark for us. But, as Edith Widder points out, it is not so for millions of creatures which make it *their* home. 'While it is true that sunlight does not penetrate below 1000 meters ... there are lots of lights –billions and billions of them.' Cited in Earle, *The World is Blue*, p. 134.
[34] Estimates of the relative proportions of the biosphere to be found in the air and in the water vary somewhat, depending on what limits are assigned to the upper reaches of sustainable life in the atmosphere. Some put the proportion as high as 99%. We have taken the more conservative estimate given by Sylvia Earle, *Sea Change*, p. 111.
[35] Earle, *Blue Hope*, p. 21.

3. Living Together / Tearing Apart

mass.'[36] At a pinch, we can perhaps name 20 kinds of fish, a few of the more famous crustaceans and molluscs, noting ruefully that the reason we know their names is primarily that (until recently) we have revelled in seeing them dead on our dinner plates. On top of that, we might be able to distinguish four or five different types of seaweed from a random search of the beach at Tathra. Beyond 'kelp' and 'Neptune's Necklace' our phycological vocabulary is dead in the water.[37]

It is wonderful to learn even this tiny bit about the astonishing life-world of the ocean and especially to understand a little of how this ocean world founds and funds life on the land and in the air. Our life too. The aquasphere seems so enormous, so stable, so life-filled as to be impervious to any actions we might take. So it is painful to be shown by the same teachers how rapidly and determinedly we are cutting away at these foundations and squandering these funds.

> Tim Flannery says that the ocean holds the 'switch' for life. Not land. Not the atmosphere. The ocean. If it switches off, life as we know it will cease to be. I feel shame as a human being standing and looking at the sea. If Flannery is right, I am looking at the switch of life right there before me. And wondering how it is poised. I am helpless and frightened. I need the ocean. In the final analysis, I am absolutely dependent on its generosity. But the reverse it not true. The ocean has absolutely no need of me whatever. It may well be in the process of deciding that it can do much better without me and my kind. The sea keeps endlessly rolling in towards the shore, towards me. I can only see this tiny little piece of it. I think to myself: 'what are you planning?'[38] [G, 23/2/15]

The fact is biological diversity 'is the key to the maintenance of the world as we know it. ... This is the assembly of life that took a billion

---

[36] Earle, *The World is Blue*, p. 135.
[37] From the Greek *phykos* = seaweed. Seaweed, the textbooks say, is a colloquial term for a wide range of marine multicellular algae—green, brown and red—which each comprise a family containing several thousands of species.
[38] For the Flannery reference see, Alanna Mitchell, *Sea Sick: The Global Ocean in Crisis* (Millers Point, NSW: Murdoch Books Australia, 2008), pp. 9-15, especially at p. 14.

years to evolve. It ... created the world that created us. It holds the world steady.'[39]

Time

The sense that in the presence of the sea we are in the presence of deep time impressed itself on us again and again.

> The sound I am hearing on this beach is a sound that has been here for 4 billion years; a sound as old as the Earth itself, or almost as old; an ancient sound, a sound that preceded any ears to hear it. And such ears as might develop the potential to hear it would have to come from the sea itself. The sea is the ur-womb of the ear. [G, 25/3/12]

What does this deep time really mean? It has taken more than 4.5 billion years for Earth to evolve from a lifeless body of cosmic dust and gases to the complex, vital system of plants, animals, insects, fungi and micro-organisms, with all their individual variations and interactions that surrounds us today. Let us imagine that this history is sketched out on a scale taking the depth of the Pacific at Challenger (11 kilometres down) as our ruler.[40] As we rise up from the ocean floor, we pass through the various geological eras, the depth indicator marking the passage of time. Somewhere around the 9.3 kilometre mark below the surface (i.e., 3.8 billion years ago), the ocean itself emerges on the face of a barren and rocky planet; the outcome of torrential precipitation from massive discharges of water vapour through volcanic eruption across millions of years. The first stirrings of life, probably a type of *cyanobacteria* or blue-green algae, appear in the primal seas at 8.6 kilometres (3.5 billion years ago). By the time we have risen to 1.3 kilometres (530 million years ago) all the main groups of invertebrates plus the earliest forms of fish (Agnathans) are present in Earth's waters. At around 1 kilometre beneath the surface, some 420 million years ago, the first pioneers of life on land (Arthropods) creep out of the ocean and become the ancestors of crabs and lobsters and insects. Dinosaurs flower in abundance at a mere 560 metres and disappear again at 160 metres (66 million years ago). Human-like creatures turn up at a depth just 50 centimetres below

---

39 E. O. Wilson, *The Diversity of Life*, quoted in Earle, *The World is Blue*, pp. 121-122.
40 Sylvia Earle suggests this way of scaling deep time, but does not spell it out, *Sea Change*, p. 5.

the surface (200,000 years ago). Indigenous Australians emerge on our continent at 15 centimetres (60,000 years ago). Writing is discovered in the uppermost 1 centimetre of the journey, 10 kilometres 999 metres and 99 centimetres from the ocean floor.[41]

In short, modern humans scarcely break the surface tension of the deep sea of earthly life. Ancient processes involving continuous interactions among living organisms in the context of the great planetary cycles of light and dark, hot and cold, wet and dry, air and water, rock and soil have shaped the history of life on Earth. The ocean is both womb and archive of that story. 'Most of the major distinctive categories of animal and plant life that ultimately evolved are still represented in the ocean, including many that are found only there; only about half have ever become established on the land.'[42] Thus, when we look out on the ocean at Tathra what we are looking at, if only from the very edge, indeed from the last micro-millimetre of an 11 kilometre journey, is the culmination of the interlocking processes of life and world through all preceding time.

'A liquid bond'[43]

Standing in the midst of such grandeur, I know myself as insignificant, almost nothing, a nanosecond in a calendar of ages. But I also know I am a part of this immensity. Through its strange fecundity I am where I am and who I am. The womb and the water. Our earliest sentient experience is of being in fluid and hearing the sounds of liquid in motion. Womb and water. My mind turns to reading about the state of the oceans: increasing acidification, rising temperature, changing nutrients. What would it mean to an embryo if the amniotic fluid around it began to acidify, its temperature rise, its nutrients fail? What

---

[41] This schema is, of course, hugely simplified. For an accessible and beautifully presented survey of deep evolutionary time and the processes of life that emerged, interacted, mutated and vanished in its stream, with special relevance to the Australian context, see White, *Earth Alive!*.

[42] Earle, *Sea Change*, p. 9.

[43] The phrase comes from a poem by Paul Claudel, "The Spirit and the Water": 'Water is the extension of spirit; it supports and feeds it;/And between/All your creatures and you is a liquid bond.' *Five Great Odes*, trans. Edward Lucie-Smith (London: Rapp and Carroll, 1967), p. 30.

would it mean if baptismal water were polluted water? What world will my grandchildren inherit? [J, 22/3/13]

The world about me is grey and dim. Rain fills the air. Water is all around. And water within: saliva, tears, blood. This brings to mind Claudel's idea of 'the liquid bond'. I feel, or think I can feel, the link between these various waters—the sea, the sky, the rain, the water within, the wet sand beneath my feet. Somehow we belong together. We are connected. [G, 10/4/14]

But how connected? There is plenty of water in the universe without life. But nowhere is there life without water. Living things need water because they are largely made up of water. Life originated in the ocean and creatures that have long since taken up residence in air and upon land retain in their bodies tell-tale characteristics of their origins. Early stage human foetuses 'depend on amniotic fluid that is a chemical replica of the marine world, and the composition of our blood plasma is astonishingly similar to the composition of sea water.'[44] Protoplasm, which is the living matter of all plant and animal cells, is largely made up of water. The average adult human being is by weight about 60% water—some 40 litres of it—moving through and within trillions of cells.[45] Our bodies are perpetual water processing factories, always striving to match intake with output.

> Water enters our bodies, circulates through it (*sic*) to the rhythms of the heart, ceaselessly carrying food, fuel, and cellular and molecular detritus to and from various organs of the body. Water seeps through our skin, escapes from our lungs as vapour and exits every opening in our body.[46]

However, like other most land dwelling plants and animals, we cannot live on salt water. Life on land is dependent on the continuous and mysterious transformation of salt water into fresh by means of the hydrologic cycle. Energy from the sun playing on the surface of

---

[44] Mitchell, *Sea Sick*, p. 25.
[45] David Suzuki, *The Sacred Balance: Rediscovering our Place in Nature* (New York: Prometheus Books, 1998), p. 59. Chapter 4 of this work, 'The Ocean Flowing through Our Veins,' pp. 52-75, is an important source for the material in this section.
[46] Suzuki, *The Sacred Balance*, p. 62.

3. Living Together / Tearing Apart

the ocean causes water to evaporate. The water vapour rises into the atmosphere to form clouds, which are then driven across the surface of the Earth by restless winds, likewise powered by the sun. The clouds release their stored moisture as rain, sleet and snow, filling lakes, rivers, billabongs and deep reservoirs of groundwater. Along the way it slakes the thirst of a billion living creatures from elephants and black faced wallabies, to sea eagles, spiny anteaters and red-back spiders. As water seeps into the soil it encounters the searching rootlets of a trillion trees, ferns, mosses, grasses and fungi. There, drawn up into branches, leaves, petals and fronds, it stimulates, regulates and sustains the chemistry of life on its magic dance through the world of space and time.

The water that flows in the blood of every person, that moves in the sap of every tree, that inflates the cells of every blade of grass, has cycled time and again from the ocean to the sky and back to earth. Each living thing enjoys its use for a while, until it moves on, eventually returning to the sea to flow again as part, say, of the Eastern Australian Current or to ride the back of a near perfect wave as it breaks on the beach at Tathra, to begin the cycle anew. All life is bound by 'a liquid bond' to the sea.

> Even if you never have the chance to see or touch the ocean, the ocean touches you with every breath you take, every drop of water you drink, every bite you consume. Everyone, everywhere is inextricably connected to and utterly dependent on the existence of the sea.[47]

> *Air*
>
> Standing by the ocean, it is perhaps relatively easy to sense the 'liquid bond', the connection of the water within and the water without. Sea and air, 'every breath you take', how are *they* linked?

> Today the line between sea and sky is as sharp as a cane cutter's scythe. The two great fluid media of life, water and air, meet there. They meet everywhere, of course. But the horizon is the place where their meeting manifests itself to the watcher unmistakeably. Dark blue meets light blue, below meets above, liquid meets gas. They touch. And interact. I know the interaction is weighted with consequences for both sea and air, but, as usual, I'm ignorant of details. [G, 11/3/13]

---
[47] Earle, *The World is Blue*, p. 17.

Today, the relative proportion of gases in the lower atmosphere is approximately 78% nitrogen, 21% oxygen, 0.93% argon and 0.04% carbon dioxide, with an exotic recipe of neon, helium, methane, krypton, nitrous oxide, hydrogen, xenon and ozone, contributing the remaining 0.03%.[48] This has not always been the case. The composition of the atmosphere has varied considerably during the 3.5 billion year tenure of life on Earth. Until about 2.3 billion years ago, the atmosphere was probably made up primarily of carbon dioxide, ammonia, methane and water vapour, derived mainly from extensive volcanic eruptions in the Earth's early crust.

With the emergence of photosynthetic organisms (e.g., cyanobacteria) in the ocean around this time, a major planetary change got under way. Photosynthetic life, drawing on the energy of sunlight, fed off carbon dioxide in the atmosphere, converting it into simple sugars and releasing oxygen into the environment in the process. At first, the oxygen released was rapidly absorbed through interaction with iron, forming vast deposits of iron oxide in so-called 'red beds', or banded-iron formations (BIF). The majority of oxygen produced over geological aeons remains locked up in these great sedimentary deposits. By about 1.8 billion years ago, all available ferrous rock was fully oxidized. The continuing photosynthetic processes in the ocean resulted gradually in a decreasing concentration of carbon dioxide and an increasing concentration of free oxygen in the air, which eventually evolved, through a series of complex and differing stages, into the atmospheric composition we know today.

Clearly, the relative proportions of gases in the atmosphere have changed markedly over geological time. However, the contemporary balance between the major gases, nitrogen, oxygen and carbon dioxide has remained pretty steady for at least the past 800,000 years. Steady at just those proportions congenial for the flourishing of life as we know it. A major factor in these favourable homeostatic circumstances remains the ancient operation of trillions of photosynthetic micro-organisms in the sea working today their transformative balancing act of absorbing carbon dioxide from the atmosphere and returning oxygen, as they have done since the beginning.

---

[48] See Suzuki, *The Sacred Balance*, p. 41.

3. Living Together / Tearing Apart

Trees, grasses, and other land plants are critically important in terms of maintaining the atmospheric gases in just the right proportions suitable for present life on Earth, including us, *but photosynthetic organisms in the sea do most of the heavy lifting when it comes to generating oxygen and otherwise holding planetary chemistry on a steady course.*[49]

This came to us as an amazing insight. We had never given a thought to the fact that more than fifty percent of atmospheric oxygen available to life on Earth comes from the ocean. In other words, every second breath we take, no matter where on the planet we live, is a gift of the sea and the life it sustains. Now we are entering a new phase, literally unknown waters. With the rapid increase of human use of fossil fuels, and the consequent release of huge amounts of carbon dioxide into the atmosphere over the past century, the mix of atmospheric gasses is changing, and with it, inevitably, the mix of life on Earth.

A planet hospitable to humankind?

We began this chapter with an uneasy sense of the tension, a tension we feel very much in our own hearts and heads, between David Hume and Uncle Max. Hume stresses the 'otherness' of the world and warns against disrespectful 'humanizing' of things, which makes them over in our own image. Uncle Max, by contrast, is concerned with our kinship with and belonging to the world. He sees disrespect in attitudes of separation from the world, with the assumption of our superiority to all other creatures, along with the presumption of our right to dominate and manipulate them to our own ends. On this pilgrimage, we have gradually discovered a remarkable convergence in both recent philosophy and recent science between the two perspectives, or rather, the two life-worlds (*Lebenswelten*). Uncle Max talks about *country*, interpreted by Debbie Bird Rose as 'a zone of connectivities organizing itself towards mutually flourishing inter-dependencies.'[50] Contemporary oceanography documents this inter-dependency of all things in space, time, water, air, and life with exquisite and amazing detail. Both know clearly that we are babes, late-comers in the scheme of things.

---

[49] Earle, *The World is Blue*, p. 179. Italics added.
[50] Rose, *Wild Dog Dreaming*, p. 91.

What *we* need to know is that for all we know, we don't really know much about the mysteries of Earth and its ways.

> Today I am conscious of the elemental contrast between being and non-being. I stand in front of all this magnificence. I am aware of it. And I am aware that I am aware of it. But none of this—the entire experience—has anything necessary or self-generated about it. I may never have walked this way in my life. I may never have had a life at all. Earth may have been radically other than it is, and life on Earth, if it were possible, radically other than it has turned out to be over millions of years of evolution. A fundamental historical gratuity stares back at me as I stare at the sea. I am part of this deep wonder. But nothing in me or in it makes it necessary or inevitable that this should be as it is, or that I should know that it is as it is. [G, 6/5/14]

It is one thing to know intellectually (Hume's knowing) that all this complex, time-laden, painstaking, development reaching back 3.5 billion years to (perhaps) a single living cell that emerged somewhere in the primal ocean, is the *conditio sine qua non* for life on Earth, our life included. It is another (Uncle Max's knowing) to feel in our bones the well-nigh miraculous combination of circumstances that make that possible.

From a dive to 300 metres below the surface of the sea, with lights out and in near total darkness, Sylvia Earle tells how she became 'suddenly mindful of the precarious nature of my existence.' Not that she was nervous about the good working condition of her diving gear. It was the contingency of *life* itself that unsettled and astonished her.

> I was sobered by the concept, looking upward through the dark sea, acutely tuned to the reality of sunlight sparking processes in the legions of microscopic plants that absorb carbon dioxide and water, churn out oxygen—and produce the basic simple sugar that in turn is transformed into other compounds munched upon by the countless creatures that have lived, died, and been reconfigured into other ingredients that make up the planet's current organic chemistry.[51]

---

[51] Earle, *Sea Change*, p. 111.

3. Living Together / Tearing Apart

Everything inter-dependent through space and time, water and air, life and death. To be able to think this thought now, to feel the pressure of the sea, to see light and dark, to breathe, to be wet, all these human things, for Sylvia Earle, balance atop a great historical pinnacle of beings and processes that might have been otherwise.

> Today is different from all other preceding days because of these ongoing processes, and tomorrow and all days that follow will be slightly changed as a result of whatever happens now, and the next day, and so on. It is about the most fantastic concept I can imagine, *the interacting processes that somehow work to produce, for now at least, a planet hospitable to humankind.*[52]

The clear message of 21st century whitefella science is that interdependence is the name of the game. Like all other sentient beings, from prokaryotes to humpback whales, we are woven into the closest relationship with Earth; enveloped, with them, by the myriad of ingredients that make life possible now, the outcome of a slow unfolding of that deep time which underwrites the story of the planet.

That this story is what it is and that it might have been otherwise, the kind of 'otherwise' that would not include us as a part of its portfolio (cf. Mars or Venus), is for Earle, 300 metres down and looking up, 'the most fantastic concept'. The fact is 'nothing in me or in it makes it necessary or inevitable that this should be as it is, or that I should know that it is as it is.'

And yet here we are.

Living together.

Increasingly, it seems, in a situation of domestic violence.

---

[52] Earle, *Sea Change*, p. 111. Italics added.

Living Together / **Tearing Apart**

We call it 'the green book'. Just a spiral notebook with a shiny green cover lying unopened on the shelf for years. These days we use it to keep a record of favourite recipes, adding new ones from time to time as whim dictates. Classification is simple; everyday (no stars), special (two stars) and very special (four stars). Only one has so far made it into the four star category. We found it early. Somehow nothing else has quite been able to measure up. The ingredients, freshly bought, are arrayed on our kitchen bench. Our eyes linger on two 2 centimetre thick slices of fish, mouth-wateringly beautiful, slightly translucent and an astonishing deep purple. Tuna. Fragrant bunches of coriander and mint, along with blood-red chillies, green-gold limes, spring onions and garlic await their fate in the blender to become an unforgettable Jamie Oliver *chilli salsa verde*. To be drizzled over the tuna at the last. And the tuna? ... well, that's to be grilled for one minute each side—no more no less—in a hot stippled pan, says Jamie. Add warm, slightly crunchy asparagus spears and we're done. Oh, and there's a layered salad to go with it: squidged-in-the-hand roasted kumara, watercress sprigs, balsamic yellow and red chunky-cut tomatoes, crumbled feta and toasted sunflower, sesame and pumpkin seeds. *Divine*!

That's a throw away word these days. What we mean is, 'try this, it's *really* good'. However, it stubbornly retains an echo of a deeper past, when the world and its bounteous life was recognised as sacred. For thousands of years and across widely diverse cultures, all life, including life in the sea, was understood to have numinous origins. Consequently, it was hunted, gathered and eaten with a sense of deep respect. Totem animals were set apart as untouchable, protected and honoured by those for whom they were totemic; living symbols of the holiness of the life that is also food. Great egg-shaped Neolithic stones (c. 5800 BCE) carved as the faces of fish have been found at Lepenski Vir on the shores of the River Danube in Yugoslavia. These remarkably human-like faces are fish goddesses. They represent one of the oldest known images portraying the wonder and mystery of regenerating life. Glimpses of this past survive in enchanted fairy tales of fish speaking to humans, in the wounded Fisher King of the Grail legends. Carvings on the portals of Romanesque and Gothic cathedrals show Christ in a fish shaped womb/egg. The fish, *ichthus*, is an early Christian symbol of Christ himself. And in some places, fish is still the ritual meal eaten on Friday, the day once sacred to the goddess.[53]

We moderns have abandoned fish goddesses and their trappings. Yet there is still something majestic, magical, and exceedingly beautiful about a great bluefin tuna fish.[54] And it's not just the taste. Though doubtless a coveted target for deep sea fishermen, a bluefin tuna is a treasure trove for marine scientists as well. They talk about it as 'the ultimate fish'.[55] Large, sleek, powerful, with retractable fins, of astonishing elegance in form and grace in movement, bluefin tuna are monarchs of the sea, and have been for millions of years. They mature slowly, live for 20 years or more and have a generation length of about 12 years. Like other members of the tuna clan, they are highly migratory, with a geographic range extending across the Atlantic, Indian and Pacific Oceans. During spawning they find their way to tropical seas off the northwest coast of Australia, returning to particular locations unerringly time and again.[56] Their motor efficiency is extraordinary. Marine engineers try to figure out how these fish succeed in harnessing for their propulsion nearly 97% of the energy they generate through little whirlpools formed in the water as they move their tails back and forth. What, they wonder, would such efficiency mean for submarines? The questions are endless.

---

[53] Anne Baring and Jules Cashford, *The Myth of the Goddess: Evolution of an Image* (London: BCA by arrangement with Penguin Books Ltd, 1991), pp. 63-64 and 414-415. Our word Friday comes from the name of the Norse goddess Freia, and in Italy, fish is eaten on the day named after Venus, *Venerdi*.

[54] The tuna family is composed of a variety of species, including albacore, bigeye, yellowfin and skipjack. These species make up most of the world market in tuna fish according to the World Wildlife Fund (see www.worldwildlife.org/species/tuna). All appear in *The IUCN Red List of Threatened Species (version 2015-4)*, and all show decreasing population trends. Albacore is evaluated as LC (least concern), the others are listed as VU (vulnerable) or NT (near threatened). But it is the largest of the tuna, the bluefin, that is of most concern, see footnote 58 below.

[55] Earle, *The World is Blue*, pp. 72-76.

[56] *IUCN Red List Version 2015-4*, www.iucnredlist.org (accessed 19 April 2016).

How is it possible for them to power their way across entire ocean basins to specific locations repeatedly, without road maps? What senses enable them to locate sources of food? How do they maintain position in amazing V-shaped formations as they move near the ocean's surface? Who leads and why? How do they rest?[57]

Bluefin are mysterious and majestic and enduring.

And we are hunting them to extinction.

Since the early 1950s, the species has been intensively fished primarily using longline fishing techniques. Worldwide reported landings show an increase from 13,552 tonnes in 1952 to a maximum of 55,200 tonnes in 1969. After that, a steep decline. Then from 1992 to 2006 catches were relatively stable at around 16,000 tonnes per year. Because of alarm over declining populations, in 2009 the global recommended take was reduced to 9,448 tonnes, but this has proved extremely difficult to enforce. Current bluefin fishing is estimated to be well above this limit.[58]

Four decades ago, when supplies were plentiful, bluefin was sold as 'horse mackerel' in the United States for cat food at 5 cents a pound. Now the total population is estimated to have declined to somewhere between 7 and 15% of the 1960 parental biomass and it currently shows no signs of bouncing back. Today, Southern Bluefin Tuna is registered as 'critically endangered' on the famous 'Red List' of the International Union for Conservation of Nature (IUCN).[59] But scarcity breeds demand. In the decades since 1960, bluefin has become a much sought after culinary delicacy. Prices have sky rocketed. In January 2016, a sushi

---

57 Earle, *The World is Blue*, p. 74.

58 These figures (obviously) do not include illegal or unreported fishing catch, which is a world-wide problem of significant and increasing importance. See the World Wildlife Fund (WWF) report, *Illegal Fishing: Which fish species are at highest risk from illegal and unreported fishing?*, October 2015. Available on the net.

59 The IUCN is the world's oldest and largest global environmental organization, founded by Julian Huxley in 1948 and now with almost 1,300 government and NGO members and more than 15,000 volunteer experts in 185 countries. The 'Red List' registers threatened species of land and marine life according to a scale which ranges from least concern (LC), near threatened (NT), vulnerable (VU), endangered (EN), critically endangered (CR), extinct in the wild (EW) to extinct (X). Bluefin Tuna presently rate at CR–critically endangered. The data referred to in this section are drawn from the IUCN red list for *Thunnus maccoyii*, Southern Bluefin Tuna at www.iucnredlist.org, (accessed 23 April 2016).

restaurant chain in Japan paid US$118,000 (AU$164,000) for a single 200kg bluefin. This is by no means a record.[60] Such prices generate high motivation for even a small catch.

Extinction looms for a 'divine' species.

'Knowing these things,' writes Sylvia Earle, 'tuna should never be consumed casually, but always with great respect, if they are to be consumed at all. Their precarious state makes eating bluefin tuna comparable to dining out on snow leopard or panda.'[61] That shiny green book contains no recipe for snow leopard steak or panda stew, with or without the *salsa verde*. And we're not looking. It's way past time for us to find some other culinary delight to put in that four star category.

Bluefin tuna is the tiny tip of a very large iceberg. 'The story of humans and fish,' writes Alanna Mitchell, 'is the story of an explosion in the human population and the systematic extermination of fish.'[62] Mitchell is referring to the work of Associate Professor Heike Lotze, a marine scientist who holds the Canada Research Chair in Marine Renewable Resources at Dalhousie University in Nova Scotia, Canada. Lotze and her team developed methods of reconstructing the changing circumstances of marine and shore systems using palaeontology, archaeology, history, fisheries science, and ecology to reveal a recurring pattern in the human-fish story. Taking the Wadden Sea (amongst other sites) as a case study, Lotze gives a brief and thoroughly disconcerting history of fish and fishing in Europe across a period from Neolithic times (when the stone fish goddesses were being carved) to the present.[63] A depressingly consistent story of serial extraction pushed from one species to another to the point of extinction emerges.

---

[60] See *The Guardian*, www.theguardian.com/world/2016/jan/05/threatened-bluefin-tuna. It is reported that in 2013 the same restaurant chain paid a staggering US$1.4 million for a bluefin weighing 222kg. See *The Guardian* 10/2/2013, at www.theguardian.com/environment/2013.

[61] Earle, *The World is Blue*, p. 76.

[62] Mitchell, *Sea Sick*, p. 129.

[63] The Wadden Sea stretches from Den Helder in the northwest of the Netherlands, past the river estuaries of northern Germany, to Skallingen in Denmark, a distance of some 500 km. It is one of the world's seas that has been, over a long period, most modified by human activity. It was inscribed in the UNESCO World Heritage List in 2009.

When humans get to the end of one type of fish we move to another, depleting as we go and moving from big, easy fish to smaller ones. We empty streams, rivers and lakes, then the shores, then the sea and finally the open ocean, a trend that takes those who fish further and further from land and deeper under the surface of the sea.[64]

Today's fishermen reach deeper and deeper below the surface, develop new technological skills and gear to go after dwindling stocks. The recent heated controversies about the introduction of Large Freezer Factory Trawlers into Australian fishing waters are a vivid reminder right on our doorstep of the way this process works; and of its potential damage to our ocean ecologies.[65]

The story of humans and fish as told by Alanna Mitchell is a story set in the context of our recent human domination of marine ecosystems, in particular the ecological effects of industrialised fishing.[66] Alongside this ongoing story, there are other stories. Many individuals and groups across the world have understood a requirement for respect and care in taking life from the sea. As Deborah Bird Rose explains, for Indigenous peoples hunting 'is set within the nexus of country and care'. 'Good hunters know when to stop hunting'.[67] Monitoring and self-regulation are part of care, not only for the present but for future generations. For Uncle Max, whales and fish are Elders. 'Everything we take from the land and sea—plants, berries, animals, fish—we ask these things permission or thank them as they are giving up their life for us to eat'.[68]

---

[64] Mitchell, *Sea Sick*, p. 129. See also the whole section pp. 129-135.

[65] See, for example, "Large Freezer Factory Trawlers in the Australian Small Pelagic Fishery," at www.et.org.au/marine; and "'Super trawler" fears unfounded', at www.afma.gov.au/super-trawler-fears-unfounded.

[66] Lotze's historical research is an attempt to provide accurate baselines for future restoration efforts. Management based purely on recent data alone can be misleading because it deals only with information about already depleted fish communities. Some understanding of the marine ecology prior to exploitation is needed to provide a standard against which to measure the effectiveness of any proposed recovery project.

[67] Rose *et al, Country of the Heart*, p. 83 and p. 88. This story, with superb photography, tells of her journey with the MakMak people of the Wagait floodplains south-west of Darwin in Australia's Top End.

[68] Harrison, *My People's Dreaming*, p. 130 and p. 88.

The complexity of the problem is baffling. We cannot return to the past. Fishing is a world-wide phenomenon. Most nations have a vital interest in it as a source of food for tens of millions and a means of livelihood for hundreds of thousands.[69] Respect for the future is undoubtedly wise. Yet, economic interests often come into conflict with ecological concerns and, as is the case in most conflicts, truth often seems an early casualty. In addition, it is difficult, especially for the non-expert, to get an accurate sense of the situation overall.

In 2003, a now famous paper entitled, "Rapid worldwide depletion of predatory fish communities", was published in *Nature*, by Ransom Myers and Boris Worm. In a climate of concern about the ecological effects of industrialised fishing and after 10 years of research, Myers and Worm conclude:

> Industrialised fisheries typically reduced community biomass by 80% within 15 years of exploitation. Compensatory increases in fast-growing species were observed, but often reversed within a decade. Using a meta-analytic approach, we estimate that large predatory fish biomass today is only about 10% of pre-industrial levels. We conclude that declines of large predators in coastal regions have extended throughout the global ocean, with potentially serious consequences for ecosystems.[70]

'Community biomass' is techno-speak for fish numbers. Myers and Worm are talking here about tuna, swordfish, sharks, skates, blue marlin, tropical groupers, Antarctic cod and other large predatory fish. The truly alarming thing about their research is that it relates not to local fisheries or regional marine areas alone, but to a decline in the amount of life ('biomass') in the worldwide ocean, not just in some areas, or for

---

[69] For contemporary statistics, see United Nations Food and Agriculture Organization (FOA), FOA 2016. *The State of World Fisheries and Acquaculture. Contributing to food security and nutrition for all*. Rome, 2016, pp. 70-79.

[70] Ransom A. Myers and Boris Worm, "Rapid worldwide depletion of predatory fish communities," *Nature*. May 15, 2003, pp. 280-283, at p. 280. Both authors are from the Biology Department of Dalhousie University, Halifax, Nova Scotia, Canada. They constructed trajectories of community biomass and composition of large predatory fishes in four continental shelf and nine oceanic systems.

some stocks, but for entire communities of large fish species, from the tropics to the poles.

Three years after the publication of this so-called 90% paper, Worm and his colleagues made public an even more worrying finding. Building on the previous research into the rate of global decline of large predatory fish, Worm made a projection of where these fish stocks were heading under a business as usual scenario.

> Our data highlight the societal consequences of an ongoing erosion of diversity that appears to be accelerating on a global scale. This trend is of serious concern because it projects *the global collapse of all taxa* [i.e., varieties] *currently fished by the mid-21st century ... in the year 2048*.[71]

That concrete number—2048—seemed to shatter the silence. This time the research captured headlines and generated fallout well beyond the scientific community. Newspaper editorials, late night talk shows, cartoonists and celebrity magazines all ran with it.

Professional response split along familiar lines, the conclusions were bitterly criticized by fisheries scientists and strongly supported by marine ecologists. Ray Hilborn, professor of Fisheries Management at the School of Aquatic and Fisheries Science at the University of Washington, Seattle, for example, called Worm's use of catch data 'incredibly sloppy' and the projection of global collapse of certain fisheries by 2048 'just mind-bogglingly stupid'. A professor Daniel Pauly of the University of British Columbia fired back with 'a thinly veiled suggestion that Hilborn and other critics of Worm's (and others') studies were "captured" by the fisheries industry.'[72] Such infighting in the community of experts makes it incredibly hard for the layperson to know where to stand and what to think, but it undoubtedly signals the fact that the issue is visceral, of fundamental importance for the future of life in the seas, and for the well-being of millions of humans.

---

[71] Boris Worm *et al*, "Impacts of Biodiversity Loss on Ocean Ecosystem Services," *Science*, New Series, Vol. 314, No. 5800 (Nov. 3, 2006), pp. 787-790, at p. 790. Italics added.

[72] For an overview of this debate see Matt Burgess, "Case Study: The Hilborn-Worm debate on the status of global fisheries," *The Téte-à-Téte*, December 3, 2014, http//theteteatete.org/2014/12/03/case-study-the-hilborn-worm-debate-on-the-status-of-global-fisheries. See also, Ray Hilborn, "Faith-based Fisheries," *Fisheries*, Vol. 31, No. 11, November 2006, pp. 554-555.

In a subsequent development, and as a fascinating example of how the scientific community moves in the process of debate (even heated debate!) towards what is hopefully a better understanding of the facts of the matter, Boris Worm and a number of his critics, including Ray Hilborn, combined to publish further research upon which they do agree. In a major paper published in *Science,* they conclude in rather more nuanced terms:

> Marine ecosystems are currently subjected to a range of exploitation rates, resulting in a mosaic of stable, declining, collapsing, and rebuilding fish stocks. Management actions have achieved measurable reductions in exploitation rates in some regions, but a significant fraction of stocks will remain collapsed unless there is further reduction in exploitation rates.[73]

In other words, the global picture is mixed, some populations of large predatory fish are stable, some declining, some collapsing, some rebuilding. This yields the conclusion that, despite the long history of radical overexploitation of many species, there is some hope that 'marine ecosystems can still recover *if exploitation rates are reduced substantially.*' What exactly does 'reduced substantially' mean? Worm and Hilborn are imprecise. It means, they say, the exploitation rate 'that achieves maximum sustainable yield (U_{MSY}) should be reinterpreted as *an upper limit rather than a management target.*'[74] The maximum sustainable yield is defined as the largest yield (or catch) that can be taken from a species stock over an indefinite period, i.e., without threatening the long-term viability of the stock.

Whether such a U_{MSY} is a sustainable goal, or even capable of sensible measurement, is itself subject to vigorous debate.[75] On top of this, Worm and Hilborn's study accounted for less than a quarter of the world fisheries area and catch, and the rebuilding of ecosystems that they studied comprised less than half of those. What of the other three quarters where systematic data are hard or impossible to come by? What of the billion

---

[73] Boris Worm, Ray Hilborn, *et al,* "Rebuilding Global Fisheries," *Science,* 31 July 2009, Vol. 325, Issue 5940, pp. 578-588 at p. 588. Available on the net.
[74] Worm and Hilborn, *et al,* "Rebuilding Global Fisheries," p. 588. Italics added.
[75] See Earle, *Sea Change,* pp. 189-197.

dollar global trade in illegal, unreported and unregulated fishing (IUU), which the World Wildlife Fund estimated in 2015 significantly impacts on 86% of global fish stocks currently being commercially exploited? In 2016, the United Nations Food and Agriculture Organization concluded (based on data from 2013) that 31.4% of global fish stocks were currently 'fished at a biologically unsustainable level and therefore overfished'; 58.1% 'were fully fished' and 10.5% 'underfished'.[76] This seems to be saying that about 90% of the current global catch is either unsustainable or on the edge of being so. Throw into the mix Matthew Evans' brilliant pioneering television program, *What's the catch?*, which confronted us with some shocking images of so-called 'by-catch waste' involved in shrimp farming in Thailand and (worse) of the grim suffering that shark-fin harvesting visits on millions of animals each year, and it is hard to know where to come down between despair and hope.[77]

As far as we are able to judge, this much is clear. Nobody who has tried to follow this discussion with any care can doubt that in the last forty years human population increase combined with industrial fishing techniques have degraded the oceanic biosphere with a range, rapidity and, if the word is not too emotive, savagery that is unprecedented.

Fish are one element in a stunningly beautiful and intricately interconnected web of life that is the ocean. In extracting millions of tonnes of fish year by year we are interrupting, removing and randomly destroying large chunks of an ancient inter-connected system that has been built up slowly over millions of years. Sylvia Earle likens this to haphazardly pulling out bits of a computer, and still expecting it to work.[78] What are the consequences? The answer is that we simply do not know. The complexity of the issues involved and the speed of change means it is impossible to predict with any certainty where this process, if unchecked, will lead.

The problem is not just that tuna are disappearing, or even that many communities of predatory fish are declining globally. We are facing a

---

[76] FOA 2016. *The State of World Fisheries and Acquaculture*, p. 38.
[77] The program was aired on SBS in October 2014.
[78] Earle, *The World is Blue*, p. 69.

systemic issue on a planetary level. Our actions are changing the way ocean biosystems function.

Changes in marine biodiversity are directly caused by exploitation, pollution, and habitat destruction, or indirectly through climate change and related perturbations of ocean biochemistry. Although marine extinctions are only slowly uncovered at the global scale, regional ecosystems such as estuaries, coral reefs, and coastal and oceanic fish communities are rapidly losing populations, species and entire functional groups. ... [Human actions are] increasingly impairing the ocean's capacity to provide food, maintain water quality, and recover from perturbations.[79]

We are on the edge of a threshold.

We are breaking bonds we do not understand.

We are 'tearing at the heart of planetary processes, vital not only for life in the sea, but for all life on Earth'.[80]

'Who hears the fishes when they cry?' asks Henry David Thoreau.[81]

---

[79] Worm *et al*, "Impacts of Biodiversity Loss on Ocean Ecosystem Services," p. 787.
[80] Earle, *The World is Blue*, p. 69.
[81] Quoted in Earle, *The World is Blue*, p. 53.

Learning a practice of attention (3)

We are part, one tiny part of an immense, living, interconnected whole. Our being—body, mind, soul—is our participation in the world. The practice of attention allows us to feel in our whole being the manifold texture of the world as it approaches us.

* * * * * *

Locating

Placing ourselves respectfully (even reverently) in *this* particular location in the world is an important preparation for attending its being. One simple way of doing this, used by many Indigenous peoples, is to 'honour' the four directions, east, north, west, south. (Sometimes the other two directions, above and below, are included as well.) This gesture acknowledges the immensity of the whole of which we are a part. Turn to face each of the compass points, think briefly about what lies near and far in that direction, and bow slightly.

Breathing

Take some long, slow, deep breaths, allowing your breath to flow through as much of your body as possible. Then simply follow the calm flow of your natural breathing. Feel your breath connecting you with Earth and everything around you.

Synaesthesia

Attending involves the use of all the senses together. Look. Listen. Smell. Taste. Touch. From time to time you may find one particular sense 'calling' for special attention: trust this.

Chanting

To our surprise, the ancient Hindu custom of chanting the sacred syllable '*om*', assisted us remarkably in aligning ourselves with the rhythms, sounds and movements of the world around us, and in joining our fleshly voices with the voices of other beings. *Om*, believed by many to 'correspond to the most intimate and holy sound of the universe', is made up of three parts (A-U-M). These are traditionally intoned as, *ah* rising from the stomach, *oo* from the region of the sternum, *mm* from the upper throat. Choose a note low in your vocal register, like the voice you use in speaking tenderly to a friend.

For those unfamiliar with chanting, this will probably seem weird or off-putting. But once we took the plunge, we found the practice well worth the initial discomfort.

4. Look! Hear! / A Wicked Problem

It requires looking more carefully at what seems only too familiar, and seeing it perhaps for the very first time.

Ian McGilchrist

On attention

Chrétien argues for a 'visible voice' of tangible things that share the world with us. Augustine claims to speak to the world by gazing at its constituent elements, and to hear by attending their insistent beauty. Uncle Max tells of *country* that 'talks'. For most of our lives we have been completely oblivious of such possibilities. Now an unavoidable question arises. Can old dogs learn new tricks?

An early journal:

> Standing is arduous. After 15 minutes pain radiates from the lower back down my legs. I need to sit. But something steels my will. I stick it out. ... The sea is beautiful; wonderful blues and dark greens out to the horizon. Beauty speaks, says Augustine. If that is true, this must be breathtaking 'language'. It silences me. I feel sort of shamed that I have waited so long to pay attention to it. I put the question to the sea: 'Are you willing to communicate with me?' Minutes pass. Then a wave, larger than its fellows, rears up and breaks with an authoritative crash right in front of me. 'Are you willing to listen?' That takes me by surprise. *Am* I willing to listen? Not to myself. Not on my terms. 'Come back when you are ready to listen', it says unmistakably; or as unmistakably as anything I have been able to discern in this enterprise to date. I break off. What does it mean to be ready to listen? [G, 11/6/13]

What *does* it mean to be ready? In a brilliant book, Ian McGilchrist argues that 'the kind of attention we bring to bear on the world changes the nature of the world we attend to.'[1] Our attention is responsive to the world,

---

[1] Ian McGilchrist, *The Master and His Emissary: The Divided Brain and the Making of the Western World* (New Haven: Yale University Press, 2009), p. 28. McGilchrist deals with the importance of attention in our engagement with the world throughout the book, but of most

but the world is also responsive to our attention. And that interaction changes possibilities. The ocean that is a recreational opportunity for a surfer, an economic resource for a professional fisherman, a scientific challenge to a marine biologist, or a dynamic, many-coloured vision for a painter, is changed by the kind of attention paid to it. The surfer, the fisherman, the biologist and the painter are themselves changed in turn by the kind of response the ocean yields to the attention they give. There is no 'real' ocean, McGilchrist contends, that can be distinguished from these various sorts of attentions, although one kind of attention may well depreciate or enhance our capacity to enjoy or even acknowledge another. A dominating interest in the ocean as economic resource, for example, may block out the aesthetic appreciation of the artist, or the scientific attention of the ecologist. What the ocean *is* depends on who is attending to it, and in what way.[2]

This becomes a primary challenge. We are drawn to attend to the ocean. The kind of attention we are trying to foster remains elusive. Somehow it always seems easier to say what sort of attention we are *not* paying.

> Even though the day is overcast, the glare from the sky hurts my eyes. I pull my cap lower, until my peripheral vision is quite restricted. As a result, I don't see the woman approaching from the south, walking a small dog. Suddenly she is in my frame of vision, hardly three metres away. Looking me straight in the eye and raising an eyebrow she asks, 'meditating?' Taken aback, I blurt out, 'yes'. 'Nice', she says, and slips from view beyond the rim of my cap. Synchronicity is an odd thing. I had spent the morning reading von Weizsäcker on meditation.[3] Now, out of the blue, a stranger uses the same word. Does 'meditation' somehow apply to this practice? Von Weizsäcker argues that the first response to such a question has to be silence. You can't say what

---

interest to us are the following pages: 28-29; 133-135; 150-153.
[2] See McGilchrist, *The Master and His Emissary*, pp. 133-135. Augustine would agree with this view. 'To the man who merely looks it [i.e., the universe] says nothing, while to another [who asks] it gives an answer.' *Confessions*, X, 6, 213. See p. 20 above.
[3] Carl Friedrich von Weizsäcker, "Gespräch über Meditation," in *Der Garten des Menschlichen: Beiträge zur geschichtlichen Anthropologie* (München: Carl Hanser Verlag, 1977), pp. 533-550.

meditation is without in the process distorting it. Sea see/hearing is not just looking at the sea (though it is that); it's not just listening to the sea (though it is that); it's not just looking at colours and observing movement (though it is that); and it's not just appreciating the whole (though it is that, too). All these 'nots' are inescapable if you try to speak to the question. But what 'yeses' do they imply? [G, 25/3/15]

Certainly not the surfer's attention to the catchable wave, though there is something of her exhilaration in the glory and power of the sea we share. Nor the fisherman's concern for the economic exploitation of the sea, though we, too, know and revere the ocean's extraordinary bounty. And not the scientist's detached and analytical investigation of the physical, chemical and biological components of sea water, though we sense how crucial such knowledge is for any responsible appreciation of the sea in our time. The artist's sort of attention seems nearer the mark, though we have no capacity to write like Mary Oliver, and even less to paint like Fred Williams.

The attention required in sea see/hearing seems to call for a disposition of patient respect, a quiet waiting on the world to declare or manifest itself in accordance with its own being or nature, and a willingness to respond with empathy, in a spirit of openness, gratitude and even love. For McGilchrist, this engaged attention to the world is 'emphatically *not* [achieved] by annexing it, exploiting it or ransacking it for congenial meanings, in a spirit of "anything goes".'[4] Rather, it looks for encounter more than possession, for participation more than exploitation, for communication more than information. We wait on something to 'unconceal' itself (Heidegger). We try to lure something into disclosing itself, encouraging it to come out of hiding, as it were. George Steiner compares such attention to that 'bending toward' of spirit, intellect and ear displayed by the astonished Mary in Fra Angelico's famous *Annunciation*. And he associates it with Heidegger's approach to truth in contrast to Descartes'.

For Descartes, truth is determined and validated by certainty. Certainty, in turn, is located in the *ego*. The self becomes the hub of reality

---

[4] McGilchrist, *The Master and His Emissary*, p. 151. Italics added.

and relates to the world outside itself in an exploratory, necessarily exploitative, way. As knower and user, the *ego* is predator. For Heidegger, on the contrary, the human person and self-consciousness are *not* the centre, the assessors of existence. Man is only a privileged listener and respondent to existence. The vital relation to otherness is not, as for Cartesian and positivist rationalism, one of 'grasping' and pragmatic use. It is a relation of audition. We are trying 'to listen to the voice of Being'. It is, or ought to be, a relation of extreme responsibility, custodianship, answerability to and for.[5]

The vital relation to otherness, in this case the otherness called ocean, is *audition* not possession. 'We are trying to listen to the voice of Being'. However, this is only possible if we allow ourselves to be 'drawn into and inextricably bound up with the world in a relation ... of "being-with" and inside, a relation of care (*Sorge*) and concern, suggesting involvement of the whole experiential being, not just the processes of cognition.'[6] In this sense, the attention entailed in sea see/hearing is a *moral* and emotional act. It places us in a relation of answerability, responsibility, custodianship and care with respect to that to which we give our attention; the ocean. This moral aspect of the pilgrimage will occupy us in detail in the next chapter, but for now we are concerned with the art of paying attention, of paying this *kind* of attention.

How do we go about it? What follows is a description of the way in which, to use Freya Mathews' words, we began to 'ask the larger scheme of things to manifest its self-meaning to us.'[7] As it is set out here, it appears more orderly and serene than was the journey that brought us to this outcome. Our stumbling attempts to learn how to be this way in the world come to light on every page of the journal. For all the stops and starts, the getting lost and having to start over again, we found there *is*

---

[5] George Steiner, *Martin Heidegger* (New York: Viking, 1978), pp. 29-31, cited in McGilchrist, *The Master and His Emissary*, p. 152.

[6] McGilchrist, *The Master and His Emissary*, p. 153. *Sorge* is the German word for 'care' or 'concern' and is used by Heidegger in his discussion of the nature of our human 'being-in-the-world'.

[7] Freya Mathews, "On Desiring Nature," *EarthSong*, Vol. 2, Issue 1, Autumn 2011, p. 13; reprinted from *Indian Journal of Ecocriticism*, 3, 2010, pp. 1-9. This whole essay has been of great significance in our efforts to shape and understand the practice we call 'sea see/hearing'.

a path here, however elusive. And it *is* worth following, however slowly. Not for the sake of some final goal, but for the surprise of the way itself. The practice outlined below condenses a mass of disparate experiences and simplifies a complex tangle of trial and error. It represents a compass more than a Google map, we might say.

Learning to attend

Place

If we are to have any chance of attending to the visible voice of the ocean (or any aspect of the other-than-human world for that matter), it is obvious that we must place ourselves in the presence of this other. At first, we just happened to be in Tathra, drawn there by the beauty of the location, and especially the beauty of the ocean. It quickly became clear that the place itself was to be foundational to our experience. Tathra is a town as well as a beach. We were happily living in it. A few minutes walk from the houses and we are outside, really outside, on the edge, the Pacific Ocean right at our feet, wide and wild.

> At the edge of the sea I feel an invitation to enter something bigger; magnificent, powerful, dynamic, changing. The intense presence of the ancient (so-called) 'elements' envelops me. *Fire*. The warmth of the sun is palpable. I feel it through my whole body. It lights up the whole world. *Air*. The wind is strong. It drives from the south pushing heavy waves at unusual angles to the shore. *Earth*. A billion grains of sand swept and washed into stunning shapes spread out all around. *Water*. Long, powerful waves roll in with urgent restlessness. The sea is intent on business. Of eternal moment. [G, 16/2/16]

In deliberately choosing to put ourselves in this wide, wild place we were responding, at the time largely without being aware of it, to a dearth of beauty in our world; to a longing for something 'magnificent, powerful, dynamic', something of 'eternal moment' that 'lights up the whole world'. We met it on the edge of the town, outside and away from the houses. This is no accident. The town is comforting and secure because its 'mirrored walls' (to use David Abram's vivid phrase) reflect our own image.[8] The town holds us in familiar ways of seeing, habits of speaking and possibilities of feeling, reassuring us of our identity. But just because of this, it also has ways of hemming us in and shutting us down. In town, the media confronts us with a relentless stream of images, most of them fleeting and many violent. A frenetic push for consumption mutes language as a vehicle of truth and dulls sensitivity to possibilities that beckon us beyond the call for instant gratification. Ceaseless development creates a vast world of houses, shopping malls, schools, roads and suburbs that often lack grace and stifle mystery. Degradation of the environment transforms more and more of the beautiful Earth into a wasteland.

This is not meant to be dismissive of the town as our human habitat. We are city dwellers through and through! But in an increasingly congested urban society, it becomes harder to escape the wall of mirrors. The human dominates. It is difficult to imagine another reality, and exhausting to try. 'Much of the stress and emptiness that haunts us,' says John O'Donohue, 'can be traced back to our lack of attention to beauty. Internally, the mind becomes coarse and dull if it remains unvisited by images and thoughts which hold the radiance of beauty.'[9]

Place is more than location, as history is more than time. We experimented with sea see/hearing in a variety of spots in and around Tathra. Gradually we were drawn to one particular place on the main beach mid-way between the southern cliff, where the famous Beach Café nestles into the dunes beneath the shady branches of a stately Norfolk Island pine, and the northern reaches of the shore, where the Bega River breaks through a massive sand bank to empty into the sea. This became 'our place'. We returned to it again and again. Memories of past experiences at this spot began to gather and consolidate within us. Early feelings of strangeness gave way to a sense of familiarity, and familiarity dissolved imperceptibly into friendship. We were starting to belong. 'I am glad to be back in the same spot as yesterday. Familiarity—

---

[8] David Abram, *The Spell of the Sensuous: Perception and Language in a More-Than-Human World* (New York: Vintage Books, 1997), p. 28.
[9] John O'Donohue, *The Invisible Embrace of Beauty: Rediscovering the True Sources of Compassion, Serenity, and Hope* (New York: Harper Perennial, 2004), p. 4.

the 'my place' feeling—is important in what happens in sea see/hearing.' [J, 6/6/13]. The living memory of these colours, these fragrances, these sounds, the familiar presence of these trees that crowd so close to the shore of this particular scallop-shaped coastline, coalesce inwardly into a story that begins to 'speak' this place to our hearts.

Nor is it only our little story that matters. Uncle Max and the Yuin Nation have called this spot 'their place' for thousands of years. Their sacred stories and ceremonies display the unique power of place and highlight the way their different ecologies call upon humans to care for *country*. Specific sites within the larger geographic area are linked with particular events or dreams. The long ridge that snakes its way down to the sea from Mount Gulaga (near Tilba Tilba) is, for Yuin people, the Rainbow Serpent whose tail is resting at Tathra. To recognize this ancient presence and to be open to the radical shift in perception, which Yuin stories and songs offer us, changes our attention to the phenomena of the sea at Tathra. We start to see and hear differently, and therefore start to speak differently.

> I remember the Indigenous greeting to 'Grandfather Sun' on the Gulaga educational weekend. I realize, with some astonishment, that we 'whitefellas', following the Elders, spoke with our voices *to* the Sun, not *about* the Sun. How did that happen? I find myself wondering today about the Yuin way of knowing the world as 'Mother Earth', 'Father Sky', 'Grandmother Moon'. And names like *Gadu* for the ocean, and *Koorah Koo-rie* for wind or spirit. When these people speak about the ocean, it is as to a person, by name—*Gadu*, not to a thing labelled 'the ocean'.[10] [J, 6/5/14]

The pull of place reaches deeper still. The longer we persist with this practice, the more we start to feel ancient stories in the rocks, the plants, the grasses, the particular birds who inhabit or migrate to *this* beach—especially the tiny (endangered) 'Little Terns' scurrying across the sand on their matchstick legs—the insects, the lizards, the kangaroos,

---

10 This comment arose after Jan had spent a weekend at an educational gathering organized by local Yuin people designed to introduce whitefellas to country around the Gulaga region. This included instruction, conversation, meals, dance rituals, courtesy protocols for entering country, and ceremonies of respect and celebration in relation to sea, sun and mountain.

the patterns of wind, the changeable clouds 'heaped on high horizons' (Stevens), the shifting sand continually remoulding the beach, blocking or freeing the river mouth, the changing course of the sun's rising and setting, the moon's white ribbon thrown gently across the water on a clear night.

> The light is beautiful. The breaking waves are beautiful. The sand is beautiful. On the beach, I try to locate myself by thinking of the continents of the world, and of ancient Gondwana Land. Am I standing on or near the edge of a break, a breaking apart, of tectonic plates? ... The ridge of the Great Dividing Range rises in the distance behind me. I am perched on land falling eastwards from it, at the place where the sea meets the sand. I try to hold in my mind the continuity of this land plunging under the sea, reaching into the depths. [J, 25/4/15]

An immensity of space and unknown depths of time coalesce here. A billion living plants with roots and branches, leaves and flowers, and countless furry things, flapping things, swimming things, crawling things, and thousands of generations of human beings have dwelt in this place. They have made it what it has been and is becoming. Now, for a brief moment in time, it is 'our place', too. Can we hear its voice? Might we join its song?

Body

The attention required of sea see/hearing is *bodily* through and through; more like the concentration of a dancer awaiting her entry on stage than a scholar preoccupied with a mathematical problem at the desk. Like the dancer, the physical situation in the moment calls forth the required bodily responses.

> Debbie Bird Rose says: 'If you put your body into the place with an attitude of attention, the place will organise you by requiring you to make changes in yourself.'[11] We are learning both things are true. Place and posture matter. We choose to put our bodies in place, at the edge of the sea. We stand upright. We pay attention. [G, 8/6/13]

---

11 Deborah Bird Rose, *Reports from a Wild Country: Ethics for Decolonisation* (Sydney: University of New South Wales Press, 2004), p. 208.

Our eyes watch over the call that rises from the ocean and our ears attend the voice that breaks from its silence because, with practice, our bodies gradually learn to engage with its presence, all senses respectfully alert to its communicative possibilities.

> Heavy waves roll toward me, tumbling across themselves in a profusion of foam and spray. Between the breaks, water roams restlessly, laced with white and green. The sky is low. Thick grey clouds threaten rain. Sound magnifies: breaking water; wind pushing against my face; gulls shrieking overhead. The world is in full voice. I try to let it flood my body. 'Natural perception occurs through our *whole body at once* and opens onto an intersensorial world', writes Merleau-Ponty. 'Synaesthetic perception [hearing, seeing, smelling, tasting, feeling, touching simultaneously] is the rule.'[12] [G, 22/3/12]

Bodily posture was also critical to the development of a practice of attentiveness. At first, we *sat* on the beach to receive whatever the sea might be pleased to offer. Meditative practices are often done sitting down. In a Buddhist context, to sit is a bodily synonym for prayer. Sitting is often, though not exclusively, the position adopted for prayer in Christian worship. However, we quickly came to feel that sitting was not the best way to approach sea see/hearing.

> Is there a difference between standing and sitting while attending to the sea? ... Sitting can easily become slouching; and slouching dozing. But dozing is much harder to manage when standing! Also, standing in our tradition is a mark of respect, an indication of attention, even deference. There is something fitting about standing—and standing still—in the 'sacred' presence of the sea. It contrasts strongly with other kinds of beach behaviour, say, sunbathing spread-eagle on a towel, or lounging in a deck chair reading the paper. [G, 11/3/13]

A Taoist practice of standing meditation reinforced our hunch. This Indigenous form of attending to the world is traditionally done standing on a mountain, beside a stream, or among trees. It aims to place the

---

[12] Quoted in Jean-Louis Chrétien, *The Call and the Response*, trans. Anne A. Davenport (New York: Fordham University Press, 2004), p. 198. The citation is from Merleau-Ponty, *Phenomenology of Perception*, trans. Colin Smith (London: Routledge, 2002), p. 266. Italics added.

practitioner upright in the presence of nature understood as a sacred whole. By repeatedly standing still, expectant and respectful in the midst of what is conceived of as a living and inter-connected web of beings, the human being slowly learns the art of close contemplative awareness of surrounding realities. This nurtures sensitivity to the 'energy of Being' that flows through everything that exists. Living communication takes place. The human self is no longer observer, still less master, of the world, but one part of a living whole.

Standing as a gesture of respect is a form of courtesy. When the world shifts from being 'stuff' to the possibility of being a communicative presence, the question of approach, of etiquette, of protocols immediately presents itself. '[A]bove all learn courtesy and how to approach the world with permission. Don't make a mine of the world, learn to wait for permission, learn how to love the world.'[13] Indigenous peoples have everything to teach about such courtesy. Their life-ways are ways of speaking, listening, acting and being with respect, grace and beauty. We have everything to learn. Standing is a beginning.

Another bodily practice—this time coming from the Hindu tradition—assumed, to our surprise, an important role in our efforts to learn the art of attending. Chanting has always held an honoured place in major religious traditions; Hindu, Sufi, Buddhist, Christian. We were familiar with the form, but unskilled in the execution. On top of which, one of us was deeply sceptical. 'I can't hold a note to save my life!' he grumbled. We had been reading Andrew Harvey, whose knowledge of mystical practices across all the great religions is truly impressive. According to Harvey, 'you don't have to have a strong singing voice or any musical talent to discover the power of chanting for yourself.'[14] He recommends chanting the sacred Hindu syllable *om*, arguing on the basis of an ancient tradition found in the Chandogya Upanishad, that this is 'the sound that the entire creation is always resonating to, and the sound that the Godhead makes as it creates reality.'[15] Hmm ... how

---

[13] Martín Prechtel, *The Smell of Rain on Dust: Grief and Praise* (Berkeley, California: North Atlantic Books, 2015), p. 157.
[14] Andrew Harvey, *The Hope: a Guide to Sacred Activism* (New York: Hay House, Inc., 2009), p. 153.
[15] Harvey, *The Hope*, p. 154.

would you know that? 'You don't,' says Harvey. 'And you won't; unless you try.'

> I decide to chant the *om*. It is a very ancient practice. I like that. It locates me in a deep time tradition, in a line of others without number. *Om* has come to mean a variety of things in different times and places. But one common aspect is that it is an attempt to align yourself with the 'essence' or 'core' of things (the heart of the matter—whatever that is!). It is like saying with your whole body, 'amen', 'I agree', 'I concur'. The chanting, Harvey suggests, is best served by choosing a note near to the voice you would use speaking tenderly to a lover. Keep this note at a uniform volume and pace. I found this easily fitted with my slow breathing. Harvey breaks the *om* into three syllables A – O – M. You generate the sound coming up from the diaphragm, through the throat, and into the mouth. ... I am conscious of joining my voice to other voices around me, especially the voice of the sea: the waves crashing and slipping, sliding and rushing, the rain softly pattering on my head. I am also very aware of other voices present with me—the wind, the birds. I don't have the same tension today that I have experienced earlier. ... I can hear the other voices around me and join with them without feeling pulled in several directions. Familiarity in the practice helps. I notice the power of the chant to quieten my mind.[16] [J, 10/4/14]

At first we felt a tension between the effort of attending to the voice of the ocean beyond ourselves while generating the sound of *om* within ourselves. With repetition we discovered the reverse to be the case. The chant enabled us to 'hear the other voices around [us] and join with them without feeling pulled in several directions'. We didn't always make use of the chant, but in the quest for the visible voice of the ocean, the engagement of the audible voice of the body proved a surprisingly valuable asset.

Listening

The attention we are trying to foster in this pilgrimage is synaesthetic, involving all the bodily senses. Thus far for us it is especially associated

---

[16] For guidance on the practice of chanting *om* see pp. 107-108.

with ear and eye. So what is involved in this particular kind of hearing and seeing? Let's begin with the ear.

Speaking of conditions under which art and literature can flourish, the novelist Saul Bellow said bluntly, 'the enemy is noise'. By noise he meant the din of urban living, 'the noise of technology, the noise of money or advertising and promotion, the noise of the media, the noise of miseducation, [and] the terrible excitement and distraction generated by the crises of modern life.'[17] Bellow's view of art holds true, perhaps more so, of the effort to pay attention to the more-than-human-world. The enemy is noise.

Internal noise.

I have a difficult time. The day is warm and the wind strong. The sea is in fine (loud) voice, which I enjoy hugely. But I can't stop myself inwardly running off in pursuit of my own interests. I think about the chapter I am working on and all the knotty problems it presents. Then I think about going to Canberra soon. All the people I need to contact. There seems no way to derail this inner chatter. I feel weary with it. I am getting nowhere. [G, 19/3/15]

And external noise.

Although we are quite a way north of the main beach area, the session is interrupted significantly by a bunch of people, adults and children, and couple of dogs chasing a pink beach ball all over the place. The party settles right in front of us. Children dart in and out of the water, squealing. Adults mill about, noisily ordering events of the moment. It is extremely hard to attend to the voice of the sea. Way too many voices of the human kind. The session falls apart. [G, 18/2/12]

If an essential requirement of listening to another human being is that we create a silence in and around ourselves in order to attend to what is being said to us—and it is—then such a silence seems even more essential in any attempt to attend to the visible voice of the world. The voice of the sea comes to us from a different order of being from that of another human person. We found that that watery voice breaks its

---

[17] Nathaniel Rich, "Bellow: The "Defiant, Irascible Mind"," *The New York Review of Books*, June 4, 2015, p. 14.

own silence only if we offer it ours. That means we must learn to achieve silence in ourselves, learn to 'derail the inner chatter' in our heads, and 'anchor our souls in a sort of serenity' (Proclus).[18]

In an impressive essay on silence in nature, Søren Kierkegaard argues that while there may be truth in the claim that 'speech is man's advantage over the beasts', unless we also learn to keep silent 'out there with the lilies and the birds, where there is silence', we will never learn to engage effectively with the deeper truths and challenges of human existence.[19] This instructive silence of nature for Kierkegaard is not the mere absence of sound, since without cease the world 'is vibrating with a thousand notes and all is like a sea of sound'. But what strikes us if we attend carefully to nature, he maintains, is a deep *background of silence* in which all these sounds of the world are held; a silence from which they emerge, a silence into which they subside.

> The sea is silent; even when it rages noisily, it is yet silent. In the first instant thou hearest perhaps amiss, and thou hearest it make a noise. In case thou art in haste to carry this report, thou dost do the sea an injustice. On the other hand, *if thou wilt give thyself time and listen more attentively*, thou dost hear—how amazing!—thou dost hear silence ...[20]

This deep background silence is never disrupted by natural sounds, Kierkegaard insists. They seem rather to enhance it and draw us into it. It is the noise of human commerce and industry—Saul Bellow's noise—that drowns it out.

Moreover, Kierkegaard is alive to the fact that it is no easy matter to learn to listen to this silence of and in nature. In a disturbingly prescient

---

[18] See Chrétien, *The Call and the Response*, pp. 62-63, here Chrétien is discussing Proclus' understanding of the 'chiasm of silences' that cross in the exchange between the human spirit and the transcendent One.

[19] Kierkegaard is here discussing words from Jesus' Sermon on the Mount, 'Behold the birds of the air'; 'Consider the lilies of the field' (Matthew 6.26 & 28). See, *Christian Discourses and The Lilies of the Field and the Birds of the Air and Three Discourses at the Communion of Fridays*, trans. Walter Lowrie (London: Oxford University Press, 1952), pp. 319-332. The original appeared in 1848-49. Søren Kierkegaard (1813–1855) was a Danish thinker, theologian and poet, widely considered to be the first existentialist philosopher.

[20] Kierkegaard, *Christian Discourses*, p. 324. Italics added.

portrayal of our own efforts to attend to the silent voice of the sea, he mocks the would-be 'poet of nature' (as he labels him) 'out there in the silence' supposedly listening to the 'lilies and the birds', but all the while 'he devises great plans to transform the world and render it blissful' or 'broods over his pain' and 'lets everything echo his pain'. Ouch!

> Suddenly I feel really other than this sea. A stand-off develops. Far from feeling akin and connected to the ocean, I feel separated and disconnected. All the things that are important to *me*—my life, my feelings, my thoughts, even our conversation in the café a few minutes ago—seem completely alien to this 'ever-hooded, tragic-gestured sea' (Stevens) coming towards me endlessly, inexorably, indifferently. The sea could just roll over me. Then keep on doing exactly what it is doing now for another eternity. And that would be that. Far from me 'anthropomorphising' the sea, the ocean seems to be 'aquaomorphising' me. I am drowning in a huge mass of water. I feel utterly destabilised and disoriented. I am very happy when the time is up and we can go home. [G, 20/2/15]

One who claims to seek the silence of nature, but really listens to his or her own voice in the silence, Kierkegaard argues, 'is never silent in the silence *with* the lilies and the birds'. Rather,

> he inverts the relationship, thinks himself the more essential thing in comparison with the lilies and the birds, imagines that he has, as the phrase goes, rendered a service to the birds and the lilies, by lending them words and speech, whereas his task was to learn silence *from* the lilies and the birds.[21]

This is a constant challenge, even battle, in attending the sea, and we fought it daily.

> I remember Harvey's suggestion to dedicate a sacred practice at the outset to 'the well-being and freedom of all sentient creatures'.[22] This is not the only, and it may not be the best, form of beginning. But it has advantages. It sets a direction. What I am about to do is not primarily for self-fulfilment, or even self-enlightenment, though both

---

[21] Kierkegaard, *Christian Discourses*, p. 330. Italics added.
[22] Andrew Harvey, *The Hope*, pp. 163, 166.

things may flow from it. The intention of sea see/hearing is *outward* not inward. It aims at placing me in the living web of being: the sea, the earth, even the cosmos. To have this orientation up front is a counter to the gravitational drag of the self upon itself; a drag which seems to make so much contemporary 'spirituality' narcissistic. I feel strongly that sea see/hearing, however vague it seems still, *must* have implications for the world, for the sea, and for my place and actions in relation to them. [J, 12/3/12]

Silence and the art of paying attention in sea see/hearing are inseparable. Without a disciplined acquisition of quietness within (a stilling of the 'monkey mind') and a deliberate seeking of a place (in Kierkegaard's words) 'far away from worldliness in the human world where there is so much talk', the needed focus of attention to nature breaks in pieces like a stream of water hitting a rock.[23] The meeting of this double silence, the silence within engaging the silence without, opens the possibility of an attentiveness 'of spirit and intellect and ear' in which the voice of nature is given hospitality; the invitation to speak and the right to be heard. In other words, this silence in and with nature is not silence in some empty absolute sense, the sheer absence of sound. It is a *liberating* silence, 'freeing the world from the agenda of the self, freeing the self from the compulsion to mastery of the environment.'[24] It is a *surprising* silence in which otherwise unheard sounds emerge and are attended to. It is a *revealing* silence, uncovering depths to our encounter with the world that often go unnoticed.

It is a silence that speaks.

Seeing

Sea see/hearing is a practice conducted with eyes wide open, in contrast to many forms of meditation, but what kind of seeing is it? Early in our efforts to engage in the practice, a guy bustled up to where we were standing and, with a puzzled expression on his face, said, 'Hey mate, you've been standing there for ages. What are you looking

---

[23] Kierkegaard, *Christian Discourses*, p. 324.
[24] Rowan Williams, *The Edge of Words: God and the Habits of Language*, (London: Bloomsbury, 2014), p. 165. The whole final chapter, "Saying the Unsayable: When Silence Happens," (pp. 156-185) is instructive for this section on silence.

at? Is there something out there I can't see? A whale? A shark?' A bit taken aback, I shook my head and muttered something about 'a spot of meditation'. He raised an eyebrow, looked out to sea, said 'Uh ha', nodded and walked off. His question, 'What are you looking at?' is a good one, but not easy to answer. We could try by picking a section from the journal almost at random.

> This place is splendid. The beauty is both powerfully alluring and at the same time partly threatening. ... Colour, sound and taste, all feel pristine. On the horizon cumulus and cirrus clouds hang in a limpid sky. Over to the right, near the edge of my vision, I swear the clouds are blue, or at least blue-grey. ... A rock formation is close by. The waves drive against it and spray flies. Around the crevices at the base of the rock, water rushes, twisting and gurgling. No tiniest corner of the complex of rocks remains unembraced by the sea that surges by, watery edges adjusting instantly to the shape of the land. [G, 10/7/13]

This seems to be a description of a panoramic vista made up of a multitude of different aspects. The eye darts here, there and everywhere, colour, cloud, wave, rock, spray. Such segmented looking is often part of sea see/hearing. Left like that, as a simple series of seemingly random observations, it doesn't do much to clarify the essence of this kind of visual attention.

In sea see/hearing we are not just looking *at* something—the ocean, the cloud, the waves—at least not as spectators, as separate observers perusing discrete objects in turn from a distance. And neither are we looking *for* something; something of particular interest; that enquirer's whale say, or the shark. The kind of seeing in sea see/hearing seems at heart neither observational nor utilitarian in these senses. We might call it, rather, *participatory* (Mathews uses the word *synergy*), a looking from *within* not without.[25] In gazing at the sea in sea see/hearing, we discover ourselves as a living part of a living whole. We deliberately try to move our point of view from outside the scene (spectator) to inside (participant). In looking at the sea, our own selves; our origins, our present hopes and fears, our ultimate ends, are somehow tied up in

---

25 See *EarthSong*, 2.1, Autumn 2011, p. 13.

the looking. That means the gaze is transactional. A genuine *exchange* takes place in the looking. It is as if this living whole is allowing itself to become manifest in the window of our eyes and in turn, and as a consequence, we are becoming aware of ourselves in the mirror of its radiance.[26]

Gaining such an interactive way of looking took patience and practice, and was not without its frustrations. In time we worked out two quite different orientations of vision which were helpful in different ways. The first, taking its cue from the Taoist practice of standing meditation outlined above,[27] suggests the adoption of a 'soft gaze' as an effective approach to the kind of seeing which promotes a genuine 'answerability to and for' the world around us (Steiner). Stand upright and look toward the sea, soften the focus of vision so that no specific object or motion holds your attention. Invite a wide and long sweep of the scene to present itself to your gaze.

> The soft gaze seems to dissolve the focal point of the perceiving eye; that perspective where the world is viewed from *my* special vantage point, and fans out from there. The soft gaze seems to let the world be seen from 'utopia', no place in particular.

But what does that mean?

> I hardly know. Trying to decide about it, or describe it more carefully, drags me back into the busy realm of particular thoughts. I try to resist that inner 'noise' … or, perhaps 'glare' is a better term. To the extent that I succeed, it feels like I am moving into a broader, less restricted, less 'mapped' inner space; a space that is 'open' to whatever is there. Grandeur, maybe. Beauty. Wonder. Infinity … or the fringe of infinity. … What should I call it? [G, 10/7/13]

---

[26] Neils Bohr, one of the founders of the Quantum Theory, consistently emphasised that this new development in science overturns the sharp separation between an object and an observing subject. Quantum Theory, he insisted, 'has emphatically reminded us of the old truth, that we are at the same time participants and spectators in the great drama of being.' See Carl Friedrich von Weizsäcker, *Aufbau der Physik* (München: Carl Hanser Verlag, 1985), pp. 526-531, at p. 527. Translation ours.

[27] See pp. 117-118 above.

This way of seeing has much to offer. It pushes to one side aspects of our ordinary interaction with the world, where everything 'is viewed from *my* special vantage point'. *Our* action is reduced to a minimum. We stand still and quiet beside the sea, the predilection for taking charge suspended. Specific perception, a looking at this and that, is blurred. The gaze is diffuse and receptive, not detailed and selecting. The result is a heightened appreciation of the scene as a whole. We see 'this ocean', not 'this wave' or 'this rock'. Metaphysical issues, as Hepburn calls them, matters which go beyond the ordinary limits of daily perception, 'beauty', 'wonder', 'the fringe of infinity', and the like, shyly make an appearance and stake a claim for our attention.[28] A 'broader, less restricted' space opens outwardly and inwardly to 'welcome' us.

A contrasting approach pushes to the opposite end of the visual scale. Poets like Mary Oliver and Indigenous teachers like Uncle Max often focus their attentive gaze on a *particular* aspect of the world that surrounds them. This 'sharp gaze' (as we might call it) deliberately tunes out the wider context of vision, which is the concern of the Taoist's 'soft gaze'. Mary Oliver looks with exquisite detail at *this* grasshopper, 'who is moving her jaws back and forth instead of up and down'; of *that* swan, trailing 'an elaborate webbed foot,/the color of charcoal'.[29] For Uncle Max watching, listening and seeing are 'the three principles of learning' and his seeing is almost always grounded locally: this tree, this rock, this flower, this echidna quill.[30] The sharp gaze looks at *this* cloud formation, not at an abstraction called 'sky' or 'ocean'.

> Out on the horizon there is a breathtaking cloud display. Like some Japanese nature-art, it is exquisite, but destined to disappear. ... The cloud is a massive blaze of pure white. Three great cumulus cauliflowers lumped together in a sky of deep and delicate blue. Across its face four or five thick streaks of cirrus, lilac/grey, are drawn as if with the stroke of a giant paint brush. The base of the cloud reaches all the way down

---

[28] See p. 49-53 above.
[29] See, Mary Oliver, "The Summer Day" and "The Swan" in *New and Selected Poems* (Boston: Beacon Press, 1992), pp. 94, 78.
[30] See, Max Dulumunmun Harrison, *My People's Dreaming: An Aboriginal Elder speaks on life, land, spirit and forgiveness* (Sydney: HarperCollinsPublishers, 2009), p. 59 and *passim*.

to the sea. There it dissolves in a misty wash of orange/grey. ... I feel as close as I will ever be to Mary Oliver's way of attending. ... A strange feeling takes possession of me. I can't quite name it. The German word *Gelassenheit* comes to mind. ... Serenity, calmness, composure. [G, 25/4/15]

If the 'soft gaze' draws us into an appreciation of the wholeness of the scene, the *one* ocean, the *one* sky, the *one* beach, spread out before us, the 'sharp gaze' brings to awareness the myriad details that compose the scene, *this* cloud, *that* wave, *this* shell. Both are essential to sea see/hearing. Without 'sharp', our gaze is somewhat empty, losing touch with the exquisitely intricate and minutely crafted texture of the world around us. Vision can become clichéd, flattened into generalities that can mask real beauty and ignore real threats. It knows one and whole; but not this and that. Without 'soft', our gaze becomes fragmented, unable to apprehend the profound unity, the wholeness and interconnection of the web of being which, in its full extent, is the cosmos. Vision stutters, breaking into pieces, losing coherence. It knows this and that; but not one and whole. Fred Williams in his Pilbara series of paintings brilliantly invites both forms of attention. At first glance, you see luminous wholes; vibrant blue sky, pulsing red earth, a thick horizon line. But come closer and you see the dobs of paint that create the texture of the canvas, here a twig, there a leaf, a tiny spider, a stick.

The parallels between ear and eye in this practice are striking. For Kierkegaard, the task of the attentive ear is to listen for the deep background silence with, in and through the myriad sounds of the natural world. This primal silence, however, is not mute or empty. It is astonishingly provocative and communicative. Kierkegaard gives it a theological twist. 'What does this silence express? It expresses reverence before God ... which affects one as if He [God] were speaking.'[31] And as we have seen, Harvey argues that chanting *om* is a way of bodily attuning ourselves to the 'sound that the entire creation is always resonating to ... the sound that the Godhead makes as it creates reality.'[32]

---

[31] *Christian Discourses*, p. 328.
[32] See footnote 14 above.

With or without such theological readings, a similar journey of surprising discovery awaits the attentive eye. In and with and through attention to the exquisite details of the ocean scene before us (the sharp gaze) we co-perceive (*mitwahrnehmen*, to use von Weizsäcker's term) the unity of the whole, the integrity of the world (the soft gaze).[33] With the radiant evening light that refracts for a moment through a breaking wave, we co-intuit the primal light, which rises from the origin of beauty itself and shines in all beautiful things. Conversely, in giving attention to the unity of the sea scene as a whole (the soft gaze) we cannot escape the awareness that this unity is in fact manifold, made up of a multitude of specifically identifiable things, which themselves are composed of smaller parts, right down to the elementary particles of quantum physics (the sharp gaze).

To begin to enter this radiant, vibrant and intricately connected reality, this 'event of the beautiful' as Chrétien calls it[34], from the inside as a participant and not from the outside as an observer, is to find oneself engaged emotionally. The beauty of the ocean calls out to us and requires a response of the whole self, a response of the heart. The seeing in sea see/hearing calls for a patient openness to whatever is before us such that (in McGilchrist's words) it 'allows us to see it as if for the very first time, and leads to what Heidegger called radical "astonishment" before the world;' an astonishment that 'drives us out of the complacency of our customary modes of seeing in the world.' McGilchrist sums it up in the striking words of Coleridge (written in reference to Wordsworth's poetry). This is a seeing that excites

> a feeling analogous to the supernatural, by awakening the mind's attention from the lethargy of custom, and directing it to the loveliness and the wonders of the world before us; an inexhaustible treasure, but for which in consequence of the film of familiarity and selfish solicitude we have eyes, yet see not, ears that hear not, and hearts that neither feel nor understand.[35]

---

[33] For a discussion of the idea of *Mitwahrnehmung* see chapter 2, pp. 47-53.
[34] Chrétien, *The Call and the Response*, p. 9.
[35] McGilchrist, *The Master and His Emissary*, p. 173. The quote is from Coleridge, S. T., *Biographia Literaria*, ed. G. Watson (London: Watson, Dent, 1965), vol. II, chap. xiv, p. 169.

It gradually dawns on us that this 'radical astonishment' is essentially just an expansion and deepening of that love for the sea which we noted in chapter 1 lives deep in the psyches of so many Australians. Sea see/hearing is a re-claiming at another level of the eyes of love that every beach-devotee already possesses.

Better done than said

What we have tried to describe here is a *practice*. Something done bodily. And done repeatedly. Trying to say what it 'means' is like trying to say what a dance means. If anyone could say what Bonachela's *Anima* means in words, why would they go to the extraordinary bodily contortions required of *dancing* it! A practice yields its meanings only to those who are prepared to undergo its disciplines. This may sound alarmingly like a plea to be excused from critique. Don't dare raise questions about this way of seeing and hearing unless and until you have subjected yourself to the (frankly) rather bizarre practice called 'sea see/hearing'!

That is not what is intended. And yet there is an element of truth in the complaint. The practice of sea see/hearing is essentially something undertaken physically. Such words as emerge from it (and we have many!) are secondary and remain accountable to the practice which gave them birth. They may and should be critiqued in conversation with other points of view, of course. But the 'knowing' involved in sea see/hearing remains practical through and through; a way of being-in-the-world rather than a conceptual-interpretation-of-the-world.

In a famous interview with a highly sceptical journalist, Carl Friedrich von Weizsäcker pushed back against his questioner's barely concealed incredulity that a first rate physicist could possibly take meditation as a serious way of knowing in the contemporary world. The interviewer, Udo Reiter, kept pressing his guest to define the essence of the meditative experience. What exactly is it that one experiences in meditation? How is that related to the experience and understanding of the world arising from physics? Von Weizsäcker remained silent for an extended period. When prodded by Reiter, he replied: 'Note first that I did not answer immediately, and that is just about the most important part of the answer.' Then he went on.

> The ... answer I must give you is that actually everything that one can say about it [i.e., meditation] is wrong, because meditation goes beyond the realm of concepts, beyond the realm of what one is normally able to say with language. Now if, in spite of this, I use language to speak about it, then everything depends on whom I am speaking to. Either I speak to someone who has these experiences, in which case he will understand largely without words. Or I speak to someone who does not have these experiences, in which case he will probably find all that I say somehow strange. Or one will feel that he has not properly understood the matter.[36]

At this stage of our experience, that feels pretty much the way it is. To know the 'visible voice' (Chrétien) or 'the eye that listens' (Claudel), at least for people with our kind of cultural and linguistic background (as distinct, say, from Indigenous people) requires a disciplined re-calibrating of perceptual habits. The habits that define the 'bell jar'. And that, it seems, cannot be achieved by just talking about it.

Look! Hear! / A Wicked Problem

The coffee shop in Lygon Street is buzzing as usual. We spot a table down the back, unoccupied and relatively quiet. It's been a while since we've seen these people, so there is catching up to do. How's the family? What are the grand kids up to? And, given our ages, how're you keeping? The essentials covered, we move on.

'You've been away, we hear.'

'Yes. Up in Tathra.'

'How long?'

'Three months. Just got back. Sigh!'

---

[36] A transcript of the entire interview, "*Gespräch über Meditation,*" is given in Carl Friedrich von Weizsäcker, *Der Garten des Menschlichen*, pp. 533-550; quotation from p. 534. Translation ours.

'So, you've joined the ranks of the grey loafers at last?'
'Hey, not loafing! Working!'
'I know, I know. It must be such hard work on Tathra beach!'
'We were writing.'
'You're writing something. Together?'
'Yes. ... Well, having a go.'
'That's great. What's it about?' The pause extends just a bit longer than it should. We exchange glances, each gesturing for the other to respond. Puzzled looks come at us from across the table.
'You *do* know what you're writing about?' Another pause.
'Yes. About the sea ... sort of.'
'The sea, sort of ... OK ... What about the sea?'
'Well, we're trying to listen to ... to pay attention to the sea.'
'Listen to the sea? Do you mean listen to the surf or something? Are we talking metaphor here?'
'Yes, but not just metaphor. Listen to what the sea might be saying. You know, at this point in history. To us. To humans.'
Silence again. It sounds dumb, even to us.
'And what does it say, the sea?'
'Beauty and wonder, for one thing. Well, two things! The ocean is very beautiful.'
'Don't suppose anyone will disagree with that.'
'But it's also changing.'
'Changing?'
'Under stress. Sick, some people say.'
'How so? What do you mean, sick?'
'Ah, you know. Pollution. Climate change. Over-fishing. That stuff.'
'Yeah. I suppose so. Have you been watching the new series of 'The Bridge'?'
The conversation collapses in mid-air. It just dies on the spot. Fortunately, we are all socially 'agile', in a Turnbullesque sort of way. The

situation is rescued with another round of coffee deftly ordered. The talk turns to the up-coming election.

This is not the first time such awkwardness has arisen. We've stumbled into it on a number of occasions before. It's not that other people are somehow at fault. We feel it ourselves. The Cambridge communication theorist, George Marshall, calls it 'an invisible force field of silence'. Without ever having being told, most people, he argues, 'have somehow learned that this topic is out of bounds. That is why they know that if someone else inadvertently enters this zone, it is a good idea to find something else to talk about.'[37] Marshall is thinking specifically of climate change, but the force field of silence applies equally, we have found, to talk about the state of the oceans. Of course, the two are deeply connected, so it isn't surprising. People don't like to talk about climate change or sea damage, even with friends and family members. 'In real life, it seems that the most influential climate narrative of all may be the non-narrative of collective silence,' Marshall concludes.[38]

Why so? If the situation is as Tim Flannery, Sylvia Earle, Boris Worm and Naomi Klein (and a host of other scientists, philosophers and commentators) describe; if we are truly facing a moment of global crisis that could threaten the state of the world—our only habitat—as we have known it, putting the lives of countless creatures at risk, and perhaps our own lives as well; if the oceans and the atmosphere are changing, and changing rapidly, in ways that portend dire things for our children and grandchildren, for tuna fish and koala bears, wouldn't that be something we would want to talk about, and quite a lot? In 2007, then Prime Minister Kevin Rudd famously stated that climate change 'is the greatest moral, economic and social challenge' of our time. But a decade later, when the 2016 election rolled around, there was hardly any serious political discussion of the matter at all. It was not that things in the air and in the ocean had drastically improved in the meantime. The reverse was the case. However, when the Labor party announced some significant goals designed to move us towards renewable energy and

---

[37] George Marshall, *Don't Even Think About It: Why our brains are wired to ignore climate change* (New York: Bloomsbury, 2014), p. 81.
[38] Marshall, *Don't Even Think About It*, p. 82.

decrease in carbon emissions, the media was instantly awash with shock ads about the reintroduction of the dreaded Julia Gillard 'carbon tax', with inevitable consequences of job losses, huge increases in electricity costs, and immense damage to the economy. The invisible force field was hammered well and truly back in place. And it's not just politicians; we all find it hard to talk about what the sea and the air might be saying in our time.

Whole volumes have been written about this eerie, socially constructed silence. George Marshall's book is one of the best. At one point, he cites an American sociologist with the wonderful name of Eviatar Zerubavel, who describes such self-delusionary silence as *disattention*.

> We have not talked about zoological gardens. That is not because we are deliberately avoiding it; the subject has simply not come up in our conversation. I would call this *inattention* because we can easily explain why we have not talked about it. But *disattention* is something very different. That is when we deliberately fail to notice something and cannot even explain the silence.[39]

We don't talk about the elephant in the room and we don't talk about the fact that we don't talk about it. It's a matter of *disattention*. It's not that we haven't paid attention, but that we wish *not* to pay attention. Disattention is the social strategy that overtook us in the coffee shop on Lygon Street that morning. All of a sudden we all discovered silence on the subject was socially and personally preferable. Much better to talk about something else.

In 1973, two Berkeley social scientists, Horst Rittel and Melvyn Webber, published a paper on social planning in which they made a distinction, since become widely known, between 'tame' and 'wicked' problems.[40] A tame problem, they suggested, is one whose challenge, while it may be complicated, is relatively clear and definite. You know (more or less) what the problem is and you can know (more or less) whether or not the problem has been solved. Blocked plumbing,

---

[39] Marshall, *Don't Even Think About It*, p. 82. Italics in text.
[40] Horst W. J. Rittell & Melvyn M. Webber, "Dilemmas in a General Theory of Planning," *Policy Sciences* 4 (1973), pp. 155-169. See also Marshall, *Don't Even Think About It*, pp. 95-96.

automobile malfunctions, mathematical puzzles, and many scientific investigations fall into this category.

By contrast, wicked problems are difficult or impossible to solve because they involve incomplete, or contradictory, or continuously changing conditions for their definition and their resolution. 'The information needed to *understand* the problem depends upon one's idea for *solving* it.'[41] Moreover, any effort to deal with the problem changes the problem's dynamics in the process of its application. So the nature of the problem is constantly evolving, and no final resolution is possible. The challenge, say, of reducing crime in the streets, or adjusting the national tax system, would be examples of wicked problems. Talking about them is hard not only because they are complex problems, but because our own deeply held convictions about life are implicated in the way we see and describe them. Tax is a tough topic, because I am (say) a market libertarian and you are a social democrat. Income tax and the reasons for imposing it look really different depending on which platform we happen to be standing on to view it.

Climate change and damage to the sea are wicked problems in this sense. 'What do you mean by the sea being sick?' Well, that's not so easy to say. Climate change means increasing the global average temperature of the air by continually pumping large amounts of heat-trapping gases like carbon dioxide and methane into the atmosphere from burning fossil fuels. This is what the science tells us. And it has been happening with increasing intensity since the start of the industrial age. All sorts of consequences flow from it. For example, increasing atmospheric temperature in turn raises the average surface temperature of the sea. And changing sea temperature leads to changing conditions for life in the sea. It also leads to melting of glaciers and the ice caps at the poles. Melting ice floods into the ocean and warming water expands the ocean, and both combine to raise sea levels. This threatens to inundate coral reefs and low lying land masses. This impacts on the animals that live in the reefs and the people who live on the lands. Animals scatter and people begin to wonder where they might go for safety. Moreover, carbon dioxide in the atmosphere dissolves in the sea and alters the acidity of the water. That

---

[41] Rittell & Webber, "Dilemmas in a General Theory of Planning," p. 161.

makes it more difficult for corals and shellfish to survive, since increasing acidity begins to dissolve their intricate carbonate houses. So they start to bleach and die, but that degrades fish nurseries and habitats. Add to that human over-fishing. This radically changes the relative density of the biomass of the ocean, and leads to extinctions of species and depleted populations of surviving fish. All this alters the marine biosphere in ways that are impossible to predict. Now throw in pollution. Plastic rubbish damages and kills fish, birds and mammals alike, everywhere. And that has knock-on effects for the intricate ocean food-web and even for the production of oxygen by micro-organisms that inhabit the surface of the water. It then has consequences for our breathing. And that ... and then ... So it goes. It's all too complicated; way too big. What can I do? Nothing. Do I want to know? Not really. It's a wicked problem.

The trouble with a wicked problem is that it only has wicked solutions. That means, as Riddell and Webber argue, what should be done about the problem depends on what you think the problem is in the first place. What you think the problem is depends on what you think a solution to the problem might look like. What you think a solution might look like depends on all sorts of personal, social and even metaphysical commitments, of which you may not even be aware. Marshall writes:

> We can define climate change [add sea sickness] as an economic problem, a technological problem, a moral problem, a human rights problem, a social justice problem, a land use problem, a governance problem, an ideological battle between left and right worldviews, or a lack of respect for God's creation.[42]

This doesn't include those who refuse to believe that climate change or serious damage to the ocean is a problem at all. Each approach to the issue calls for a different sort of response, singles out different culprits as the 'real enemy' in the fight, argues for different ways to share the costs involved in rehabilitation—if in fact rehabilitation is what is needed—and uses different language and warrants to justify what is thought to be the appropriate action. It's a jungle out there. How do you know where those who are sitting opposite at the coffee table fit in this complicated mess? You innocently raise the delights of standing on the beach at

---

[42] Marshall, *Don't Even Think About It*, p. 96.

Tathra and before you know it you're up to you neck in politics, science, religion, carbon tax, coal exports to India, multinationals, the budget deficit, illegal immigration and border protection. It's a wicked problem. Who needs it?

A disattention strategy is reinforced in us because we all know or intuit that buried somewhere in any talk about ocean health or climate change lurk implications that immediately, and probably adversely, affect us. The talk turns to climate change in the coffee shop and a red light immediately starts flashing in my brain. I don't say it out loud. Inside, however, a passionate speech in defence of the status quo begins to play out in me. It runs something like this:

'Look, fossil fuels have been the drivers of advanced economies for two centuries or more. Coal is one of Australia's best and most abundant export commodities. And vast natural gas deposits are now being discovered off the coast of Western Australia near the Kimberly. You can't just ignore that. It's economic suicide. Our cars, planes, trains, trucks, ships, factories and homes all depend on fossil fuel to function. Half the most helpful items in our society are made of plastics. They come from fossil feedstocks too. And now you're saying this very thing, the thing that makes Melbourne the 'most liveable city in the world' and Australia such a desirable destination for travellers (and asylum seekers!), is the thing we have to curb or maybe dismantle all together. That's not going to happen. China, India and South Korea won't stand for it. And look at the US, Japan and the EU, for heaven's sake! How can something, which has been so brilliantly successful, so enriching for everyone, suddenly become the bogey-man? Anyway, when is this catastrophe supposed to happen? 2050? 2075? Maybe the turn of next century? The scientists can't agree. The politicians won't agree. Nobody knows. So let's not rush to turn the lights off just because someone yells the sky is falling in! We've heard it all before.'

In George Marshall's words, 'dealing with climate change requires that people accept short-term costs and reductions in their living standards in order to mitigate against higher but uncertain costs that are far in the future.'[43] And that's a wicked problem if ever there was one.

---

[43] Marshall, *Don't Even Think About It*, p. 57.

Talking about it only embroils us more and more in language that seems evasive and self-serving, driven more by emotion than reason. Nobody likes that.

How can we respond to a situation like ocean acidity in the Great Barrier Reef, or over-fishing in Thailand, or plastic junk in the North Pacific? None of it, or almost none of it, we can see for ourselves. Tathra beach looks fantastic. What could possibly be amiss here? If we do believe there is a problem, we have to believe it on authority. Science tells us this, science tells us that, but few of us have read that science for ourselves, and if we have, most of us are ill-equipped to evaluate it critically. How can we get our heads around such an avalanche of material? Even if we had the time to research it—which we don't—how do we weigh priorities? If we open our mouths on the subject, we're left muttering vague statistics we have read or heard somewhere else. If someone challenges us in the coffee shop, it becomes a my-authority's-better-than-your-authority tug of war. Then there's the little matter of guilt. Talk about a sick sea or a heating planet always, well almost always, seems accusative. Somehow we're to blame for the plight of polar bears in the Arctic. Or penguins on Phillip Island. That just makes us feel helpless, or depressed, or angry, or all of the above. Yes it's true, we live a carbon heavy lifestyle compared, say, to rice farmers in Sulawesi, but what can we do about it in mainstream Australian society? Perhaps recycling throw away stuff and fitting low energy light bulbs helps. We can do that. But if the Carmichael mine goes ahead, what's the point? We feel the problem in our guts. It's not hard to see why Marshall's 'force field of silence' swings into play at the coffee shop, or the family reunion, or the office staff room, or the RSL club.

Disattention in relation to the ocean is a 'wicked' phenomenon arising in response to a 'wicked' problem.

There are some really good reasons for *not* paying attention to the ocean.

Learning a practice of attention (4)

Faithfulness

You may already be in love with the natural world and spend time hiking, canoeing, surfing, walking or gardening. This is a different way to attend, but it is true to the same love, and seeks faithfully to honour the same 'call'.

Repetition

Like learning any new skill, acquiring this kind of attentiveness takes time, dedication and practice. Like any genuine ritual, repetition is the path to transformed vision and deepened sensitivity. If you already have a spiritual practice—prayer, meditation, Tai Chi, contemplation, Yoga—you will already know the value of a regular commitment. Consider re-allocating some of the time you already set aside. If a practice is a new idea, you may need just to plunge in and see what happens.

Persistence

Like a growing plant this work is slow, organic, unfolding quietly. We suggest you commit yourself to keeping the practice for at least three months. At first it can feel quite strange. Take time to become familiar with this way of being in and attending to the world. Half an hour each day, or even once or twice a week, would be a place to start.

Community

Transformative learning is essentially a communal endeavour. Our community was each other, Indigenous teachers/elders, living human beings, but also books.

This is a deeply counter-cultural practice in our present context. One friend is an invaluable support and encouragement. Find a pilgrim companion.

5. Heartbreak / Coalophobia

The human race is being brought to the moment where it must choose connection, if we choose connection, what we are bound to choose ... is heartbreak.

Andrew Harvey

Our love affair with the sea, called by beauty, was deepened in our practice of attention. The call of beauty is love's call, our response an answering love. Connection. The question of decision in the quotation above, of needing to *choose* connection and a relationship between such a choice and heartbreak, emerged only in fits and starts and over time. There was a dark side to this call to love. The second part of each chapter begins to give expression to this; beauty, but also disfigurement; connection, but also breaking of bonds; a practice of attention, but also a wicked problem. This chapter now turns more directly to the struggle, to deepening layers of confrontation. Our pilgrimage proved to have an ethical dimension, calling us to recognise the need for decision, for our hearts to break open, for grief.

What does it mean to choose connection? For the ancients, the three great transcendentals—beauty, truth and goodness—are *inseparably* connected. Mythologically expressed, beauty is sister to truth and goodness. As sibling, she demands from her devotees as much courage as her sisters. 'She will not allow herself to be separated and banned from her two sisters without taking them along with herself in an act of mysterious vengeance'.[1] With von Weizsäcker, we had to learn again the reality of this sisterhood.[2] The separation, or at least the independence, of beauty from truth is deeply ingrained in us. To love the beauty of the ocean at Tathra was nourishing, restorative, a homecoming, and did not at first require anything much of courage. Truth, however, did. The 'worldwide catastrophe that threatens the survival of the planet demands

---

[1] John O'Donohue, *Beauty: The Invisible Embrace* (New York: Harper Perennial, 2004), quoting Balthazar p. 4.
[2] See chapter 2, footnote 13.

of us unparalleled openness to horrifying facts'.[3] We are overloaded with facts, already knowing more than we can bear. A huge force-field is in place silencing these truths. Illusions need to be shattered. We will not survive unless we 'go through this final ordeal', this 'savage awakening'.[4] Truth, goodness and beauty are sisters. Honouring these daughters of the one Mother requires courage and choice: a decision.

Occasionally, it has been the appearance of a patch of yellowish, greasy foam that visually jolted us. At first our response is to want to move away, but we learn to attend.

> I am disturbed by the eerie coloured water and the 'alien' yellowish froth running on its surface. I feel moved by the capacity of the sea to 'forgive' and 'absorb' all the polluting substances we pour into her. The sea is a vast being that for thousands of years has taken what we have chosen to dump in it. It still looks so lively and beautiful. But are we coming to the edge of that capacity and that patience? What will that mean to our grandchildren? Once I would have been tempted to walk away from that ghastly pollution and find some place where I didn't have to put up with it. But now I can't. I am part of the cause of this damage. I want to stand here as part of the awful truth. [J, 6/4/14]

Beauty and pain. Disturbance and sorrow. We look. Beauty is marred, disfigured. We stand, choosing to stay and become aware of the graciousness of the sea, and of our culpability. Standing face-to-face shakes open deep places; primal questions surface about the future of life itself, the heritage we leave for coming generations, heartbreaking questions.

To turn and face the other, the ocean, seems such a small gesture. Yet Deborah Bird Rose argues the choice to 'turn toward' is the essence of a possible response in our times. In conversation with Levinas, for whom the human 'face' and human 'call' are critical terms, Rose asks what will happen when the face of the other is other-than-human, for example an animal, and the call a bark or a howl? Rose is clear. This implies 'an ethics of motion toward encounter, a willingness to situate one's self so

---

[3] Andrew Harvey, *The Return of the Mother* (New York: Jeremy P. Tarcher/Putnam, 1995), p. 182.
[4] Harvey, *The Return of the Mother*, p. 186.

as to be available to the call of others. It is a willingness toward dialogue, a willingness toward responsibility, a choice for encounter and response, a turning toward rather than a turning away'.[5]

We stand face to face with the ocean, seeking to listen to her call. That facing confronts us with a world being unravelled. And this truth is hard. To choose to be open to connection is a beginning. Is there hope of mending some of the damage? What of the grandchildren, of all species? We cannot answer the questions that arise. However, we can try to remain open where the face of the other is not only the human face, but the face of the ocean, where the call is a crashing wave, or a swathe of greasy yellow foam.

Breaking open – the self

Moments of ecstasy or intense pain can be gifts, 'diamonds' to be held in the hand, turned over and over slowly over time, learning to appreciate their value and beauty.[6] Occasionally for us there have been such sudden moments, unanticipated, piercing. Gifts. Coming to know ourselves to be 'part of the awful truth' crystallized in the following journal.

> A beautiful day. Tathra at its sparkling best. The sun is out. Golden light all around. The light on the water is breathtaking, lively, alluring blue-green. I think to myself, 'this is what I have been looking for! This is how I remember it! I'll be able to get into this easily today!' But it just doesn't work like that. I can't settle inwardly. It is not that there are extraneous conversations in my head. But somehow I can't give myself over to the practice as I intend. The ongoing unsettlement of spirit persists, lasting most of the session. Near the end of the time, I decide (a bit desperate) to put the question: 'Are you willing to communicate with me?' to the sea. Nothing came back to me. I stand for quite a while—disappointed. Then suddenly it is said to me, or anyway it becomes clear to me: 'this is a session of restorative justice'. Just like that. I know what restorative justice is. The criminal has to come face to face with his/her victim, and in the presence of a mediator, listen to the victim's side of the story; what

---

[5] Deborah Bird Rose, *Wild Dog Dreaming: Love and Extinction* (London: University of Virginia Press, 2011), p. 5.
[6] Harvey, *The Return of the Mother*, p. 200. This image is part of a discussion of the Sufi way of heartbreak—a three stage system of purification, expansion and union.

the crime has done to the victim. I felt the list of crimes being read out to me as a representative of the human race. 'You have torn the heart out of the web of life I have laboured to create. You have trawled and dug and drilled and sucked the floor of my world, a world that has taken billions of years to build. You have poured hundreds of millions of tons of your sewage, garbage, poisons and plastics into me until the very last corner of my world is polluted by you.' The litany then went on. 'In your (human) legal world these actions go by the following names: rape, the violation of the most intimate parts of another; grievous bodily harm, the violent wounding of the being of another; murder or mass murder, the taking of the life/lives of others wantonly and wilfully; theft, the forceful taking of what does not belong to you; breaking and entering, the violation of another's home. That is what your behaviour does to me. I am interested in what you have to say in your defence.' And ... I had nothing to say. I felt really horrified at myself. And that was the end of the session. [G, 3/3/15]

If we were in danger of indulging the pleasure of attending the sea without accepting the demand, the moral imperative, this session exploded it for all time. The encounter moved information about the plight of the ocean from the mind to the heart, dragging it down deep into the gut. Here, factual descriptions of damage (arising from a paradigm of disconnection) shift to profound discomfort, self-knowledge, culpability and vulnerability.

There are some parallels perhaps with moments known in a psychotherapeutic process when, after maybe months of circumambulation, a moment of sudden clarity arrives, a painful self-revelation where what was deeply hidden emerges and is recognized. 'At such a time ... it is as though all of one's life, and the patient's life, passes before one. Such a moment may not be long but much is packed into it.'[7] The difference, however, is dramatic. The language here is not that of the therapist's deeply concentrated reverie and attention, or not only that, but of the courtroom, and the voice that of the judge. The language used includes the words justice, victim, defence, criminal; the

---

[7] Craig San Roque, "On *Tjukurrpa*, Painting Up, and Building Thought," *Social Analysis*, Volume 50, Issue 2, Summer 2006, p. 166.

crimes are listed, rape, murder, grievous bodily harm, theft, breaking and entering. What happens? In the beginning there is a sense of anticipation; the sea is sparkling, quintessential Tathra. Yet expectation turns to disappointment and then frustration. Far from the sea evoking a matching response, and far from a transference of an inner mood onto the sea, today they are opposed. Unsettled within, peaceful golden light without. Almost at the end of the session the question of a courteous approach comes to mind and is put, there is a choice to keep waiting in the face of silence and finally a response.

The session is concerned with justice, though not the punishment and sentencing of the one accused of crime; it is a session of *restorative justice*. For restoration to occur, the perpetrator must grasp that he has committed a crime, that his actions had consequences that were deeply injurious to others, and he must begin to feel and know this. 'What have you to say in your defence?' This is a moment where there is nothing to say; a moment of seeing the world (the ocean) and the self with new and 'horrified' eyes; an unveiling.

The encounter above then moved to a second stage, deepening the distress even further.

> Walking back out along the beach, feeling very stressed, the sea spoke again. 'And, by the way, what have I done to you?' My mind ran through the reading I had done earlier. I breathe 15 times per minute, i.e., 24 x 60 x 15 = 21,600 breaths per day. More than 50% of the oxygen in those breaths comes directly from the sea. When I woke this morning I shaved, had a shower, a cup of tea, avocado on toast, etc. Every drop of water involved in that consumption (and for the whole day) came from the sea. I have lived this day comfortably in a temperature range that ran from 17° to 24°C, which is a direct result of the 'air conditioning' provided by the ocean. And in this very moment, I am walking in the sun on the wonderful sand of the beach, listening to the waves, looking at the colours all around. This is what the ocean has done to me. [G, 3/3/15]

The question from the sea, 'what have I done to you?' evoked an overwhelming sense of our immediate, intimate and total reliance on the abundance of gifts, given freely. The complete reversal of the litany of our taking. An awareness of bounty breaks open the tough shell of our normal existence even further. Coming face to face, facing the self, seeing our own face anew and being horrified. In what sense is this restorative?

Through the ages such moments of self-exposure have been linked with the 'stirrings of conscience'. (Chrétien). Though this is no gentle flutter, more a gale force wind tearing up roots. Among the various stirrings of conscience, 'repentance is the one whose characteristic is to judge and concern itself with our past lives'.[8] While the journal entry does not specifically refer to repentance, it clearly deals with judgement and our past life. Conscience, repentance. Uncomfortable words we moderns prefer to push aside. Indeed some modern philosophy sees repentance as merely a negative, a highly uneconomical, even superfluous act, a disharmony of mind arising from lack of thought, or even sickness.[9] It carries a sense of useless deadweight, or a morbid dwelling on the past (the 'black armband' view of history). For Nietzsche repentance is an inner deception, that arises when passions of hate, revenge or cruelty, once allowed free play, come to be condemned by State, Law and Civilisation and so turn for satisfaction elsewhere.[10] Repentance for Spinoza is a pointless echo of earlier times, no virtuous thing and certainly no offspring of reason. The one who 'repents a deed is doubly oppressed and incapable'.[11]

In his landmark essay, Max Scheler argues powerfully against such views. Scheler (1874-1928) lived in Germany, writing after the first world war, and like Husserl, was a pioneer of phenomenology which he used to investigate 'spiritual' realities. For him, repentance is a dynamic phenomenon analogous to medical conditions where the body is attempting to heal itself. When the world is torn apart by violent acts, unjust choices, lying talk and the like, repentance is the name of the tough

---

[8] Max Scheler, *On the Eternal in Man*, trans. Bernard Noble (Connecticut: Archon Books & SCM Press, 1960), p. 35. The whole chapter, "Repentance and Rebirth" (pp. 35-65) is foundational for this section of our argument.

[9] Scheler, *On the Eternal in Man*, p. 36.

[10] Scheler, *On the Eternal in Man*, p. 37.

[11] Spinoza quoted in Scheler, *On the Eternal in Man*, p. 49.

remedial process which seeks to undo, or at least diminish, the damaging effects which such behaviours project into the present from the past, and prolong into the future, for the individual and society alike. Repentance, we might say, is a common work of the inseparable sisters; a striving for truth, goodness and beauty in the face of their betrayal. It is the costly effort undertaken by morally damaged life to heal itself. Thus Scheler asserts, 'repentance ... has, together with, and even in consequence of, its negative, demolishing function, another which is positive, liberating and constructive'.[12] It is 'the most *revolutionary* force in the moral world', killing only to create, annihilating only to rebuild.[13] The voice of the sea could not have been clearer. 'This is a session of restorative justice'. The litany of crimes relentlessly pursued, breaking the heart open to create the possibility for change, for amendment of life.

Whether we have the courage to entrust ourselves to this 'demolishing function' in the hope that we can awaken to what is 'positive, liberating and constructive' in this radical call to change remains a work in progress. And no easy one. This is to say nothing of the possibilities for our politics and society in a brave new world of 'alternative facts' and 'fake news'. Nietzsche and Spinoza appear merely beginners. A repentant Trump seems a truly serious oxymoron!

The power calling us is infinitely tender and at the same time 'runs through illusions with a knife', a power that is an immense love with 'a ferocity calm at its core'.[14] A heartbreak. A diamond.

> A heartbreak shakes yellow leaves from the branch of the heart
>
> So fresh green leaves can go on and on growing. ...
>
> Heartbreak pulls up the roots of old happinesses
>
> So a new ecstasy can stroll in from Beyond.
>
> Heartbreak pulls up all withered, crooked roots
>
> So no root can stay hidden.[15]

---

[12] Scheler, *On the Eternal in Man*, p. 36.
[13] Scheler, *On the Eternal in Man*, see pp. 51-57, quote at p.56 Italics in original.
[14] Harvey, *The Return of the Mother*, p. 207.
[15] Rumi quoted in Harvey, *The Return of the Mother*, p. 179. Jelaluddin Rumi (1207–1273) was a Persian Muslim poet, jurist, theologian and mystic. His poetry is revered worldwide

Breaking open – our story

A second moment broke us open in an even more startling way; breaking open our cultural mythology, opening our hearts in ways that were unexpected, surprising and life-giving. 'The wonder of the Beautiful is its ability to surprise us. With swift sheer grace, it is like a divine breath that blows the heart open'.[16] The restorative justice encounter can be readily understood within our 'normal' framework of interpretation; our story of the ways we make meaning and order in our society. This second moment blew open the framework itself. We will make an approach from the edge, as we have been seeking to do throughout this book, an edge provided by Indigenous teachers who see from this vantage place what we in the midst cannot, assuming 'our' world is *the* world. A central feature of this vantage place is what is referred to in English as the 'Dreaming'. From here comes a quiet but devastating statement: 'You, whitefellas have lost your Dreaming'.[17] Warlpiri man, Andrew Japaljarri Spencer who uttered these words, intended them as a gift.[18] What is being offered? How shall we hear?

Can we gain a glimpse of the meaning of this 'Dreaming'? Craig San Roque, a psychoanalyst, has worked for many years with Indigenous peoples of the Australian Central Desert, particularly the Warlpiri and Pintubi. Attending with a psychoanalytic ear and eye to what happens between Indigenous and Caucasian persons, he began to attune to the immense power and psychological significance of the 'Dreaming'.

> "Dreaming". You hear them talk about it, this sweet thing. "The Dreaming" an approximation for the English language speakers, sometimes in Arrernte they call it *Altjerre* or in the Western Desert language *Tjukurrpa*, or the Warlpiri, *Jukurrpa*. What does this really mean, this state of things which brings tears to Paddy Sims' eyes, seated cross legged before a canvas, singing quietly, painting "The Milky Way Story"? This thing which women depict and men define in

and translated into many languages.
16 O'Donohue, *Beauty: The Invisible Embrace*, p. 17.
17 San Roque, "On *Tjukurrpa*, Painting Up, and Building Thought," p. 153.
18 They are part of a conversation with Craig San Roque in April 1990, at a meeting of the Healthy Aboriginal Life Team (HALT).

5. Heartbreak / Coalophobia

sand-drawings, deft fingers moving upon canvasses stretched on the bare ground, or smudged on a backyard cement slab near the Todd River? *Tjukurrpa*, land claims, faraway looks, marking this rock and that, casually. Reverence, breaking into song in creek beds, shrugging, walking off. *Tjukurrpa*, lightly held, with a gravity so exquisite, so solid, so omnipresent. *Tjukurrpa*, perhaps the most misunderstood, most ignored, most beautiful, most mysterious, most exploited, most obliterated phenomenon in this country. This strangely provocative phenomenon seamlessly sewn into the Australian landform, sown as seeds in the mind of a country a long time ago, today.[19]

We cannot, as non-Indigenous white people claim to understand let alone to live this 'Dreaming'. We are among those who misunderstand, exploit and obliterate, though we long for this not to be so. San Roque is concerned with the failure of white people to appreciate 'this sweet thing'.[20] In a conversation with singer-songwriter Bob Randall, he is told about 'Dreaming' as laws set down from the beginning, passed on through generations, and absolutely inseparable from care and responsibility. There is value in this glimpse of the strange mystery and power of 'Dreaming'. Another Indigenous speaker puts it this way.

> My father said this, 'My boy, look! Your Dreaming is there; it is a big thing; you never let it go [pass it by]. All Dreamings [totemic entities] come from there.' Does the whiteman now understand? The blackfellow, earnest, friendly, makes a last effort. 'Old man, you listen! Something is there; we do not know what; *something*.' There is a struggle to find words, and perhaps a lapse into English. 'Like engine, like power, plenty of power; it does hard work; it *pushes*.' [21]

The speaker is working very hard here to try to help us understand. We feel the effort, and feel the alien strangeness of what is being said.

---

[19] San Roque, "On *Tjukurrpa*, Painting Up, and Building Thought," p. 152.
[20] His context is one of cultural trauma, particularly around the use of alcohol, and the persistent failure to find 'solutions' that endure. Some understanding of the structure and content of 'Dreaming', through anthropological and psychological analysis of intercultural conversations might, he hopes, enhance the effectiveness of the work.
[21] Quoted in San Roque, "On *Tjukurrpa*, Painting Up, and Building Thought," p. 152. (The speaker was an informant of Australian anthropologist William Stanner.)

Loss of connection with their Dreaming is experienced by these Indigenous speakers as an alarming loss of strength. 'You separate me from that and you've made me weak'. San Roque's conversations revealed the desire to pass on this knowledge, even to uninitiated Westerners. Uncle Max similarly felt a responsibility to try to make us understand. He sees, all too heartbreakingly, our disconnection from this knowledge. 'Forgetting it or ignoring the psychological significance of 'Dreaming', may be ... a form of dissociation which mentally weakens us all'.[22]

This is the view from the edge. 'You whitefellas have lost your Dreaming'. 'Dreaming' which is respect and care. We have not shown respect. We have not lived care. We act as if we are lost or mad, destroying our own habitat and, it seems, unable to stop even when we know it. Not only this, we have already violently desecrated and destroyed Indigenous Land that is belonging and home, and to our deep shame continue to do so. Is this the weakness Bob Randall refers to? If we have lost our Dreaming, we have lost the matrix from which responsibility, sanity and meaning might flow; a place where 'the continual becoming and rebirth of human life' might occur.[23] We did not know how to find our Dreaming, not even really grasping that we had lost something, though the feeling of lostness was as familiar as the air we breathe.

One day quite early in our pilgrimage, an encounter occurred that has taken, as do some dreams, several years to assimilate. It happened on the day of our visit to the 'Sapphire Coast Marine Discovery Centre' where we had been so shaken by the information about the length of time debris, especially plastics, remain in the ecosystems of the ocean.[24] The practice of the approach again created an opening, a gateway, for unthought thoughts, fresh images and accompanying strong feelings. After putting the question, 'Are you willing to communicate with me?' I wait to see in what form the 'you' in the question may appear.

> An image slowly gathers. A woman rising from the sea. She is draped in seaweed, dripping water. Plastic and other debris, like garbage caught in the foliage along the Merri Creek after a heavy flooding, cling to

---
[22] San Roque, "On *Tjukurrpa*, Painting Up, and Building Thought," p. 157.
[23] San Roque, "On *Tjukurrpa*, Painting Up, and Building Thought," p. 157.
[24] See chapter 2, p. 60.

her.[25] The skin on her face and arms appears blotched and unhealthy. I feel shocked. From somewhere in my memory, the figure of Mary superimposes itself on the diseased figure. It is Mary of the Magnificat. A woman of transformative action for justice; a woman clothed with the Sun (the Book of Revelation).[26] Those two readings of Mary have been in my memory for some time now. They sit uneasily beside the image of the seaweed woman. I don't know what to make of it. Are the women 'speaking' for the sea in some way? How? Are they parts of me? Is there a call here? I am unsure. And unsettled. [J, 11/6/13]

That this is a moment of portent was unquestionable. The reflections that follow are the outcome of a journey in which we found ourselves taken into deep time and strange places. A similar journey may await you.

What is going on here? This woman is draped with human rubbish that, as she rises up, clings to her along with the seaweed. Her unhealthy skin indicates that she is sick. I was not expecting this, and my response is deep shock. As I am struggling with the impact of what is happening, a second image overlays the first. Another woman, a figure of immense power, magnificence and passionate for justice, and called by the name of Mary in the Christian tradition, appears. Mary, whose name means the sea (*mare*). I am shaken yet again. I know it is significant, but how?

The seaweed woman

The first woman is a heart-breaking figure. The question of where she appeared from is, we believe, ultimately unanswerable. I am attempting to attend to a speaking world, to put on hold the paradigm of disconnection in which I have lived. The shocking juxtaposition—rubbish draped on a female figure—clearly relates to my experience earlier in the day. I saw the destructiveness of our current relationship with nature. That I found this distressing is a sign of a sense of connection, of myself as part of a

---

25 The creek in our home-place, Melbourne, a tributary of the Yarra River.
26 I am grateful to Andrew Harvey among others for a critique of readings of Mary in which she is a passive, compliant figure. These texts provide alternative biblical sources for recovery of a more faithful image of a historical Mary stripped of a patriarchal overlay, and an invitation to attend to a Cosmic Mary. See, Andrew Harvey, *Son of Man: The Mystical Path to Christ* (New York: Jeremy P. Tarcher/Putnam, 1998), pp. 180-186. Biblical references are to Luke 1.46-55 and Revelation 12.1.

whole, the living web of life. Two selves. I am a destroyer of life (rubbish creator) and wounded by the knowledge of this. How then might we approach these two women and the gifts they may hold?

A female figure associated with waters is an ancient mythic image, persisting across civilizations in the ancient and modern worlds. Botticelli's astonishing painting, *The Birth of Venus*, immediately comes to mind, and seems to offer a beckoning call, a call of beauty![27] Who is Venus? How is it that Botticelli is painting her birth? Where does the image of her rising, being born from the sea come from? Might this help our understanding of this other woman her skin no longer smooth and clear, her garments draperies of human rubbish, her beauty so damaged?

Botticelli's painting is inspired by the 'First Homeric Hymn to Aphrodite' dated between 8th and 12th centuries BCE.[28] Aphrodite is the name given by the Greeks to a goddess who became Venus in Roman times.[29]

> Golden crowned, beautiful
>   awesome Aphrodite
>   is who I shall sing,
> she who possesses the heights
>   of all
> sea-wet Cyprus
> where Zephyros swept his moist breaths
> over the waves
>   of roaring sea
> in soft foam.[30]

---

[27] *The Birth of Venus*, Sandro Botticelli, c. 1485. See Appendix 3.
[28] This excerpt is the first stanza only. The complete poem is part of a collection of Homeric hymns. Dating, oral and written transmission and authorship are widely debated. See Anne Baring and Jules Cashford, *The Myth of the Goddess: Evolution of an Image* (London: BCA, 1991), p. 349.
[29] Venus, the morning and evening star, the brightest star in the heavens.
[30] Aphrodite's name comes from the manner of this birth—*aphros* means foam in Greek. Baring and Cashford, *The Myth of the Goddess*, p. 355.

5. Heartbreak / Coalophobia

Botticelli creates an Aphrodite truly awesome in her beauty, a masterpiece in the Western tradition. He sings her into being with his colours, his paints. In the Neoplatonic tradition in which Botticelli painted, Aphrodite was 'an image of the dual nature of love, the sensuous and the chaste'.[31] The passionate Zephyros (on the painting's left) blow her towards the shore scattering roses, while the Hour (on the right of the painting) moves swiftly to clothe her, bringing her a flower strewn garment. Venus (Aphrodite) herself rising from the sea, with her abundant long hair, is stepping from an exquisite scallop shell. In earlier myths the womb of the sea gathered and nurtured the semen of heaven, but in the fourth century BCE was reconceived as a shell. (*kteis*, the Greek word for scallop shell is also the word for female genitals).[32] 'Aphrodite' appears again and again in our pilgrimage, rising up wherever beauty awakens our hearts with a gasp of joy; beauty 'ever ancient' is 'ever new'.

To understand the diseased woman we need to reach behind Aphrodite to earlier myths. The stories and images that across the centuries gather around Aphrodite hold a glimpse of a more distant lineage, that of the Great Goddess. These are her truly ancient origins. All the Great Mothers in this tradition, (including Aphrodite), are born from the sea, 'from the primeval ocean or the watery abyss, the primordial womb of life from which all created forms emerge'.[33] She is an ancient goddess but taking a new (and diminished) role in Olympia. But why consider it here?

This tradition concerns our Caucasian roots, our own indigenous beginnings (our Dreaming?), in the parts of the world where our culture came to birth, including what we now call Europe, the near East, Asia and Africa. Anne Baring and Jules Cashford in their book *The Myth of the Goddess*, investigate these beginnings, drawing on a vast range of modern scholarship.[34] Their research unexpectedly unveils the presence

---

[31] Baring and Cashford, *The Myth of the Goddess*, p. 356.
[32] Baring and Cashford, *The Myth of the Goddess*, p. 355. The seashell sacred to Aphrodite was the image by which the initiates of Eleusis recognised each other, and became in the Middle Ages the talisman of pilgrims journeying to the great shrine of Santiago de Compostela in northern Spain, p. 558.
[33] Baring and Cashford, *The Myth of the Goddess*, p. 557.
[34] In this pioneering research Baring and Cashford draw on a huge range of understandings including archaeology, art, mythology, history, poetry, literature and psychology.

of a striking pattern across vast ages and apparently unrelated cultures. This pattern is that which prevailed in the Palaeolithic and Neolithic Ages and Bronze Age Crete (that is from about 40,000 years ago until 1250 BCE), almost 40 millennia.[35] It reveals an underlying vision, (that is called 'the myth of the goddess'), a vision of life as a living unity.

> The Mother Goddess, wherever she is found, is an image that inspires and focuses a perception of the universe as an organic, alive and sacred whole, in which humanity, the Earth and all life on Earth participate as 'her children'. Everything is woven together in one cosmic web, where all orders of manifest and unmanifest life are related, because all share in the sanctity of the original source.[36]

Everything is part of her living substance, animated with soul. There is no division between mind and matter, spirit and nature, soul and body, and nature and humanity thus share a common identity.[37] Why would a female figure have been so consistently created and depicted in this way? One interpretation is that the mystery of birth was for these our ancestors numinous. To ascribe the name goddess is simply to recognise this numinosity; the mystery of birth, the mystery of life, a universe nourishing and alive with regenerating power. Approaching the figure of Venus in Botticelli's painting with this astonishing evidence in mind requires a reappraisal of history, a history that reaches back through tens of thousands of years.

---

[35] Archaeological sites in Germany, Czechoslovakia and Russia abound with small figurines of female figures. The strange power and beauty of these images is impossible to convey, but a picture emerges of a divine being who alone gives birth to the world from her own body. As the last era of glaciation began its long retreat the frozen tundra became steppes. Between 20,000 and 15,000 BCE these grasslands then gave way to flourishing forests, and hunters moved further east following the herds. Some, however, remained behind making homes in caves in the fertile river valleys. This is the period of the figurines in human form and the paintings in the great caves in northern Spain and SW France. Baring and Cashford, *The Myth of the Goddess*, pp. 3-6.

[36] Baring and Cashford, *The Myth of the Goddess*, p. xi.

[37] Baring and Cashford, *The Myth of the Goddess*, pp. 7-8. One example is the Goddess of Lespugue (France 20,000-18,000 BCE), a delicate statue only 14cm in height with a flattened upper chest, a small almost serpentine head, and neither hands or feet, carved from the ivory of a mammoth. The whole emphasis is given to her capacity to give birth and nourishment. Large pendulous breasts merge with her swollen womb and rounded buttocks—like eggs in the nest of her body. Beneath her buttocks ten vertical lines are etched suggesting the 'waters of birth falling profusely from the womb like rain.'

5. Heartbreak / Coalophobia

Who then is this diseased woman rising from the sea? She seems to belong in this ancient lineage. Yet something has happened. Her sanctity is not honoured, but desecrated, her life-giving power sickening. How has this happened? This is a vast topic, and only the briefest summary is possible here. Evidence shows that the myth of the goddess, whilst a story of a vision uncontested over millennia, is also a story of slowly diminishing power.

The Iron Age Babylonian epic *Eneuma Elish* finally cemented the changes begun in the Bronze Age. (The Bronze Age began about 3,000 BCE and the Iron Age about 1250 BCE).[38] Numinosity was gradually transferred from the Mother Goddess to a Father God. In all the myths of the Iron Age, a sky god conquers a giant serpent or dragon. (It is thought to have arisen from the people's experience of water in the annual flooding of the Babylonian plain.[39]) In this story, the Mother Goddess named Tiamat is killed by the god, her great-great-great grandson Marduk. It is from her dead corpse that the world is now made, by splitting her in half, one part becomes earth and the other part heaven. Marduk, the wind-and-fire, sky-and-sun god, takes up and wields a now superior power.[40] Creation is dissociated from the creative source, and the world is no longer a living being, a sacred entity. Such a reversal could hardly be more dramatic. From the perspective of Marduk, the world is now inert, inanimate, dead matter to be shaped and ordered by his spirit. This, however, did not remain a local nature myth. Its popularity was immense and influential, and finally it was known all over the ancient world (even though less ferocious creation stories existed at the time).[41]

The slaying of the goddess can be read symbolically as a story of the evolution of consciousness in the Western tradition, understood as

---

[38] In the Bronze Age pictures, hieroglyphs, words and images appear on stone columns, the walls of temples, tablets of clay and strips of papyrus. Gods and goddesses abound, all of whom 'take their being from one Primordial Goddess who is the origin of all things.' She is recognisably the Great Mother Goddess of Palaeolithic and Neolithic eras, but now words have appeared—she has many names and her many stories are accessible to us. Baring and Cashford, *The Myth of the Goddess*, p. 145.

[39] The myth was ritually remembered as people waited for spring, for the re-appearance of dry land from watery chaos, for it was land that brought life, as earth for planting grain.

[40] Baring and Cashford, *The Myth of the Goddess*, p. 661.

[41] Baring and Cashford, *The Myth of the Goddess*, chapter 7, pp. 273-298.

a necessary murder, as we separated from our identification with the Mother.[42] From this position, we moderns can be seen to have taken one stage of an ongoing story as '*the* story'. We are trapped mythically in an era now past, in a developmental stage appropriate for its own time but now proving deeply destructive. No longer do we need to separate from too close a symbiosis with nature; our problem is rather the reverse. The diseased woman rising from the sea could be understood as an image of the outcome of this living with a one-sided, distorted or inadequate story. 'You whitefellas have lost your Dreaming', slaying the Mother, living without respect.

The figure of Mary

'From somewhere in my memory the figure of Mary superimposes itself on the diseased figure'. 'Superimposed' implies that the two figures need to be understood together, that they have a close relationship. Who is Mary here? Mary the mother of Jesus in the Christian tradition, whose name means 'the sea', and who traditionally is depicted wearing a blue robe, appears. Classically Mary is an obedient, often a submissive or passive figure, held in a golden cage of obsessive purity by a patriarchy intent on controlling feminine power.[43] In the New Testament her significance is secondary. Yet in paintings, icons, sculptures, hymns, music, not to mention the titles accorded by the Catholic Church after the closure of the canon, her significance is far reaching. Biblical word and later art speak different stories, a difference that Baring and Cashford suggest represent a deep yearning in human consciousness.

The Mary who appeared overlaying the diseased woman is Mary of the Magnificat and the woman clothed with fire from the Book of Revelation. The Magnificat, is a Song of Praise that wells up from Mary's heart. 'My soul doth magnify the Lord . . . ' . She feels the unborn child in her womb 'leap for joy' when visited by Elizabeth who has also

---

[42] Baring and Cashford, *The Myth of the Goddess*, p. 660. The assumption of Baring and Cashford's work is that one way 'humans can apprehend and know their own being [is] by making it visible in the images of gods and goddesses.' Coming from a Jungian position they neither romanticise the past nor argue for a return to it (were that even possible).
[43] Harvey, *The Return of the Mother*, p. 341.

miraculously conceived.[44] The song is in praise of a God of mercy and justice, one who 'scatters the proud', who has 'brought down the powerful from their thrones, and lifted up the lowly', who has 'filled the hungry with good things, and sent the rich away empty'.[45] The Magnificat is no sweet, interior prayer, but a fierce call for the transformation of society, a metamorphosis 'of this world into a living mirror of God's beauty, justice and love'.[46] The woman clothed with fire appears in the Book of Revelation as a cosmic figure, 'clothed with the sun, with the moon under her feet and on her head a crown of twelve stars'. The Virgin, the Divine Mother is calling us to respond to the messianic truths of the Magnificat, that she might bring the Christ consciousness to birth. Both these images together evoke a Mary of passion, tenderness and power.[47]

By re-entering our deep history we can begin to glimpse something that has been almost completely obscured by the church and our culture. Joseph Campbell notes that Mary holds almost all the titles of the goddess tradition.

> And so it came to pass that, in the end and to our day, Mary, Queen of Martyrs, became the sole inheritor of all the names and forms, sorrows, joys, and consolations of the goddess-mother in the Western world: Seat of Wisdom . . . Vessel of Honour . . . Mystical Rose . . . House of Gold . . . Gate of Heaven . . . Morning Star . . . Refuge of Sinners . . . Queen of Angels . . . Queen of Peace.[48]

The rich and beautiful tapestry of this poetic vision of Mary carries the unrecognized Mother in all her 'silent unvoiced majesty', who has appeared across cultures and times, rising again whenever she is neglected or suppressed.[49]

The superimposing

Mary of the Magnificat, the Cosmic Mother, and the sea-woman, diseased and blotched, ailing and suffering are held in relationship in

---

[44] Elizabeth is cousin to Mary in the biblical text.
[45] The Magnificat draws on a deep religious heritage. See the Song of Hannah, I Samuel 2.1-10.
[46] Harvey, *The Return of the Mother*, p. 342.
[47] Harvey, *Son of Man*, pp. 180-186.
[48] Joseph Campbell, quoted in Baring and Cashford, *The Myth of the Goddess*, p. 549.
[49] Harvey, *The Return of the Mother*, p. 351.

the palimpsest woman. How might this 'superimposing' be interpreted? The prophetic voice, passionate for justice, now extends beyond the poor in the *human* world. This Mary's arms are open to the diseased woman, to the living ocean (and all its creatures), her body. She, clothed in the sun, the one whose love pours forth in the power that creates the world. A theological reading of this and of Mary and her relationship with Jesus is far beyond the scope of this work.[50] Confusion, splitting and oppression linked with interpretations of Mary that rob her not only of her revolutionary power for justice, but spiritualize her, can be clarified by re-claiming this deep history. The step still to be taken is for her to be given, along with the titles listed above, the one still missing: Queen of Earth.[51]

As we stand at the ocean's edge at Tathra, we find our cultural story broken open, and a deeper story unveiled. References to the ocean in our journals show a slippage between 'it' and 'she', an oscillation between mythological histories that live on in our own psyches. The space between Hume and Uncle Max is a new threshold. Might we learn to discriminate between misleading and insightful humanizations, and re-instate what has been long suppressed and/or undervalued? We do not need to speak the language of 'goddess' or 'Mary' (perhaps *yin* and *yang* are more accessible for us) but we can reclaim our own indigenous mythic past, a deeper and empowering story.[52] A 'Dreaming' that pushes?

Grieving

The two 'diamond' moments described above opened questions of loss and grief in visceral form. Our sadness over what is happening to the ocean was at times overwhelming, beyond our capacity to name, let alone hold or express. As the criminal in the restorative justice session we were broken open; to grief. As the diseased woman, blotched and

---

50 See Harvey, *The Return of the Mother*, pp. 339-434; *Son of Man*, pp. 131-193.
51 Baring and Cashford, *The Myth of the Goddess*, p. xi. We note the Papal Encyclical, *Laudato Si': On Care for Our Common Home* (2016), begins with St Francis' Canticle of Praise, including to Our Sister, Mother Earth (para 1) and pleads with us to hear her cry (para 2). Mary's grief for a world laid waste (para 241) is named in chapter 6, section viii entitled *Queen of All Creation*!
52 *Yin* and *Yang* parallel the 'sacred marriage' of god and goddess, a developmental stage that awaits us. Baring and Cashford, *The Myth of the Goddess*, chapter 16, pp. 659-681.

5. Heartbreak / Coalophobia

sick, we were broken open to a devastating sight of ourselves and of our culture; to grief. And this figure, the ocean herself, weighted with rubbish now almost beyond bearing, perhaps terminally ill, is she, too, grieving?

In our pilgrimage, sorrow appears time and time again.

I feel huge sorrow as I stand looking at the beautiful, stunning ocean, knowing at the same time that we, the species of which I am a part, have already decimated so much of life, and seem not to realize, or not to want to know. I feel, too, a sense of lostness. I am floundering in the presence of the little bit I *can* grasp. ... Two people come into the water to surf. I try not to watch them, but every now and again I can't help it. I watch them falling off their boards. The leaden grey sea—sometimes it seems beautiful—today seems congruent with my mood of heaviness. I let the raw crash of the waves wash over me. [J, 25/2/15]

Heavy, lost, falling off something secure, awash in raw crashing waves. Grief is a response to loss. It manifests in a range of ways, including numbness and denial, shock and anger, yearning and sorrow, disorganisation and despair. Grief is a process. It takes time. If allowed to follow its natural course, eventually the grieving self can reorganise and begin to heal. But grief can also be arrested. A self (or a culture) can rigidify, with unlived or incomplete grieving surfacing in destructive behavioural patterns or addictions. What are we doing with our grief?[53]

There are many fine studies of the dynamics of grief. For us, few have the originality, compassion and insight of the sometimes hilarious and always provocative book, *The Smell of Rain on Dust: Grief and Praise*.[54] Martín Prechtel, native of New Mexico, believes that in the deepening crisis of Western civilization, it is vital to promote a 'search for the Indigenous soul in all people'.[55] His work, like Uncle Max's, is a sustained effort to find ways to help us live ancient wisdoms afresh in

---

[53] For a more detailed discussion of grief in the prophetic tradition in the context of ecological crisis, see Jan Morgan, *Earth's Cry: prophetic ministry in a more-than-human world* (Melbourne: Uniting Academic Press, 2013), pp. 113-145.
[54] Martín Prechtel, *The Smell of Rain on Dust: Grief and Praise* (Berkeley, California: North Atlantic Books, 2015).
[55] Prechtel, *The Smell of Rain on Dust*, p. 171.

modern times. One of these wisdoms concerns grief. We were surprised and deeply challenged by what was so forcefully presented. Not that the basic anatomy of grief as sketched by Prechtel was unfamiliar. Feelings that arise when we lose what we love are common the world over, and not only in human beings. What was new was Prechtel's hermeneutics of grief; what grief *means* and the way it finds expression in personal and social living. His is a picture of grief as an essential work of love. This grief is not only heaviness, sadness and depression. It is that too, but this grief creates beauty out of desolation. This grief 'metabolises' pain into new life. This grief is praise.

> Grief expressed out loud, whether in or out of character, unchoreographed and honest, for someone we have lost, or a country or home we have lost [or a lost Earth], is in itself the greatest praise we could ever give them. Grief is praise, because it is the natural way love honors what it misses.[56]

We could see how such a framing of grief, if it is realized, might lift some of the grey heaviness associated with grief's sorrow. How might it happen in practice?

In the village where Prechtel lived for many years, the Tzutujil town of Santiago Atitlán, grief was expressed aloud and understood to be as natural as eating, peeing and laughing. It was 'an obligation to the life one has been awarded, an *obligation to life to make more life*', and should never be avoided or postponed. Failure to do what was necessary had cosmic consequences, for it would mean 'the world would cease to renew itself; the world would cease to exist'.[57] Grieving, Prechtel argues, is a sacred art; movement not stagnation, creativity not depression. It needs intentionality and time for its messy watery life to spill out. As it does, grief makes a sound; it is storytelling, weeping, making beautiful poems, and singing. Above all, grief is praise. Praise of life. Praise of love. Praise of what has been given. Indeed, grief is 'the great prayer of praise singing the world back into life'.[58] With some wonderfully humorous stories, themselves a healing balm to sorrow, Prechtel suggests that

---

[56] Prechtel, *The Smell of Rain on Dust*, p. 31. The words in brackets are our addition.
[57] Prechtel, *The Smell of Rain on Dust*, p. 3. Italics added.
[58] Prechtel, *The Smell of Rain on Dust*, p. 6.

5. Heartbreak / Coalophobia

modern westerners have learned to repress and hide their grieving, to present to the world an unemotional flatness that leaves them stranded in a spiritual vacuum.[59] Knowing our own culture (and selves!) as we do, this seems a pretty persuasive diagnosis.

Such active, open and natural unfolding of grief, allowing it to flow freely, looks inviting—and also impossible. Prechtel knows this. To grieve in this way, a tribe is necessary, a real community 'a resilient non-judgemental human basket against which the griever is able to thrash'.[60] The basket holds, keeps safe, allows the person to do what is needed, however irrational or uncharacteristic it seems at the time. Our problem is that most of us do not have such a community. We were stunned then to read of his 'solution'. 'For people ... who have no community or an extended family of like mind, but might have one real friend to watch over them while they go splashing through grief's messy and ecstatic route to beauty, the best thing to do is get both of you down to the sea'.[61] The natural world, Prechtel claims, has the best and most capable communities anywhere; but the very best of all is the ocean, the great Mother, the womb of the entire earth, her salty water the tears of all the grief of all the world's losses. On a stretch of sea coast with no people 'she, the ocean, can pull and suck down grief, converting pain into life, in a way only very few people can. ... The sea speaks in a million ways, but the waves always lick the face of our hurt until our real face reappears from beneath'.[62]

This is something we are only just beginning to explore. To choose connection is to choose heartbreak. If we allow ourselves to be broken open, we need to learn more of the 'sacred art of grieving'. Looking back from our present vantage point, we can see that Prechtel's point of view gives voice to a dimension of our pilgrimage that was always there, though we did not always recognise it. To turn towards, to stand face-to-face with a damaged ocean, we need our 'real face' restored to us, if we are not to remain mired in the secret grey heaviness of despair. Unlike

---

[59] Prechtel, *The Smell of Rain on Dust*, p. 32.
[60] Prechtel, *The Smell of Rain on Dust*, p. 37.
[61] Prechtel, *The Smell of Rain on Dust*, p. 47.
[62] Prechtel, *The Smell of Rain on Dust*, pp. 47-48.

the loss of a human friend, the loss that is the despoiling of the ocean is ongoing. To commit ourselves to grief as a sacred responsibility, a spontaneous expression of the integrity of love, is therefore an on-going challenge. We are just on the edge. If Prechtel is right—and we (shyly) hope that he is—the challenge itself is already the birth of new life.

> Grief that praises life shows the depth of our appreciation for having been given life enough to begin with to experience both love and loss and that with all the mistreatment we humans give to the earth, we still have this amazing unlikely opportunity to actually speak and bathe in the Divine.[63]

We take up this theme in chapter 6.

Heartbreak / **Coalophobia**

The light is softening at last, the windows open to catch any late afternoon breeze. Time to prepare the evening meal. The day has been hot, glaring bright. It is February 2017 and temperatures this summer have continually broken records. I glance out the window and back to the worn surface of my chopping board. Ginger, garlic and onion, pungent, fragrant and tearing up my eyes. The TV is on and I hear the word 'coal' and walk over to look, Chinese chopping knife in hand. There, in the Australian parliamentary House of Representatives, is the Treasurer, Scott Morrison, Member for Cook, a large chunk of black coal in his hand. He holds it up, with a look of triumphant, mocking glee and says:

'This is coal.

Do not be afraid.

Do not be scared.

It will not hurt you.'[64]

---

[63] Prechtel, *The Smell of Rain on Dust,* p. 59.
[64] Commonwealth Questions Without Notice, House of Representatives, 9th February 2017, p. 54, www.aph.gov.au/Parliamentary_Business/Hansard/. Questioner Andrew Hastie, MP. All subsequent citations of Mr. Morrison's words in the House come from this same source.

5. Heartbreak / Coalophobia

What is this? We can't quite believe our eyes. Behind him on their green leather benches, his colleagues are laughing, and when the Speaker reprimands him for bringing 'props' into the chamber,[65] the Treasurer turns and, with a flourish, hands the lump of coal to the Deputy Prime Minister, who passes it on to the Minister for Energy, who passes it along the front bench and then on into the ranks of the government backbenchers. As the lump of coal travels from hand to hand, Mr. Morrison, at the dispatch box, continues his assault. This coal 'was dug up by men and women who work in the electorates of those who sit opposite' (i.e., the Labor Party) and it has ensured the prosperity of Australia for over 100 years. Those who oppose the continuing use of coal as an energy source are suffering from a serious 'malady'—he lets the word linger a moment, relishing the suggestion of illness and weakness it exudes—'a pathological fear of coal.' A pause and he continues, 'There is no word for "coalophobia" officially, but that is the malady that afflicts those opposite'; a 'pathological, ideological opposition to coal.'

Watching the screen, a dark incredulity gathers to a knot in our guts, bewilderment and astonishment. He can't be serious. At one level he isn't. He's playing for the cameras. He knows there will be people all over the country, just like us, watching this on the evening news in their lounge rooms. This is a way to grab their attention. At another level he is deadly serious. Morrison is not speaking to the House, but to an edgy electorate. The political context here is blackouts in South Australia, which the Federal Government attributed to the South Australian State Labor Government's investment in wind and solar, though the minister's own department was clear that this was not the case.[66] Morrison knows people are worried. He knows jobs are insecure. He wants this pain to go away, or at least to be deflected onto the opposition, and he sets about doing just that.

We needed time to lay our incredulity aside in order to decipher the different threads cleverly interwoven here.

---

[65] It is a tradition of the House that no props be used by members in their speeches to the Parliament during normal debates on policy or the answering of questions without notice.
[66] The primary cause was extreme weather events.

Pantomime

One commentator likened the Treasurer's performance to 'show and tell' time at the local primary school.[67] The unspoken script runs something like this. 'Look children, here is a lump of black stuff, hard and shiny and dark. See (waving it about)? It's called coal. Some people feel scared that it might hurt them. But it won't. Really it won't. Lots of people, just like your mummy and daddy, have worked hard for a long time to get this coal for us. And it really helps. Coal makes electricity for our lights so we can see when it's dark, and our air-conditioners so we can be cool when it's hot, and our stoves so we can have lovely meals when we are hungry. We need it every day. So don't be frightened. It won't hurt you!'

The show and tell has a double aim. At one level, Morrison wants to make a simple point that any child *could* understand. Coal has been a great boon to our lives for a long time. Now all of a sudden some people are saying it's bad and dangerous and should be stopped. Really? And do you also think the moon is made of gorgonzola cheese?

A second thing the pantomime intends is more subtle. Mr. Morrison, like a teacher speaking soothingly to alarmed children, declares, 'don't be afraid, don't be scared, it won't hurt you'. In other words, there is absolutely nothing to worry about. This is the message the Treasurer wants *us* to hear, standing with Chinese chopping knife in hand in front of the tele. All this agitation about coal is basically a distraction. Let's cut to the chase. I'm the adult in the room. I know how to handle this stuff, because I am not driven by irrational fear. 'On this side of the House, you will not find fear of coal any more than you will find fear of wind … you will not find fear of sun, you will not find fear of wave energy, you will not find fear of any of these sources of energy.' By contrast they—all those coalophobes—are just scaredy-cats; big, frightened kids, sitting there hand-wringing and heartbreaking over coal and climate change, but offering you nothing. They're a bunch of 'bleeding hearts', who have no understanding of the *real* world and of the way it *really* works. I know what to do. And I'm not scared. Why should you be?

---

[67] www.facebook.com/theguardianaustralia/videos, accessed 1 March 2017.

Politics

When the pantomime is over, the Treasurer gets down to more serious business. He stops pretending to be a teacher talking to children. He's made that point, and no one in the House or in the lounge room has missed it. Coal is benign, indeed hugely beneficial, in the right hands. *Our hands.*

In real life everyone knows, the Treasurer included, it's not a lump of coal waving in his hand in the House of Representatives that's the problem. It is *burning* huge quantities of it in coal-fired power stations across the land. That's the problem and that's the fear. That fear is what Mr. Morrison now goes for. The gloves come off. Morrison is now talking as adult to adults. The 'show and tell' lump of coal has gone to the backbench. I will tell you what you *really* need to worry about. The thing you ought to fear, and with a genuine grownup's fear, is *not* burning coal. The real world is the world of business, and money, and jobs, and security. If we do not burn coal Australian businesses will 'fizzle out in the dark' because 'affordable energy is what Australian businesses need to remain competitive.' And without coal that affordable energy just isn't available and won't be secure. Precisely what *we* aim to give you is cheap, available and secure energy. While 'those opposite' (the coalophobes), 'just like the South Australian Labor Government are switching off jobs, switching off lights and switching off air conditioners and forcing Australian families to boil in the dark as a result of their Dark Age policies.'

The political blow lands with practised precision: get your fears right. We have been burning coal for a century and more. Our present prosperity is a direct result. And burning coal is still delivering the same benefits and promises more. Why change? Alternate paths are patently unreliable. Look at South Australia.

Grow up.

Philosophy

Pantomime and politics are not the final points the Treasurer wishes to make to an edgy nation. The bed-rock issue is philosophical. Morrison is concerned with the basic narrative that has founded and guided western civilization for the last three hundred years: the story of ever increasing human mastery of the natural world through science and technology. The unavoidable physicality of that lump of coal in the chambers of parliament held an immediate and eerie fascination. Here, a piece of the natural world, a real part of one of our nation's most plentiful 'natural resources', is brought right into the heart of *our* world, the centre of our human control. Parliament is the symbol and the focus of our best efforts at ordering our lives in the world. Here human power concentrates. The black lump in the Treasurer's hand is dense with a different kind of power, a chemical power accumulated over millions of years, with tons and tons of ancient plants, gathered together, compressed, heated, slowly transforming into black magic: coal. In the last few centuries, humans have learned with increasing efficiency how to find this magic, dig it up in huge quantities, and use it as fuel to drive massive generators that power an entire economy and run everything from computers to trams, from hot water systems to beer-bottling machines. Now the scientists (the same scientists who taught us how to harness coal in the first place) are saying coal, the way we are using it, is a primary source of emissions that are causing dangerous climate change. Earth, it seems, is suddenly fighting back against our known and cherished ways of dealing with it. That is a clash of powers.

It is a clash of mythic proportions. Marduk faces off against Tiamat in the House of Representatives.[68] That ancient battle is played out again in front of us; with the same result. Morrison (Marduk) triumphantly brandishes a fragment of Nature, the Mother (Tiamat), demonstrating by his action that he holds her power in his hand and can control it as he wishes for his own (and our) enrichment. If there is some kick-back from Earth, we will master that in turn. Nor is it just coal that we will master. Morrison has no fear of wind, or sun, or wave, or 'any of these sources of energy.' Tiamat's secrets, whatever they may be and wherever they may be, remain so many material assets to be exploited, lifeless reserves for us to manipulate to our own ends. This is *our* story. There is no need to change it. Rather every reason to re-tell it, louder.

---

[68] For a detailed discussion of the Tiamat and Marduk myth see above, pp. 155-156

5. Heartbreak / Coalophobia

The Treasurer resumes his seat, clearly well satisfied with his presentation, but the shadow of Naomi Klein has been hovering in the chamber the whole time the Treasurer was speaking. 'What the climate needs to avoid collapse is a contraction in humanity's use of resources; what our economic model demands to avoid collapse is unfettered expansion. Only one of these sets of rules can be changed, and it's not the laws of nature.'[69]

Tiamat is rising. Waving a lump of coal in the Parliament is as good a sign as any that, though we may not like it, somewhere deep down we know it.

We turn back to the kitchen bench, switch on the cook top, and enact the battle ourselves.

---

[69] Naomi Klein, *This Changes Everything: Capitalism vs. The Climate* (United Kingdom: Penguin Random House, 2015), p. 21.

Learning a practice of attention (5)

Beginning and ending matter. The first prepares us for what will follow. The second gathers up and integrates what has taken place.

* * * * * *

Approaching

Entry. We make the transition from whatever matters have occupied us during the day to come to a special place for a special period of time for a special practice of attention. We acknowledge this transition as we step out onto the sand (our practice being on the beach) by lightly brushing ourselves down with our hands—head, arms, chest, back, legs—symbolically flicking off the ordinary business of the day and taking up the special business of sea see/hearing.[1]

Silence. Silence is essential. We found that the visible voice of the world broke its silence only when we offered it ours. Preparing for this, we walked separately and in silence along the beach for about half an hour to reach the selected spot for the practice.

Greeting. Acknowledge the place with a gesture of respect. Take a moment to gather and attend to all your senses.

Dedication. As a way of 'unselfing' ourselves and turning outward to the other-than-human-world, we dedicate the time silently to the flourishing of all beings, and especially to those in our immediate vicinity, and to bearing witness to the loss they are suffering. If you belong within a particular faith tradition (Buddhist, Muslim, Christian, etc.) you can adjust this dedication appropriately.

---

[1] We are grateful to our friend Susanna Pain for drawing this gesture of approach to our attention.

Departing

Offering. We found that a way to bring the time to an appropriate end is to make a simple offering of gratitude. A beautiful small bottle of fresh water poured out on the sand, for example, as a symbol of the centrality of water to all life and acknowledgement of the sea as its source.

Taking leave. Honour the compass point directions as previously described.

Returning. Walk back home in silence.

Journal. Once home we take a few minutes to tell each other about the salient features of the experience and to write down what is said. It is quite remarkable what this discipline brings to light, not only in the moment of its being recorded, but in the growing weight and interconnection of the insights gained as they build up over a period of time.

6. Adoration

There is a worldwide famine of adoration, and we are all visibly dying in it.

Andrew Harvey

The star jump

> I am struggling with the effort of standing still. My back hurts. My mind rushes hither and thither. When will this be over? ... All of a sudden a little girl, four or five at the most, appears in front of me. Her back is toward me as she faces out to sea. A wave breaks in front of her and foaming water gushes over her feet. She squeals in delight. The wave retreats. As it does, she performs a perfect star-jump; arms and hands stretched upward and outward, legs and feet off the ground and splayed outwards to mimic her arms. A gesture of pure joy. She runs into the waves, splashing and calling, turning round and around, flinging spray over herself and others. Spontaneously the child reaches out to the sea with all her life-force. She knows exactly what to do. I marvel at her capacity to be seized by such wonder. She has a live connection with the ocean I seem to have lost. If ever I had it. [G, 18/3/13]

Wonder is the beginning of philosophy, Plato said. Philosophy is the love of wisdom. The love of wisdom is the love of life. The little girl by the sea knew wonder. No one could miss it. That she loved life was obvious in her every move. Did she have wisdom too? Insight and understanding that eluded us? Looking from our present vantage point, there is not much doubt.

In what does it consist? Why do we note it with a kind of nostalgic envy? The child meets the world with uninhibited immediacy. She is not thinking of what needs to be done for lunch, or whether the ASX remains 'volatile'. The ruminations of ageing adults behind her are of no slightest concern. She is caught in a moment of delight that absorbs her completely. Unable to contain her feelings, she squeals, dances, jumps and throws her arms and legs in all directions, drenching herself in a spray of sun-lit drops. The child leaps to embrace what Tathra beach has to offer and is dazzled and delighted by what she receives. Spontaneously, she gives voice to her joy in shrieks of laughter and shouts of glee.

As we age, it seems, we lose this natural sense of the immediate and amazing 'thereness' of things, and the generosity with which they offer themselves to us. Familiarity blunts wonder. The practical demands of living crowd out any sense of astonishment at the strange *being-present-with-us* of the world, which once we may have had. A child's star jump by the water's edge awakens a dim echo. 'From deep in my memory, as far as I can reach back into childhood, my love for the sea floods in to me.' [J, 12/3/13] Such moments, when they come, are precious. The rare and fleeting awareness of the world's amazing strangeness in the midst of its daily familiarity, argues David Bentley Hart, is not some childish confusion or passing emotional flurry, 'but a genuine if tantalizingly brief glimpse into an inexhaustibly profound truth about reality.'[1]

> One realizes that everything about the world that seems so unexceptional and drearily predictable is in fact charged with an immense and imponderable mystery. In that instant one is aware, even if the precise formulation eludes one, that everything one knows exists in an irreducibly gratuitous way ...[2]

We noted in a previous chapter that the discipline of paying careful attention to the ocean has certain distant but not unhelpful parallels with the processes of psychoanalysis. A careful and extended exchange in the presence of a patient and attentive other, albeit in this case a non-human other, has the capacity to open a way for us to re-enter events and experiences that we have always known, but with which we have long since lost touch. The grief of buried trauma and the grief of a child's wonder lost, alike, can stalk and constrict our on-going lives, as long as they remain unacknowledged and unlamented in the hidden depths of the unconscious. It is a taxing labour both on the couch and on the edge, as anyone who has tried it knows. However, the truth that comes to light

---

[1] David Bentley Hart, *The Experience of God: Being, Consciousness, Bliss* (New Haven: Yale University Press, 2013), p. 90. Pages 87-94 are a brilliant analysis of the experience of childlike wonder at the world. The whole of chapter two (pp. 84-151) spells out powerfully some of the philosophical and theological implications of this experience.
[2] Hart, *The Experience of God*, p. 88.

in the process, and the truthfulness it subsequently requires of us, bring some surprising gifts in their train.

> This is like a wonderland. The ocean is on brazen self-display. A lyrebird with its tail-feathers up. This is what the beach 'really is'; the Platonic Idea (*eidos*) of beach. Every beach in the world longs to be just like this. ... Well, steady on! ... But it's true. This presence, lit up and lively, filled with colour and sound, lifts my spirits. It forces me out of myself into a wider space. Yes, it's Tathra beach. Same old. I've seen it a hundred times. But today it feels like an alarming, inexplicable wonder. Not so much *what* it is—this wave, this sand dune, this blue horizon. But *that* it is at all. Any of it. All of it. And on top of that: here it is, pouring its magnificence gratuitously into my insignificant awareness. Schleiermacher says somewhere that all events in the world are really miracles, only we're so used to them we've forgotten how to see them for what they are. There are ten banks of waves, reaching way out into the deep ocean. Again and again they heave their great bodies skyward. Sunlight pours through them and bounces back in a flare of blue. The surf is a thunder roll. White energy boils through the water. I feel it. Plato says philosophy begins with wonder. Worship does too. Am I a philosophical worshipper today? [G, 12/4/14]

This is no star jump, to be sure. Our adult gestures are well under control. Acutely aware of beach frolickers around us, we defer to accepted protocols. A still and upright stance, an occasional shallow bow, perhaps the quiet intoning of a guttural *om*, is about as much as the casual observer might detect of anything out of the ordinary. With time and practice, we have grown bolder in our gestures, seeking ways to give bodily expression to a changing consciousness within. For the child it is spontaneous and natural. For us it is learned and laboured. It feels like struggling to wake up from some deep and dream-plagued sleep. We know this world well, and yet we don't know it. In this journey we have certainly been jolted awake.

> That sudden instant of existential surprise is ... one of wakefulness, of attentiveness to reality as such, rather than to the impulses of the ego or of desire or of ambition; and it opens up upon the limitless beauty of being, which is to say, upon the beauty of being seen as a

gift that comes from beyond all possible beings. This wakefulness can, moreover, become habitual, a kind of sustained awareness of the surfeit of being over the beings it sustains ...[3]

That is the hope, anyway; to wake up and to stay awake to the 'limitless beauty of being'. But what does that mean? Is there an adult equivalent to the child's star jump? If there is, with us it is sadly reigned in. Which says something about us, no doubt, and about the society we live in.

> This session is messy and unsatisfying. The beauty of the ocean is immediate and pressing. It demands attention. My instant response is exhilaration. I am running towards something alluring, captivating, welcoming. ... A cluster of words comes to me. Grandeur, glory, splendour. All seem apt. ... What are their opposites? Take 'grandeur'. Opposites: narrow, constricted, mean. Something shrunk down or dried out. To call all this 'grandeur' seems to point to its largeness. Its inexhaustibility. A wide and abundant space. As for 'glory', to my mind it tilts towards transcendence. Radiance, brilliance, energy. Light that lends colour to things. 'Tyger, tyger burning bright'. Antonyms: limp, lifeless, colourless. ... 'Splendour'. Splendour is the manifestation of the essence of something. The real thing. It's opposites, well ... dull, mediocre, 'not up to it'! ... Where am I? [G, 16/3/15]

Abundance, largeness, brilliance, colour, energy, life, essence, the real thing. Is this the star jump for grown-ups? A way of being in the world that recognizes in astonishment what is given, acknowledges it gratefully, and responds with gladness of heart?

Immanuel Kant is the philosopher for grown-ups *par excellence*. He is all for humanity 'come of age'. Traditional authority—religious, political, intellectual—is to be cross examined vigorously in the court of experience and reason. Think for yourself! In a remarkable passage, Kant comes close to finding words which, we might argue, uncover what lies hidden in the gesture of a little girl leaping with delight in the waves of the sea. This matter, which a child can give such expression to, is in fact a matter which belongs to all ages and possibly to all cultures, religions and philosophies. It touches the human condition *per se*, yet

---

[3] Hart, *The Experience of God*, p. 151.

6. Adoration

encapsulates a mystery that shakes off any language that attempts to grasp it.

> ...the consideration of the profound wisdom of divine creation in the smallest things and of its majesty in the great whole, such as was indeed available to human beings in the past but in more recent times has widened into the widest admiration—this consideration not only has such a power as to transport the mind into that sinking feeling called *adoration*, in which the human being is as it were nothing in his own eyes, but is also, with respect to the human moral determination, such a soul-elevating power, that in comparison words, even if they were those of King David in prayer ... would have to vanish as empty sound, because the feeling arising from such a vision of the hand of God is inexpressible.[4]

Kant uses religious language here. God even makes an appearance at the end. This raises questions in our time, of course, and we will take them up in due course. For the moment though, it is enough to note the disposition that Kant identifies as implicit in and fitting for human beings when they confront the world ('creation') around and within. The incredible dynamic cohesion, both in the tiniest details ('smallest things') and in the majestic scale ('great whole') of the universe, has been intuited by people since time immemorial. In more recent times, with the astonishing explorations of science, this wondering awareness, Kant asserts, has been informed, deepened and amplified immeasurably ('widened into the widest admiration'). The immediate sense of the 'great whole' in the 'smallest things', and the 'smallest things' in 'the great whole', if given due attention ('consideration'), draws us forcefully ('such a power to transport us') towards a strange ambivalent sentiment. On the one hand, there arises a humble feeling of our own insignificance in the face of grandeur ('nothing in his own eyes'). On the other, an exultation of being ('soul-elevating power') that seizes us by the throat,

---

[4] Immanuel Kant, "Religion in the Boundaries of Mere Reason," in *Religion and Rational Theology*, Allen W. Wood and George di Giovanni (eds) (Cambridge: Cambridge University Press, 1996), p. 212 (emphasis in the original). Cited in Jean-Luc Nancy, *Adoration: the Deconstruction of Christianity II*, trans. John McKeane (New York: Fordham University Press, 2013), p. 16.

rendering us speechless (words—'even ... those of King David in prayer ... vanish as empty').

Kant calls this sentiment '*adoration*'; a word which again, at least until the relatively recent past, has had strong religious overtones, implying profound regard or love for God. Intriguingly, he describes adoration as 'that sinking feeling'. For a pilgrimage concerned with water, this is a fascinating image, if at first sight counter-intuitive. Isn't adoration essentially an elevation, an uplift of spirit, not a deflation or descent? Yes, and Kant notes carefully its 'soul-elevating power'. It is not sinking as opposed to rising that is at issue here. It is sinking as in being inundated, overwhelmed or swamped by the intensity of the situation. Adoration is a flooding experience. At once both uplifting (I am a part of this great whole) and humbling (I am nothing in comparison). Exactly this tension creates the liquid turbulence of spirit Kant calls adoration; a turbulence which, at times, threatens to carry us away in its flood.

This, or something like it, is what the child knows and we have forgotten. Andrew Harvey believes such forgetfulness is extracting a deadly price in our time. 'There is a worldwide famine of adoration, and we are all visibly dying in it', he says.[5] To put it another way, wonder-blindness, a lack of profound respect and love toward the 'great whole' and the 'smallest things', is as big a danger to the future of the planet as unbridled commitment to growth without limit and consumption without sustainability. They are two sides of the same coin. If we do not see and love beauty, we will probably find it easy enough to live with defacement and destruction. If we don't know reverence, there is a good chance we won't recognize profanity when it comes along. If we have no feeling for wonder, it is more than likely we won't feel grief at its loss. Adoration is a flooding disposition ('that sinking feeling'), which loves beauty, cultivates respect, and rejoices in wonder. In our noisy, anxious, violent, consumption-driven world it is in short supply.

---

[5] Andrew Harvey, *The Return of the Mother* (New York: Jeremy P. Tarcher/Putnam, 1995), p. 169.

6. Adoration

Does beauty say adieu?

We have been on the trail of beauty from the start. Beauty is the word that appears more frequently than any other in our journal. St Augustine's famous conversation with the earth, the sea, the stars, the sun, the air and the animals, was pivotal for our decision to embark on this journey. He is crystal clear. The visible voice of the world is heard in the fundamental speech of beauty. 'I asked these questions simply by gazing at these things, and their beauty was the answer they gave.'[6] Where does this answer take us *finally*? The answer the beautiful things give to Augustine somehow falls short. They say 'no' to his enquiry. 'We are *not* your God. Seek what is above us.' In other words, we are *not* what you are (finally) looking for. This negative response, Chrétien argues, 'dispossesses us of any possibility of being satisfied with them [i.e., the beautiful things] and stopping at them.' In short, 'the visible manifests in its responsive inadequacy the excess of origin over itself.'[7] The voice of the ocean, it seems, declines any claim to be the beginning and the end. It sends us on, looking for that which exceeds it. But looking where?

Here Chrétien poses his central question. Does beauty say adieu?[8] Adieu in French means 'goodbye'. Also, literally, 'to God' (à Dieu). Does the world in its beauty simultaneously point us beyond itself, that is, say 'goodbye, don't stop here;' *and* 'press on,' commending us to what exceeds it, à Dieu? A long tradition of meditation on the experience of beauty, which runs from Plato, Plotinus and Augustine to Dostoevsky, Barth, and David Bentley Hart leans in this direction.[9] Kant finds a place in this illustrious pedigree. The adoration which the 'smallest things' in connection with the 'great whole' calls forth from the attentive participant, Kant claims, is directed finally not toward beautiful things themselves, though certainly not without them, but 'to the vision of the

---

6 Augustine, *Confessions*, trans. R. S. Pine-Coffin (Harmondsworth, Middlesex, England: Penguin, 1961), X, 27, 231. See also chapter 1, pp. 14-17.
7 Jean-Louis Chrétien, *The Call and the Response*, trans. Anne A. Davenport (New York: Fordham University Press, 2004), p. 37.
8 Chrétien's brilliant essay entitled, "Does Beauty Say Adieu?" is found in *The Ark of Speech*, trans. Andrew Brown (London & New York: Routledge, 2004), pp. 77-110.
9 Chrétien traces this history in his essay.

hand of God' understood as the origin of all 'creation', great and small. Beauty is always in excess of itself, an envoy of its origins.

Secular naturalism—the belief that there is nothing apart from the physical order of the world, and certainly nothing supernatural—finds this suggestion simply incredible. There is no 'beyond' to refer to. No 'elsewhere' to take account of. God is dead. The world is the world is the world. Such naturalism has no quarrel with Augustine's beautiful things exclaiming, 'we are not your God'. *Naturally* not! But, 'seek what is above us', is a vain and futile demand, whatever its pedigree. It has no reference and so it has no meaning. This is an important issue in our culture. Thus far we have tried in our discussion not to presume a theological perspective, anyway not too intrusively. Loving and respectful attention to the Earth is obviously not the prerogative of believers alone, as anyone familiar with nature writing in our time or with Indigenous understandings will testify. Religion, and particularly Christianity, has been rightly and robustly criticized for its contribution to an attitude of human dominance over and exploitation of the world (Gen. 1.28), but Chrétien's question has a way of asserting itself. Not merely from consideration of a venerable tradition, but from everyday experience. A child's star jump nudges the mind.

From our personal perspective a theological account seems the more comprehensive and satisfying in response to the experience of beauty in all its mysterious excess, splendour and gratuity. This is not the culture's 'house opinion', however. In our contemporary Australian context, such a theological view is likely to be looked upon as a minority, if not eccentric, option. Big issues are at stake across this divide, of course; the reality or unreality of God being just one of them. To go into detail would take us well beyond the scope of this book. However, in relation to the question of adoration as a possible, and in our times perhaps necessary, disposition toward a world threatened by our human excesses and brutalities, there is more common ground to be found here than might at first glance seem possible. At any rate, it is a question worth exploring. We will take up first a theological perspective on adoration, and then move to a non-theological one.

6. Adoration

Adoration: a theological reading

We began this journey in response to a text from book X of Augustine's *Confessions*. Having now explored the drama of beauty to the point where the question has emerged, 'does beauty say adieu?', it is instructive to listen to him once again, so as to gather a more precise idea of what is at stake. Later in the same book of *Confessions*, Augustine gives voice to his encounter with beauty in a passage of 'most blazing intensity'.[10]

> Late have I loved you, beauty (*pulchritudo*) so old and so new: late have I loved you. And see, you were within and I was in the external world and sought you there, and in my unlovely state I plunged into those lovely created things which you made. You were with me, and I was not with you. The lovely things kept me far from you, though if they did not have their existence in you, they had no existence at all.[11]

Augustine cries out to beauty as 'you'. He is in the presence of 'lovely things', the sun, the moon, the stars, the sea and so on, but it is not these he now addresses. They are there. Yes. And through their impact on him he is moved to cry out, but not to them. At least, not to them alone. In his encounter with beautiful things, Augustine senses, not as an element added later, and not as an inference subsequently thought out, but as intrinsic to the experience itself, a presence that is not contained within the beautiful things themselves, not singly, and not as a unified whole. He cries out to this beauty which is not *a* beauty, but the infinite source of all finite beauties; the living well without whose continuous overflow they would have 'no existence at all'. He calls *à dieu*, 'to God'. Augustine is famous for his capacity to argue a case, and that at a high level of philosophical sophistication, but here in no way does he scrutinize or analyse this beauty. His speech is nearer a gasp than a doctrine. More invocation than instruction. More prayer than debate.

---

[10] The phrase is Chrétien's, *The Ark of Speech*, p. 90. We gratefully acknowledge the importance of his masterly discussion of this section of *Confessions* for our reflections at this point. See pp. 90-93.
[11] Augustine, *Confessions*, X, 27, 38, trans. Henry Chadwick (Oxford: Oxford University Press, 1991), p. 201.

Moving ... beyond

The pressure that beauty exerts does move us. It transports us from the place and state we were in to another place. This movement is often felt as a step from the ordinary to the extraordinary, from the predictable to the surprising, from the mundane to the exulted. Beauty awakens us to its nearness, its presence. It 'pushes' us to respond; to sing out.

> It is wonderful to be here. An awesome place. I want to give thanks to something or someone. It doesn't feel right just to stand and gawk. This beauty calls for an answer with physical urgency. It pushes and pulls. It clamours for expression and acknowledgement. I wish I could sing it out. But I don't know how. It reminds me of Afro-American congregations when the singing really takes off. The music sings you rather than the other way around. That's what it's like here. Being sung. I look at these wonderful waves. And I can't even say what a wave is. It has to be seen to be believed. Thomas Farber says that, 'to name the qualities of ... Earth's oceans ... reveals our hungers. Takes us to the limits of our capacities. And beyond.' Yes. ... beyond. ... beyond is what it feels like.[12] [G, 12/4/14]

Kant is right. This is hard to put into words. Not because there is nothing to say, but for the opposite reason. The 'clamour' of the event, which might better be called an *advent*, is flooding. It swamps you. You find yourself swept up in (to use Chrétien's vivid phrase) 'a kind of catastrophe',[13] which is not something that can be described from the view point of an onlooker. 'The music sings you rather than the other way around.'

If beauty says à Dieu, as Augustine claims, it does not reveal itself to us as the kind of spectacle we can look down on or grasp as one more feature of the world before our eyes. This is not *a* beauty like the 'wonderful waves'. They defy description too. This is the advent, the drawing near, of beauty itself; that beauty which precedes all finite beauties, as the source and energy of their radiance; that beauty which precedes the eye that beholds it, and indeed creates the forms that give

---

[12] For the Farber reference, see James Bradley (ed), *The Penguin Book of the Ocean* (Camberwell, Victoria: Hamish Hamilton, Penguin Books, 2010), p. 5.
[13] Chrétien, *The Ark of Speech*, p. 91.

meaning to the eye's beholding. In this moment, we are not observers of beauty, but something more like its victims. We undergo it, like a surfer tossed from her board by a powerful wave.

'So old and so new'

If a first dimension of 'excess' is that of beauty over beautiful things, a second has to do with temporality. Having addressed God as *pulchritudo* (beauty), Augustine immediately qualifies this in temporal terms as being 'so old and so new'. At first glance, this seems to be a biographical reference. 'Late have I loved you' (mentioned twice) refers to his conversion at the age of 31 (in 386 CE), which he reports in detail earlier in *Confessions* (VIII, 12, 175-177). Only then, in the midst of his life, did he come to respond to beauty/God with the love that is called for, and he regrets the years spent in ignorance and opposition to this beauty and its claim on him.

This certainly has its parallels for us. A sense of having left it late appears in the very first records of our journey. 'The sea is generous, willing to share. We only have to open our eyes, our ears, our mouths. And there is sorrow too. Where have you been? How old are you that it is only now you take time to come?' [J & G, 14/2/12] We have regrets that it is only now, in our seventies, that we have begun to wake up to the call of the ocean. Why has it taken so long? Where have we been all this time?

Personal circumstances do not exhaust the meaning. '*Sero te amavi* (late have I loved you) has something universal about it; it is a matter of principle, for the response of our love is necessarily belated with regard to the splendour of God.'[14] God is eternal, therefore the 'splendour of God' is always before us, with us, and after us. Before ever we can become aware of it and respond to it, that splendour has already approached us and touched us.

> The sea is in front of me. In this very moment it says to me: 'Way before you came along, I have been faithfully present, rolling onward, showing myself regardless of who is looking, and mainly with no one looking.' ... The sound I am hearing on this beach ... is a sound that has

---
14 Chrétien, *The Ark of Speech*, p. 91.

been here for 4 billion years; a sound as old as the Earth itself, or almost as old; an ancient sound, a sound that preceded any ears to hear it. ... I drift into a von Weizsäcker-like series: I am older than the business of sea see/hearing; the church is older than me; humanity is older than the church; the sea is older than humanity; the earth is older than the sea; the cosmos is older than the earth. Something in me wants to go on: God is older than the cosmos. But that is the wrong way to put it. God is *ontologically* prior to the cosmos and all its evolution, *not* its temporal first cause. [G & J, 25/3/12; 16/4/14][15]

The way-before-you-came-along feeling refers to deep evolutionary time. Earth time. Attention to the ocean, we found, faces us with the unimaginably vast temporal priority the Earth has over human history, and over our own tiny lives in particular. On a scale which compresses the 4.6 billion years of Earth's evolutionary history into one year, James Cook arrives at the coast of Australia at one second to midnight on December 31st.[16] We humans are always late in coming to appreciate and respond to the beauty of the sea. Even the star jumping child is 'late' in her exultation. The ocean is always ahead of us and the ocean will always outlast us. Our utter dependence on the prior actuality and continuing generosity of the sea is implicit in that 'way before'.

If this is true of the sea, it is doubly true of God. God is not the temporary first cause of the cosmos; though this seems to be the (mis) understanding of many of the popular anti-theists of our time. God is the *ontological* condition of the world; the ground of both time and cause. God is *creator* and *upholder* of anything and everything that is. Augustine understands this deeply and discusses it at length in book XI. 'For the will of God is not a created thing, but comes before [*not temporally but ontologically before*] the creation—and this is true because nothing could be created [*including time*] unless the will of the Creator came before it.'[17]

---

[15] This citation is a combination of two journal entries recorded some months apart. Their common theme, we feel, justifies the amalgamation at this point.
[16] See chapter 3, pp., pp. 86-87.
[17] Augustine, *Confessions*, XI, 10, 252.

6. Adoration

We cannot be contemporaneous with what is always already there. In this sense it is always 'late have I loved you.' When beauty approaches us in beautiful things, it brings with it its own absolute precedence, 'the fact that it comes before us and that it was shining forth long before we opened our eyes to it.'[18]

This ancient beauty is also new; 'so old and so *new*'. The beauty, which in meeting we discover has always preceded and anticipated us, yet comes, when it comes, like an 'avalanche of light'.[19] The shock of the new is at the same time the shock of recognition. Beauty is old when we find it has gone before us and already echoes in the depth of our being. We recognize it instantly. No one told the star jump girl Tathra beach was beautiful. She already knew it and danced toward it in joy. But beauty is also new. We can never quite anticipate it, and when it comes it always surprises us, breaks open our mind and heart, renews us.

> The thing that strikes me like a blow is a sense of strange familiarity and familiar strangeness. The wonderful form of the waves, rising, breaking, running to the beach is utterly familiar. I have watched it a thousand times. And yet there is a surprising newness about it all. The beauty of a well-formed wave rolling over into a dancing throng of white capped ripples seems as pristine as ever it was. I know it. But I don't know it. I need to be shown all over again. ... This strange familiarity is uncanny. It is a gift that keeps on giving. But all this talk seems petty. You have to be here ... and here again ... and again ... to know it. [G, 17/2/16]

The new 'strikes' like 'a blow', *because* it is old and 'utterly familiar'. We know it and have known it from the beginning. Yet we don't know it. Such newness is not the emergence of a novelty, something that, with repetition, gradually ceases to be new and loses its capacity to fascinate and feed. 'It is the radical newness, safe from all ageing, of eternity springing into time.'[20] Truly à Dieu.

---

[18] Chrétien, *The Ark of Speech*, p. 91.
[19] Chrétien, *The Ark of Speech*, p. 91.
[20] Chrétien, *The Ark of Speech*, p. 92.

Two realms?

All this is complex and tantalizing and difficult to describe. In the phenomenology of beauty there is a taking leave (adieu) and a going on (à Dieu), but does the one displace the other? Does goodbye mean good riddance? Augustine struggles with this tension. 'You were within and I was in the external world and I sought you there ... You were with me, and I was not with you.' It is as though he assumes the existence of two separate regions, the inside and the outside. Augustine searches in one, 'the external world', the outside. The place of beautiful things. The sun, the moon, the stars, the sea. He misses what he seeks. For God, it seems, is 'within', on the inside. Is to be with the one necessarily to be away from the other?

> I am having a struggle. I feel acutely the sense of a gap between spirit and matter that I have inherited. I want to be inside not outside; to think and feel the sea as I used to when we were here last. As I used to as a child. But I can't seem to get into it. I remember something Andrew Harvey said on the phone. I was struggling to find language to use. If I say 'God', it seems as if God is separated from creation. Harvey interrupted me: 'You already love all the Mother has made, so you love the Mother!' He said it better than that. But that's the gist. I am struggling with the split that I've often tried to name: my love for the natural world, on the one hand and, on the other, love of God. These two have been different parts of my being. I have responded passionately to both. But separately. I find it very distressing now when I feel it again. [J, 23/2/15][21]

Such a split is familiar enough, both from the religious and the secular sides. The one, the religious side, fearing to collapse the reality of God into the beauty of 'those lovely created things', is tempted to turn away from the world into a 'spiritual' realm within or above. Adieu means saying goodbye to all that. The other, the secular side, fearing the

---

[21] The citation from Andrew Harvey comes from a conversation of 'spiritual direction' he offered by telephone link-up. Harvey often refers to 'the Mother' where we might use the word 'God'. He does this to try to redress the patriarchal usurpation of language and imagery in reference to the transcendent that has plagued western theology (and not only western!) for centuries. The divine feminine needs to be retrieved.

6. Adoration

depreciation of the concrete beauty and call of the world, embraces it as a self-sufficient reality, complete in its own right. Adieu means saying goodbye to God.

Augustine does not always get the balance right. He is infamous for his suspicion of sexuality as somehow inherently sinful, a drive that is prone to alienate us from God, but even in this text he seems to adopt a 'two realms' view of experience. This side. That side. 'The lovely things kept me far from you.' He knows this is ultimately incoherent. For without 'you' 'they had no existence at all.' In trying to make and honour the distinction, it is hard, manifestly, not to fall into separation.

The problem is a 'search' for God, as for something we do not have and need to find, 'out there' somewhere, or 'in here' somewhere, will only carry us further away from our intended goal, which is to know and love the world we really live in. The truth of the matter is that we need to let ourselves *be found* by that which is already always there both within and without. 'You already love all the Mother has made, so you love the Mother.' God is not God without the world. The world is not the world without God. We cannot seek the one by turning our back on the other. In a striking image, Jelaluddin Rumi gives expression to such re-visioning of a two realms kinds of thinking.

> I have lived
> on the lip of
> insanity, wanting to
> know reasons, knocking
> on a door.
> It opens.
> I've been knocking from the inside![22]

'*You called...*'

Augustine concludes his meditation with words that vividly chart some of the fundamental dynamics of the experience of beauty/God.

---

[22] *The Illuminated Rumi*, trans. Coleman Barks, illuminations by Michael Green (New York: Broadway Books, 1997), pp. 36-37.

You called and cried out loud and shattered my deafness. You were radiant and resplendent, you put to flight my blindness. You were fragrant, and I drew in my breath and now pant after you. I tasted you, and I feel but hunger and thirst for you. You touched me, and I am set on fire to attain the peace which is yours.[23]

Augustine has been concerned with his own efforts to 'find' God in 'the lovely things' around him. It's been a game of cat and mouse to this point. He always seems to be in the wrong place. 'You were within and I was in the external world'. Or looking the wrong way. 'You were with me, and I was not with you.' This now suddenly changes. With shaking clarity, he learns he is not the one who does the looking. He is the one who is found out. God, not Augustine, creates the conditions which make possible God's manifestation in his human awareness. And it is hardly a polite knock at the door. More a break in. A rout. 'You shattered my deafness.' 'You put to flight my blindness.' God 'does not come to fulfill or satisfy a desire that is already ours', writes Chrétien, 'but he himself comes to rouse its flame within us.'[24] 'I am set on fire to attain the peace that is yours.'

And this is a *bodily* experience. There is no talk now of an inner and outer realm. The advent of God happens through the arousal of the five senses. Augustine uses metaphorical language to be sure. He is not literally deaf. He can hear the sound of the wind in the forest And his physical eyes can see well enough. He clearly perceives all 'those lovely things'. Later theology referred to the 'spiritual senses' as opposed to bodily, but Augustine makes no sharp distinction here. 'Beauty so old and so new' that comes upon him with such shattering force, is not a disembodied ideal existing in the mind alone, separated from the sun, the moon, the stars, the sea with which he physically communicates. God approaches and seizes him in and through real sounds that he hears, radiant sights that he sees, strong fragrances that he smells, sweet tastes that he swallows, and soft touches that sets him aflame.

It isn't a brilliant day. Misty grey skies hang over everything. Yet it is amazingly beautiful. The sight of the waves with their wonderful

---

[23] *Confessions*, X, 27, 201.
[24] Chrétien, *The Ark of Speech*, p. 93.

greens and whites is exhilarating. The surf is singing in a strangely human way. It moves me, like the voice of a friend. The air is heavy with sea fragrance, slightly salty, damp, a hint of shellfish. If I open my mouth I can taste the sea, like the flavour of oysters we had last night. A gentle wind embraces my entire body. The beauty of Tathra comes at me through all sensory channels. A surge of longing for the Earth rises in me. Not in the abstract. But now and here. This is a sacred place. Sacred long before I got here. [G, 3/3/16]

A child's star jump senses beauty well before she has words to give it limping linguistic expression. But any speaking of God that is not ultimately accountable before what is revealed in that jump is almost certainly blinkered. In his astonished sensory clash with divine beauty, Augustine does not so much speak *of* it as *to* it. And speaking to it, praises its transformative impacts. 'You were radiant and resplendent, you put to flight my blindness.' 'I tasted you, and I feel but hunger and thirst for you.' Beauty calls forth the speech of longing, the speech of adoration, the speech of prayer. This is the first and basic language of theology. It never loses sight of the fact that wherever we are, God is always in advance, which means 'late have I loved you.' Whatever is offered in this belated love can never be other than what beauty itself has 'set on fire' within. 'Beauty ... says adieu and commends to God because it arouses, as the only possible response to its manifestation, a prayer, a speech that itself says adieu and itself turns towards God.'[25]

Adoration: a non-theological reading

What if beauty does not say *adieu*, for the simple reason that there is no *Dieu* to say it to? God is dead. That has a double meaning. It means that the word God has lost relevance in contemporary life. It adds nothing to what we can meaningfully say about the world, and it means the word has no referent beyond itself. There is no God. What then of adoration as a way of living in the world at this time of widespread destruction of the natural order? Can real reverence for the world survive in a godless cosmos?

---

[25] Chrétien, *The Ark of Speech*, p. 93.

The history of western sensibility since the 17th century seems to be the story of an increasingly confident 'no' in answer to this question. The mechanistic worldview of Newtonian science conceived the world as composed of physical bodies operating in relation to each other according to universal laws of motion, inertia and force. Purpose, intentionality, feeling, consciousness, will all become the sole prerogative of human beings. God, if the idea of God survives at all, becomes a 'demiurge', a sort of master craftsman who sets creation in motion at the beginning, then leaves it to run according to Newtonian (or Einsteinian) law. Consequently, the world appears increasingly de-sacralised. Cut off from the source of holiness, its sanctity drains away. Along with this, and in lock-step with it, the myth of human mastery seems ever more convincing. To know the world is to learn to control the world. To control the world is to learn to turn it evermore obediently to our human advantage. The world as 'standing reserve' becomes a dominant feature of contemporary political, economic and metaphysical conviction.

The distinguished philosopher, Jean-Luc Nancy, challenges this view vigorously. In 2013, Nancy published a difficult but impressive work entitled simply *Adoration*.[26] That it intends a non-theological treatment of the subject of adoration is clearly indicated in the subtitle, *The Deconstruction of Christianity II*. The book is part of a major project to think through the implications of a genuinely post-Christian, indeed post-religious, society. 'In truth, I'd like to speak of it [Christianity] as little as possible', says Nancy. 'I'd like to move toward an effacement of this name and of the whole corpus of references that follow it ... [toward] an exit from religion and of the expansion of the atheist world.'[27] Not much ambiguity there!

The world 'comes about'

For Nancy the world is self-subsistent. The world does not derive from, nor does it need, some prior, more fundamental reality to ground its being or determine its meaning. '[O]ur world proceeds only from its own fortuitousness ... It takes place, it is there, it could not not be

---

[26] See footnote 4.
[27] Nancy, *Adoration*, p. 22.

6. Adoration

there or not be, it does not derive or stem from anything.'[28] There is no founding relation to an 'elsewhere', no 'back world', as Nietzsche called it, of which this world is a kind of envoy. The universe is built up of relations between its constituent elements. In fact, such relationships are its essential being as cosmos. No divine energy established the world, and no divine word speaks into the world. The 'world is a totality of echoes', says Nancy, 'but it does not echo [*renvoie*] anything else.'[29]

In answer to the question of the origins, Nancy is blunt and unapologetic. The world 'comes about'—from *nothing*.

> A distance comes about [*survient*], comes into play within homogeneous, undifferentiated nothingness. Whether it comes about "at a given moment" or "during all eternity" comes down to the same thing, and yet it *comes about*. It is the very fact of coming about. This gap opens the world.[30]

It is pointless to ask *how* this 'distance' comes about in nothingness, because its coming about *is* the 'gap' which 'opens the world'. The world *is* its coming about. From a theological perspective this looks a bit like a sheer assertion, accompanied by a blank refusal to address what seems to be an irresistible question: What do you mean by 'comes about'? This is an old argument. Important issues hang on its outcome, no doubt, but these are not our present concern. The world is here, for Nancy, without ultimate foundation. The urgent question is how we are to live in it at this critical juncture in history.

Nancy is as clear as Augustine, and as bold. We should live in this world with *adoration*. Adoration is what the world *requires* of us. Nancy is thoroughly alive to what Hart calls 'that sudden instant of existential surprise', the sheer gratuity, or gift, of the world as it meets and gives itself to our awareness. 'The gift of this: *that there are some things, things, all beings [étants]*'. He wants us to be clear that he is not flirting with the old metaphysical question, 'why is there something rather than nothing?' since, as he puts it, 'precisely *nothing* is what there is'.[31] The

---

[28] Nancy, *Adoration*, pp. 10-11.
[29] Nancy, *Adoration*, p. 12.
[30] Nancy, *Adoration*, p. 14. Italics in the original.
[31] Nancy, *Adoration*, p. 14. Italics added.

basic *thereness* of the beings that constitute the world, including our own 'being there', is a fundamental datum of consciousness. To be aware of anything at all implicitly includes the awareness of this primal gift.

The form of the spirit

It *is* primal. At the head of his book, Nancy quotes Ludwig Wittgenstein.

'The form of the spirit as it awakes is adoration.'[32] This could refer as well to history as a whole as to individual biography. In the beginnings of western thought, the awakening of the spirit, understood as the coming to awareness of our being in the world, is identified by both Plato and Aristotle as *thaumazein*. *Thaumazein* is often translated 'to be astonished'. Since the English word astonishment can be neutral as to what evokes it—one can after all be astonished at evil and horror—it is perhaps better, Nancy argues, to render it as 'to wonder' or 'to marvel'. *Thaumazein* is 'to gaze in wonder at'.[33] As we have had cause to note, the emergence of the spirit in the child, the star jump, for example, is an expression of the same elemental response to 'some things, things, all beings'. Wonder may not yet be full adoration. Adoration calls for a response of gratitude and praise. But it is certain there can be no adoration without wonder.

Nancy is also fully aware that we *forget* what we once knew in the awakening of the spirit. The child is delighted, but the adult ponderously wonders at her wonder. 'We know all this,' says Nancy. 'We know it, and we forget it.'[34] The task is to retrieve it; to recover the call of the world and to respond appropriately. 'The gift of the world calls for adoration. It invites us to adoration, commits us to it, arouses it.' This invitation, commitment and arousal are not something added onto the approach the world makes to us. They are integral to it. 'The gift opens the possibility, if not the necessity, of adoration.' Nancy underlines (again!) that this gift is a 'gift without a giver'. The gift 'is simply equal to the event of

---

[32] Nancy, *Adoration*, p. 1.
[33] See Chrétien, *The Ark of Speech*, p. 116. Details of the references to Plato and Aristotle can be found on p. 160, note 9.
[34] Nancy, *Adoration*, p. 2.

the world'. This event 'already itself constitutes a gesture of adoration'.[35] This is a remarkable statement. The world, gift though it is without a giver, *already in itself* constitutes a gesture of adoration. This is strongly reminiscent of Augustine's 'late have I loved you'. In calling us to wonder and adoration, the world calls us to enter what already constitutes its true nature as world, prior to our participation in it.

To what is this adoration directed? The answer is to the world itself, understood as an infinite web of living relationships, self-organizing and self-sustaining.

> The world = all the beings [*étants*] that are near or neighbouring one another, that thereby relate to one another, and to nothing else. In this way establishing relations between one another, and to nothing else. "God" was a name for the relation among all beings—therefore, for the *world* in the strongest sense.[36]

If there is any remnant sense of Christianity, it is exactly this. The Word became 'flesh' and 'dwelt amongst us' (Jn. 1.14). That is to say 'God' becomes this *among*. 'He is the *with* or the *between* of us, this *with* or *between* that we are insofar as *we* are in the proximity that defines the world.'[37] This perspective on the fundamental inter-connectedness of all aspects and entities that make up and constitute the world brings us remarkably close to our earlier discussion of beauty.

> The long slow process of the formation and evolution of life, beginning with the tiniest of single cell creatures and leading to the brilliant abundance of a million different life forms, arises in and continues to depend on the fecundity of the seas, which in turn depends on all the other great interlocking natural cycles. All this, and everything else that belongs to the web of being that makes up the planet Earth, is implicate in the spectacle that the sea presents to our senses. ... Thus when we perceive this balance as beautiful ... '*we perceive the harmony without which we cannot live.*'[38]

---

[35] Nancy, *Adoration*, p. 14.
[36] Nancy, *Adoration*, p. 30.
[37] Nancy, *Adoration*, p. 30.
[38] See chapter 2 above, pp. 52-53.

The difference is that, for Nancy, this world of mutually sustaining relationships rests on nothing. And, he insists, 'that *the empty place must not be occupied.*'[39]

'Salut!'

What does adoration in and of this 'between' amount to? For Nancy it can be described basically as an *address*. *Adoratio* is a word spoken (*oratio*), a solemn word, addressed to (*ad*) another. It is no ordinary word. The word adoration, he says, is 'maintained by the entire speaking body.' Adoration demands the unconditional response of our whole being. It is an 'elevated language' that calls, honours, and attends to its addressee. Provocatively using religious language in his thoroughly non-religious context, Nancy describes this elevated language as 'a prayer, invocation, address, appeal, plea, imploring, celebration, dedication, salutation ... and not one or another of these registers, but a composition formed from them all.' Following Derrida, he describes its simplest and most basic form as a greeting, '*salut!*', but (naturally!) a salutation without salvation:

> When Derrida writes, or rather cries out, with all his might, "*salut!*—a salutation without salvation," he indicates the following: that the word addressed, the address that barely contains anything beyond itself, bears the recognition and affirmation of the existence of the other.[40]

Unlike Augustine's cry 'late have I loved *you*', this cry, '*salut!*', is not taken into a higher register (God), but is directed precisely to the being-there of the countless 'in-betweens', close and far, small and large. It is a 'recognition and affirmation' of their sheer existence alongside us, and of their sufficient right to adoration, with no need 'to exit from the world.'

This '*salut!*' is not the prerogative of humans alone. All beings participate. 'Do not the morning sun, the plant pushing out of the soil, address a "salut" to us? Or the gaze of an animal?'[41] A 'salut' that is an exchange of greeting; a recognition of dignity; a reciprocity of belonging; a caring for the other. This is Augustine alive and enamoured amid 'the

---

[39] Nancy, *Adoration*, p. 33. Italics in text.
[40] Nancy, *Adoration*, p. 18.
[41] Nancy, *Adoration*, p. 18.

6. Adoration

lovely things' of the world, only without God. Beauty says 'hello', not 'adieu'.

Nancy also has a keen sense of the 'excess' that beauty has over particular beautiful things. He knows well Kant's 'sinking feeling' when one's senses are assaulted, 'shattered', 'put to flight' by the lovely things of the world. It is hard in this context to avoid the word God, but Nancy is a skilled demythologiser.

> "God" could be understood as "what joy!" or "what grandeur!"—a salutation to the incommensurable not designating any sort of being, designation only itself as salutation ... a nomination of the unnameable or of what is nameable par excellence—through excess, through the profusion hidden within each name.'[42]

This sense of excess, 'the profusion hidden in each name', something exceeding all measure and scope, induces a joy that is 'unnameable', beyond speech (even the speech of King David at prayer, perhaps?). At the same time, it brings that sense of humility of which Kant spoke, 'in which the human being is as it were nothing in his own eyes'.

'To bow down'

In a truly remarkable passage toward the end of the book, Nancy recognizes adoration as a response to that which 'infinitely surpasses' us. Adoration, as he understands it, and as a philosopher practices it, is not just an acknowledgement of the dignity and worth of those numberless beings that stand in mutually sustaining relations with us. It is that, too, but more. Adoration is 'a gesture recognizing a passage that infinitely surpasses, passes beyond.' For an author who has made so much of rejecting any 'elsewhere' or 'back world', this language comes as something of a surprise. The consequences Nancy draws from it are even more surprising. 'What is at stake here,' he writes, 'is ... the fact that it obliges me to bow down. In bowing down, I open the finite to the infinite.'[43]

Nancy goes so far as to use the word 'prostration', fully aware that this skirts, and perhaps even crosses the border of what is unmistakably

---
[42] Nancy, *Adoration*, p. 77.
[43] Nancy, *Adoration*, p. 79.

religious territory. For, he acknowledges, 'religion—let us say, the religious, observant disposition—is finally alone in opening the possibility of prostration.' Despite this paradoxical admission, Nancy argues that the logic of adoration, the adoration which this world, built as it is on nothing, 'calls' and 'commits' us to, is a logic that leads to prostration, a bowing low in the presence of the other.

That this creates ambivalence in the philosopher, at least in a philosopher of Nancy's metaphysical persuasion, is understandable. 'The philosopher, he who understands in conceptual terms the truth that only religion represents, knows how to do everything except prostrate himself.' This is so because the condition of his thinking is that there is no God, no Lord, before whom to bow. 'Yet,' he insists, 'the philosopher must prostrate himself.' Why? Because '*as a philosopher*, he must know that reason prostrates itself before what in itself surpasses it infinitely.' Only 'a reason that adores is fully rational and reasonable.'[44] What is it in reason that surpasses reason infinitely? Nancy takes his cue from Kant. 'Two things awe me most, the starry sky above me and the moral law within me.' Just such Kantian awe, which arises in us in the presence of wondrous worldly things, without and within, names 'the infinite opening of reason' for Nancy.[45] The non-religious and the religious readings of adoration seem tantalizingly close at this point. It is hard to think that such language doesn't have a hint of Plato, or even Augustine, about it!

The honesty with which Jean-Luc Nancy, avowed atheist, follows to this conclusion the logic of adoration as a fundamental response to the call of the world, is impressive and unsettling. It is impressive. Does Nancy really mean to lay himself flat to the ground in the presence of the ocean, or the forest, or the stars as a 'recognition' and 'acknowledgment' of the surpassing value and dignity of these 'neighbours'? Probably not. More likely he intends an inward prostration, the adoption of a humble, attentive, reciprocal attitude toward fellow beings who share the glory and fragility of being-in-the-world-together in the sheer gift of the universe. This could be a reflection of our hesitation rather than

---

[44] Nancy, *Adoration*, p. 79. Italics in the original.
[45] Nancy, *Adoration*, pp. 79-80.

6. Adoration

Nancy's! In any case, in a world dominated by the drive for maximal human possession and control, this is a strikingly counter-cultural stance. A wake up call, whether a body is flat on the ground or not.

It is unsettling. At least from our perspective. The non-religious interpreter, without a shred of sentimentality or compromise, lays out the implications of adoration. Bluntly, it means being 'put in our place'. That phrase has come up time and again in our journals. Yet with all our religious entanglements, we lacked the wit and the courage to speak of 'prostration'. Yes, we agree; we must be in solidarity with 'the others', our neighbours, in this world. Not above, with. But flat on our faces with? Does respect for the world mean reverence in this extreme?

> I have a renewed appreciation for approaching sea see/hearing in a respectful way. It comes from reading Prechtel's piece on the ocean. My walk in is more than usually careful. I am in the presence of greatness. Tread gently. Moses by the burning bush took off his sandals. Holy ground, the voice said. But the sand here is too soft, so I keep mine on! ... The sea is fairly calm. The wind is blowing from the north-east. The sound presses on me the vibration *om*. I join in, feeling a part of the great chorus around me. ... Then from nowhere, a phrase from one of Leonard Cohen's songs leaps at me: 'Forget your perfect offering!' It stings like a rebuke. I was pretty pleased with my offering. And I am told: 'Get back in your box.' What to do? Prechtel suggests kneeling in the presence of the sea, as before true majesty. We have talked about this from time to time. But I have always felt way too self-conscious to try it. With my composure in tatters, and Prechtel prodding me, I look up and down the beach. No one nearby. Gingerly, I get down on my knees. I feel foolish—really silly—down here. Very glad no one can see me. This is out of line. In church, maybe. But you don't do this on the beach! It suddenly occurs to me that on my knees I am placed where a child is. Down here I have the child's perspective. The sea is much closer, and the sand. I feel its grit pressing into my skin. ... I remember the star jump. And the words: 'Unless you become as little children, you cannot enter the kingdom of heaven.' [G, 22/2/16][46]

---

[46] See Martín Prechtel, *The Smell of Rain on Dust: Grief and Praise* (Berkeley, California: North Atlantic Books, 2015), pp. 47-59. Prechtel is adamant, if we are to offer this kind of respect to the more-than-human-world, it is vital to find a place without people (p. 57).

In place of a conclusion

We began this pilgrimage in Tathra sitting on the beach looking out to sea. Now it ends in Tathra kneeling on the beach looking out to sea. Geographically we have gone nowhere. Yet the journey that took us from sitting to kneeling has been a long one, and often arduous. Tathra is still beautiful, yet everything is different. The words are so well known as to be a common place. But they say what is to be said.

> We shall not cease from exploration
> And the end of all our exploring
> Will be to arrive where we started
> And know the place for the first time.

After all the 'exploration' we called sea see/hearing, we are starting to know this place for the first time. This means starting for the first time to have an understanding of what our initial motivations involve.

Our hearts have been opened to beauty, the beauty of the ocean, and beyond that, the beauty of the natural world all around us. A beauty that at times takes the breath away. We have been confronted with time. Deep evolutionary, Earth time. The time in which the astonishing inter-connection of all things great and small, that 'harmony without which we cannot live', has been knit together to make and maintain the oceans, indeed the entire planet, as we know it today. We have tried to pay attention, to look and to listen with, if not unbiased care, at least with a care that is as open as we can make it. Tried to listen not just to other human beings and their voices, important though they are, but to the voices of the more-than-human world, and in this case, especially, to the voice of the 'veritable ocean' (Stevens). Sadness and grief, anger and guilt have been our companions on the way. The seaweed woman, draped in rubbish and deathly pale, rose from the waves as we watched and joined us. Profound and brutal changes we discover are taking place, changes that are deadly for the life of the ocean we say we love. And we are complicit in them. All this is what it means 'to know the place for the first time.'

6. Adoration

Something else remains. Beyond those famous lines, T. S. Eliot continues with words that are less well known.

> Through the unknown, remembered gate
> When the last of earth left to discover
> Is that which was the beginning;
> At the source of the longest river
> The voice of the hidden waterfall
> And the children in the apple-tree
> Not known, because not looked for
> But heard, half-heard, in the stillness
> Between two waves of the sea.[47]

'Between two waves of the sea', as it were, sitting for us became kneeling and love became adoration. What was 'not known, because not looked for' slowly took shape in our minds. Things 'half-heard in the stillness' little by little became audible. An 'unknown gate' was 'remembered' and the 'last of the earth left to discover' revealed itself as 'that which was the beginning.' Not the beginning which is the start of our pilgrimage. Not even the beginning which is the start of the oceans. The ultimate beginning; that which lies at the origin of all things. Sea see/hearing is a pilgrimage that finally takes us to 'the hidden waterfall' that rises at the 'source of the longest river'; to that mystery which 'the children in the apple-tree' (and in the star jump) know and we have forgotten. Chrétien speaks of God. Nancy of a self-relating world. Chrétien of praise. Nancy of prostration. Both of adoration.

Is this a journey worth taking? In a time like this, what use are adoration and praise, prostration and kneeling? Will they impact on our economic bottom line? Can they contribute anything helpful to the violent politics of global terror? What of justice and the ever growing gap between rich and poor in the world? What of violence against children? These brutalities fill the news and we go sea see/hearing? Talk of adoration? What's the point?

---

[47] T. S. Eliot, *Four Quartets* (London: Faber and Faber, 1986 [1944]), "Little Gidding," section V, p. 48.

There is no point. Not in that sense. Sea see/hearing is not a policy. Not an action plan. Not a business strategy. It is a way of seeing and hearing the world. Adoration is the cultivation of a disposition; the nurture of a way of being in the world. Adoration is about loving the world before using the world. Uncle Max understands what that means. So does the star jump child. The beach lovers of Tathra intuit it somewhere deep down as well. Our culture at large seems to have forgotten, or deliberately obliterated it. The state of the oceans is a brutal reminder. If the oceans die, or turn against us, the outcome will be terrible. No blue, no green. Something needs to change. First of all, our hearts.

Chrétien sees adoration in theological terms. It means to look upon the world as God's loved creation; to see the world as it were with the eyes of the Creator and to praise it as that.

> To see that this [world] is good can surely be nothing other than to praise what one sees by gazing at it. The fact that this praise is inseparable from a safeguarding, a benevolence, a blessing of the time in which what we see is transformed and develops, teaches us exactly how urgently we are required to praise. What would a praise be if it did not watch over what it praises, which would not keep vigil over it? All human praise of the world as God's work is inscribed and accomplished in this first gaze, this gaze that follows the behest of the Spirit, which does not show itself but shows other things. To evade praising the world, however imperfect our praise might be, would mean leaving, as it were, the divine gaze without reply and without a future, leaving God as the only one in the world who sees things, as if no mind could see in its turn what he himself sees and shows. God's gaze is always a word: it calls for a response, a sharing, even if the nature of this latter still remains to be defined.[48]

Jean-Luc Nancy rejects the theology point blank. Yet his sense of being in the world is astonishingly congruent. Chrétien's theological hymn of praise might be translated into the naturalist's song of adoration as follows.

---

[48] Chrétien, *The Ark of Speech*, p. 116.

To grasp the fact that the world is a vibrant network of relationships without which we cannot live demands that we respond to it with a heartfelt *'salut!'*; a *'salut!'* uttered with our whole being, which is an expression of true adoration. The fact that this *'salut'* is inevitably linked to a protective responsibility, an attentive care, a deliberate nurturing of the intricate and unending inter-dependencies of all things that constitute the world, reminds us how urgently we are required to render it. What would adoration be if it did not watch over what it adores, if it did not defend against harm what it salutes? Adoration of the world is initiated and made possible by the fact that the event of world itself is already a gesture of adoration. To evade giving a loving echo to this gesture, however inadequate it may be, would mean failing to respond to the gift inherent in the world's gracious action in bringing us to being in the first place. The splendour of this world, our world, is always a summons: it calls for a response of love, even if the nature of this response still remains to be defined.

Theological praise is inseparable from safeguarding, watching over, keeping vigil. Secular adoration means protective responsibility, attentive care, defending. Both positions echo ancient Indigenous wisdom. Much remains to be defined. Much has already been lost. This is sure. Religious or not, we seek to save what we love.

Where there is no love, there is no salvation.

Concluding unapologetic postscript - A way with the ocean

She sang beyond the genius of the sea.
                                                Wallace Stevens

It is abundantly clear that our pilgrimage has been undertaken in community, not in isolation; primarily in community with the great other of the ocean and all her creatures, along with the sky, the wind, the sun and the rain. Also with an array of human companions, some contemporaries (Uncle Max, Jean-Louis Chrétien, Andrew Harvey, Sylvia Earle, among them) and some ancestors (Plato, Augustine, Kant, Hume, and so on). Early in the journey (as noted in chapter 1) we stumbled into the company of another companion, previously unknown to us, the 20th century American poet, Wallace Stevens. Flushed with enthusiasm, we had purchased on impulse a fat volume entitled, *The Penguin Book of the Ocean*, which consisted of 46 selected readings taken from a wide range of sources beginning with the book of Genesis and winding up with David Malouf's *Fly Away Peter*.[1] When we got to selection 7, we ran full tilt and unsuspecting into Stevens. There on the page was a poem in 7 solid stanzas with the title, 'The Idea of Order at Key West'. Sitting on the deck overlooking Tathra beach, a glass of red in hand and with no idea of what to expect, we plunged into reading the words aloud. At the end we shook our heads. The poem was about the sea, clear; but *what* about the sea? The words came at us like a force of nature. Chiselled, powerful, incomprehensible, and yet strangely alluring. We hadn't a clue, but we were hooked.

Try it.

> *The Idea of Order at Key West*
>
> She sang beyond the genius of the sea.
> The water never formed to mind or voice,
> Like a body, wholly body, fluttering

---

[1] James Bradley (ed) *The Penguin Book of the Ocean* (Camberwell, Victoria: Hamish Hamilton, Penguin, 2010).

On the Edge: A-Way with the Ocean

Its empty sleeves; and yet its mimic motion
Made constant cry, caused constantly a cry,
That was not ours although we understood,
Inhuman, of the veritable ocean.

The sea was not a mask. No more was she.
The song and water were not medleyed sound
Even if what she sang was what she heard,
Since what she sang was uttered word by word.
It may be that in all her phrases stirred
The grinding water and the gasping wind;
But it was she and not the sea we heard.

For she was the maker of the song she sang.
The ever-hooded, tragic-gestured sea
Was merely a place by which she walked to sing.
Whose spirit is this? we said, because we knew
It was the spirit that we sought and knew
That we should ask this often as she sang.

If it was only the dark voice of the sea
That rose, or even coloured by many waves;
If it was only the outer voice of sky
And cloud, of the sunken coral water-walled,
However clear, it would have been deep air,
The heaving speech of air, a summer sound
Repeated in a summer without end
And sound alone. But it was more than that,
More even than her voice, and ours, among
The meaningless plungings of water and the wind,

Theatrical distances, bronze shadows heaped
On high horizons, mountainous atmospheres
Of sky and sea.
          It was her voice that made
The sky actutest at its vanishing.
She measured to the hour its solitude.
She was the single artificer of the world
In which she sang. And when she sang, the sea,
Whatever self it had, became the self
That was her song, for she was the maker. Then we,
As we beheld her striding there alone,
Knew that there never was a world for her
Except the one she sang and, singing, made.

Ramon Fernandez, tell me, if you know,
Why, when the singing ended and we turned
Toward the town, tell why the glassy lights,
The lights in the fishing boats at anchor there,
As the night descended, tilting in the air,
Mastered the night and portioned out the sea,
Fixing emblazoned zones and fiery poles,
Arranging, deepening, enchanting night.

Oh! Blessed rage for order, pale Ramon,
The maker's rage to order words of the sea,
Words of the fragrant portals, dimly-starred,
And of ourselves and of our origins,
In ghostlier demarcations, keener sounds.[2]

Wallace Stevens, 1879-1955

---

[2] Wallace Stevens, *The Collected Poems of Wallace Stevens* (New York: Vintage Books, 1982), pp. 128-130; reproduced in Bradley, *The Penguin Book of the Ocean*, pp. 43-45.

Something tugged at our sleeves. The poem talks of the sea and its interaction with humans. It seemed to know all about the 'visible voice'. Stevens speaks directly of the 'voice of the sea'; and is aware that it is no easy voice to interpret. It is a '*dark* voice of the sea that rose'. The tension between the human and the other-than-human, the town and the sea, is also strongly present. '[T]he glassy lights' of Stevens' town '*mastered* the night and *portioned* out the sea' (italics ours). Town tames, or tries to tame, ocean. So for all his being beyond us, Stevens was shaping up as, if not an ally, then perhaps a critical guide, in the journey we were setting out upon. We read and re-read his words until we had them by heart. Across the months, the poem informed our way of attending the sea, and sea see/hearing shaped the way we read the poem.

Stevens was born in Reading, Pennsylvania in 1879 and died in Hartford, Connecticut in 1955. For most of his life he worked as an insurance executive for the Hartford Accident and Indemnity Company, writing poetry in his spare time. His mother was a devout member of the Dutch Reformed tradition, but Stevens rejected the faith, agreeing with Nietzsche that ours is a time of the death of gods. He wrote this poem in 1934, the year he became Vice President of the Insurance Company, and well before the ecological crisis hit home to the public mind. Yet his work has a prophetic dimension that seems to speak to our situation some 80 years on. We came to the poem with minds full of Plato, Augustine and Chrétien, a faith-shaped hermeneutic of which Stevens might well disapprove. So be it. Great art transcends the limits of its origins and the intentions of its maker.

A way in

(i) *The title*. The poem is about order and lack of order in the world. The setting is Key West, an island city on the southernmost tip of the Florida Keys, surrounded by sea; the Gulf of Mexico on one side, the Atlantic Ocean on the other. Key West is a place where town meets ocean. Stevens used to holiday there.

(ii) *Agents*. The most significant figure in the poem is called simply 'she'. 'She' is the first word of the poem and 'she' dominates from that point on. Then there is 'the spirit', which makes a brief appearance in stanza 3, but seems somehow to hover over the whole. 'We' includes the poet and perhaps a friend alongside him by the shore. It also invites *us*, the readers, to identify ourselves with the poet in the drama. 'Me' appears once in stanza 6 and refers (presumably) to the poet. 'The sea' is a primary character throughout. Along with the wind, the clouds, the sky, the sea has a distinctive (yes, dark) voice to be attended to. Lastly there is one called 'Ramon Fernandez'. He bursts on the scene in stanza 6 (and emerges again in 7). No introduction. No biography, but given a name, as no other participant is.

(iii) *Place*. The main action of the poem takes place on the sea shore. The poet, his friends, and us (if we so imagine ourselves) are by the sea, surrounded by the great sweep of sky, air, cloud and sand. We see, hear, feel, taste and touch these 'theatrical distances' with their 'bronze shadows heaped on high horizons'.

(iv) *Structure*. The poem is constructed in three main sections. The first (stanzas 1-5) is the longest and most complex. It deals with the human/sea encounter. The second (stanza 6) brings a dramatic shift. We turn from the sea to the town. Finally, stanza 7 returns to the mysterious 'she' of part one as, through the poet, she makes a final address, first to the sea and then to us.

Stanza 1 – listening to the sea

Obviously *she* is central. Opinions vary as to her identity. Some believe Stevens intends the poet's *muse* or inspiration; the 'spirit of poetry' we might say, the mysterious origin of the creative word that fires the poet's imagination. Others are more down to earth. She is simply an anonymous busker plying her trade near to where Stevens and his friends are standing. Her song interrupts and shapes his seaside reverie. Both suggestions can make sense of the poem, but for us, coming from our starting point, it is hard to escape the sense that she is rather more than these. There is a brooding sense of deep presence in the poem. She is shaper of worlds, architect of time, and a maker of meanings. Like the creator Spirit, the great feminine *ruach*, that moved on the face of the waters in the creation story of Genesis 1, she hovers over this water world in all its splendour and mystery. If that seems way too theological, perhaps think of she as Jean-Luc Nancy's 'name for the relation among all beings', or von Weizsäcker's 'harmony without which we cannot live', or even of Aphrodite rising from the sea! We will use 'Spirit' as shorthand for this presence, however understood.

'She sang beyond the genius of the sea'. The first line states what the poem is about. She and the sea. It concerns her *voice*, what the Spirit is saying, or rather, singing. She sings by the sea. And she sings 'beyond the genius of the sea'. The idea that places—rivers, rocks, trees, mountains—were inhabited and protected by a local spirit, or 'genius', much like a guardian angel, was widespread in medieval times. Places had a spiritual quality that gave them dignity, depth, meaning. Our modern Cartesian view of matter as essentially lifeless, so much stuff to be analysed and used for human purposes (Scott Morrison and his lump of coal), has undercut much of that early sensitivity. Stevens reminds us of it with the word 'genius'. The song he wants to hear by the sea is not that of a local spirit or angel. It is 'beyond' that.

The word 'beyond' is a crucial signal, a literary move, which Stevens employs time and again in the poem. He wants us to see more than what at first meets the eye on the beach; to hear more than what first attracts the ear. But, and this is important, he does not think we can meet, or become aware of this 'beyond' directly or immediately. We only have access to the song from 'beyond' by attending to what is there in front of us; by attending to the sea. The sea *at first sight* (at least to western eyes) is water, a great pile of it, and water doesn't speak. 'The water never formed to mind or voice,/ Like a body, wholly body,' meaning *only* body, body without *spirit*, Descartes' *res extensa*, 'fluttering its empty sleeves'. The image that springs to mind is one of those blow-up figures at service stations that flutters its arms as if it were a person beckoning us to come in, but really it is no more than heaving air. We often see the ocean just so, empty, meaningless motion. Then, another of Stevens' 'there is more to it' signals: 'And yet …'; it might *seem* like meaningless motion, 'and yet' there is more to it. 'And yet its mimic motion …', that endless repetition of waves rolling toward the shore—*speaks*. It '[m]ade constant cry, caused constantly a cry'. The sound of the sea that we know so well is a *cry*. Stevens chooses his words carefully. To cry is to weep or lament. To cry is to call out to attract attention urgently. To cry is to express pain or suffering. For those coming from a biblical tradition, the word 'cry' has strong resonances. The enslaved Israelites in Egypt cry out to God for deliverance. Job in his affliction laments to God, 'Even when I cry out "violence", I am not answered; I call aloud, but there is no justice'. (Job 19.7). John the Baptist is described as 'a voice crying in the wilderness'. (Matt 3.3).

The sea 'caused constantly a cry'. In our times, the sea is staggering under the assault we are making on it. There is a cry, if we can hear it; a cry of abuse, suffering, death; a cry for help. And the sea's cry, says the poet, is the *sea's* cry, not ours; 'caused constantly a cry,/ That was *not* ours although we understood,/ Inhuman, of the veritable ocean.' The sea does not belong to us. It is itself. It is 'inhuman', not in the sense of being cruel, but in the sense of being 'other-than-human', a being in its own right, with its own integrity. This cry belongs to the 'veritable ocean'; the ocean in itself and for itself; not the ocean as our possession.

Stanza 2 – the sea and 'she' inseparable

Having strongly asserted that the ocean has its own integrity, Stevens now reveals how this 'veritable ocean' and 'she', the Spirit singer, are related. This is complex and takes the next three stanzas to work through. Stanza 2 says essentially that the voice of the sea and the voice of the Spirit are *inseparable*. For anyone familiar with sacramental thinking, this is recognisable territory. The sacramental imagination requires a receptivity of mind and heart which appropriates the presence of Christ in and through the material elements of bread and wine in the Eucharist, or the water in Baptism. Stevens is working here with something like that imagination.

'The sea was not a mask.' That is crucial. Stevens is not pretending that the sea is a disguise for something else, a temporary stand-in for God or the Spirit or what have you. It is the sea. That's stanza 1. But ... 'No more was *she*.' The singing Spirit is not a disguise either. The Spirit is the Spirit. The sea and the Spirit each have their own voice. But here the sacramental-like imagination kicks in, 'The song and water were not medleyed sound.' A medley of songs is a string of stand-alone songs tacked together one after another. That is *not* what is going on here. We don't have the song of the Spirit *here* and the cry of the ocean *there*, the two voices separate from each other and simply lumped together arbitrarily.

What then? Well, here's another of Stevens' signals of 'something more'. '*Even if* what she sang was what she heard,/ Since what she sang was uttered word by word.' What did she hear? What if not the cry of the ocean set out in verse 1? *Even if* that is so, Stevens goes on to repeat the point so as to underline it for us. 'It may be that in all her phrases [all her song, that is] stirred/ The grinding water and the gasping wind'. In short, when we stand by the sea and attend to its presence, the first thing we see and hear is the sea itself, water grinding, wind gasping. We need to attend to and respect it as such. Although all that is true, if that is *all* we see and *all* we hear, we are missing something of deep significance about the world. 'But it was *she* and *not* the sea we heard.' The song of the Spirit sounds in and through the sound of the sea. Their voices are distinct, but they cannot be separated. They are not 'medleyed sound'. Yet neither can they be collapsed into each other. They are not masks, but real voices. Like the two natures of Christ, divine and human, the voice of the Spirit and the cry of the sea are joined without separation but also without confusion. This brings us to stanzas 3 and 4.

Stanzas 3 and 4 – 'she' and the sea distinct

In stanza 2 the *inseparability* of the Spirit and the ocean is highlighted. In stanzas 3 and 4 the *distinction* between them is drawn.

'For she was the maker of the song she sang.' Not the sea, *she* was the maker of the song. The word *maker* is central to the poem. Stevens uses it five times in all and each time in reference to the singer. For those with even a passing acquaintance with the Christian tradition, this inevitably recalls the words of the creed. 'I believe in God the Father Almighty *maker* of heaven and earth.'[3] The singer is the maker of the song she sings. And the song is really distinct from, really other than, the cry of the sea. 'The ever-hooded, tragic-gestured sea [extraordinary

---

[3] The Creed was formulated in an historical period in which a mythology of 'She' as Maker had been almost completely obliterated.

phrases!]/ Was merely the place by which she walked to sing.' In the previous verse, the sounds of the sea, the grinding water and gasping wind, are all caught up with her song. But here the distinction between them stretches almost to breaking point. The sea seems now just the backdrop, the stage, upon which the singer produces her glorious music. The image seems to echo again the story of Genesis, where the Lord God walks in the garden of creation at the very origins of the world. 'They (Adam and Eve) heard the sound of the Lord God walking in the garden at the time of the evening breeze ...', says the text. The Spirit present in the breath of the wind. 'And the man and wife hid themselves from the presence of the Lord ...' (Gen. 3.8). They knew they had transgressed. This has been our experience attending the ocean, too. Standing by the sea, aware of the damage that we humans are causing to its life, the voice asks 'where are you?' and 'what have you done?'

Then the central question of the first section of the poem. 'Whose spirit is this? we said, because we knew/ It was the spirit that we sought and knew/ That we should ask this often as she sang.' This is an important question in any form of meditative attention. The search for the Spirit is not necessarily easy or self-evident. In our efforts at sea see/hearing, all kinds of thoughts, feelings, ideas, impulses flooded through us. How do we know if the voice that is moving in us is authentic, and not some 'genius of the sea', or, more likely, some self-interested prompting of our own too, too human spirit? Remember Kierkegaard's 'poet of nature', out there amid the lilies and the birds, but all the while 'devising great plans to transform the world'.[4] We can be mistaken.

Stevens wants us to understand at least this much; that the Spirit's song, the song sung as she walks beside the sea, is really the *Spirit's* song and not just the sounds of nature. Here comes another one of those 'there is more' sentences. 'If it was *only* [but, of course, it is not *only*] the dark voice of the sea/ That rose, or even coloured by many waves;/ If it was *only* the outer voice of sky/ And cloud, of the sunken coral water-walled,/ However clear, it would have been deep air,/ The heaving speech of air [remember the fluttering of empty sleeves] a summer sound/ Repeated in a summer without end/ And sound alone.' It is possible,

---

4 See chapter 4, pp. 121-123

indeed we do it all the time, to walk, play, swim, sleep on the beach, to see its varied colours and hear its manifold sounds, but to see and hear *only* that. 'A summer sound'. Aussies know that sound; the sound of warm and lazy days, of lolling on the sand with a book and the brolly. It is wonderful, but if that is all it is, says Stevens, 'it is sound alone'. It mediates no further depth.

'But it was more than that,/ More even than her voice, and ours, among/ The meaningless plungings of water and the wind,/ Theatrical distances, bronze shadows heaped/ On high horizons, mountainous atmospheres/ Of sky and sea'. What we are seeking in our journey by the sea is more than an appreciation, however deep, of the beauty that surrounds us; the water and the wind, the spectacle of huge distances and changing colours, those 'mountainous atmospheres' of sky and the water. It is more even than a personal encounter between my spirit and Aphrodite: 'More even than her voice and ours'. Sea see/hearing is not just appreciation of nature's grandeur. It is also not just private devotion to 'beauty so old and so new' (Augustine) or 'the relation among all beings' (Nancy), that happens to take place by the sea. It is something more than either. Which brings us to stanza 5.

Stanza 5 – the sacramental imagination

This is the climax of section I. Having examined the sea and the Spirit for their separate and distinct integrities, Stevens now fuses them together in a form of sacramental, or at least conceptual, inseparability. 'It was her voice that made/ The sky acutest at its vanishing.' The song the Spirit sings does not just celebrate the sky, it *makes* the sky, and makes it acutest, sharpest, at its vanishing point. On the beach you look out to the horizon, that amazing blue line between water and air, and then your eye is drawn on and on until it can reach no further, and the sky disappears into the infinity of space, filled, as we know, with billions of stars and millions of planets. The song of the Spirit *makes* all this vastness, the glory of the universe beyond understanding.

It is not just space that the Spirit sings. It is also *time*. 'She measured to the *hour* its solitude.' A magnificent line! When we stand on the shore and gaze at the great ocean before us and listen to the sounds of its endless breakers, we are seeing a sight and hearing a sound that has been in play on Earth for 4 billion years. It embodies the whole astonishing process of evolution, unfolding its creative energies across huge tracts of time. All this the Spirit measures, 'to the hour'. Space and time the Spirit sings into being; sings into the astonishing order we see all around us. The world is the solid music of the Maker, or the Goddess, or the Evolutionary Process. However we see it, 'She was the single artificer of the world/ In which she sang.'

Now the climax. The song that calls forth the world becomes *accessible* to us in relation to the sea before which we stand. *Here*, not in the depths of the vanishing sky. *Now*, not in the far reaches of evolutionary time. Here and now a sort of miracle occurs. 'And when she sang, the sea,/ Whatever self it had, became the self/ That was her song, for she was the maker.' In sacramental terms, this is the parallel to the moment of consecration in the Eucharist. 'This is my body.' 'This is my blood.' However we understand those mysterious words, they mean to realize, that is, to make real, the presence of Christ in and with the material elements of bread and wine. These become the means by which we, in the unity of body and soul, encounter the living Christ. Something like that is what Stevens is claiming for the spirit quest by the seaside. If we have the ears to hear and the wit to attend, when the Spirit truly sings, the sea 'whatever self it had', that is, whatever else we may say about it in poetry, or know about it in science, or feel about it in our summer haze, whatever 'dark voice' it may possess, whatever plungings and grindings it may make, when the Spirit hymns her creation, the sea 'whatever self it had, became the self/ That was her song, for she was the maker.' In that moment the maker meets, shapes, enlivens, speaks, sings through the creation, and in so doing reaches out to touch and communicate with our spirits, if we have the imagination to receive it. If that does happen, we see and know the world in a new way. We understand not with our heads but with our hearts that this is a sacred world, and the Spirit sings all of it, the whole world of space and time, ourselves included, into the song of her own making. We hear it. 'Then we,/ As we beheld her striding there alone,/ Knew that there never was a world for her/ Except the one she sang and, singing, made.'

Stanza 6 – the turn toward the town

Stanza 6 rings a dramatic change. The shift is signalled by the first words, 'Ramon Fernandez'. Where on earth did he come from? It seems there was a real person, a literary critic, of that name known to Wallace Stevens, but he always denied that he had a specific individual in mind here.[5] The name seems to function as a transition from the world of nature—sea, sky, wind—to the human realm. Ramon Fernandez is the beachcomber, the fisherman, the surfer, the swimmer, the sunbaker. Ramon Fernandez is everyone and anyone. Ramon Fernandez is you and me. The poet challenges *us*. 'Ramon Fernandez, tell me, if you know'. Tell what? Tell '[w]hy, when the singing ended and we turned/ Toward the town …'. The beach-party is going home; moving away from the sea with its 'bronzed shadows heaped on high horizons', and heading for the town. The town is civilization. The town is human technology, industry, buildings, lights. As the beach-goers turn toward the town, three things happen.

(i) The singing ends. The creative voice of the Spirit stops. In the previous 5 stanzas the creative word is everywhere … voice, singing, speaking, sound … everywhere. The sea, indeed the whole universe, seems to gather into a great choir of communicative intention. That now ceases. The town shuts out the song. Tell me, Ramon Fernandez, why?

(ii) Night falls. Three times in four lines the word 'night' is used. 'As night descended, tilting in the air,'; 'Mastered the night and portioned out the sea …'; 'Arranging, deepening, enchanting night.' Night. Night. Night. Darkness is descending on the human town; a darkness that, although it is 'enchanting' in many ways, is deepening, tumbling over itself, 'tilting in the air', which suggests that the night is somehow out of balance, tipping over, spilling out, deepening as it goes. In St John's narrative of the Last Supper, Judas is dramatically revealed at the table as intending to betray Jesus to his enemies. John writes, 'after receiving the

---

[5] 'Stevens pointed out to two of his correspondents that in choosing this name he had simply combined two common Spanish names at random, without conscious reference to Ramon Fernandez the critic: "Ramon Fernandez was not intended to be anyone at all."' *The Norton Anthology of Poetry*, third edition, Alexander W. Allison *et al* (eds), (New York: W. W. Norton & Company, Inc., 1970), p. 935, footnote 4.

piece of bread, he [Judas] immediately went out. *And it was night.*' (John 13.30) Darkness descends, 'tilting in the air'. Jesus, the 'light that shone in the darkness', is about to be engulfed in night.

The oceans are under serious threat and Ramon Fernandez is largely to blame. Rising temperatures, acidification, mining, melting polar ice sheets, over fishing, destruction of habitats, and plastic waste finding its way into every last corner of the world. The sea is sick. Night is tilting in the air. Tell me, Ramon Fernandez, why?

(iii) Control. The town is the place where humans are in control, in contrast to the wide ocean where the singer walks and sings. In the town *we* 'master the night' with our 'glassy lights' and 'fiery poles'. We 'portion out the sea' with our 'fishing boats at anchor there,' ready to ply the waves with our radars and our sonars. Stevens isn't suggesting that technology and industry are bad things. He knows we need our fishing boats and our glassy lights, but he sees danger in our incessant drive to 'master' things, 'fixing' them for our own purposes alone. It is *harder* to hear the song of the Spirit in our technologically ordered cities. We get fish from the supermarket, but we don't ask how it was caught or whether the catch is sustainable. We turn on the glassy lights, but don't ask how the electricity was generated and whether it is renewable. We jump in the car, but don't think about how the oil that powers it was extracted. We throw out plastic bags, bottles and toothbrushes, but don't ask will they wind up poisoning another albatross on King Island, or sticking in the gullet of a penguin waddling up the beach at Phillip Island.

Ramon Fernandez, tell me, if you know ... why? To attend to the sea is to begin to feel in our bodies the urgency of this question. It is to begin to realize that there is no Planet B; that 'there never was a world for her/ Except the one she sang and, singing, made.' This world.

Stanza 7 – blessed rage for order

Now to the final section of the poem. Stevens returns to themes of the first section (1-5). He doesn't refer to 'she' or to the 'spirit', but picks up the other title, 'maker'. He also links together the second section of the poem, the section dealing with the town, by referring to Ramon (Fernandez) again in the first line of this final verse. 'Oh! Blessed rage for order, pale Ramon,/ The maker's rage to order….'. The poet confronts Ramon Fernandez—the town dweller, the light producer, the fishing boat owner—with the maker's passion, even anger; her '*rage* to order'. This is a rage that arises from and intends in its utterance a *blessing*. In the famous words of beatitude in the Sermon on the Mount, Jesus recounts a series of blessings for those who order their lives in a way that aligns with the just and peaceable order of God's kingdom. 'Blessed are the pure in heart …' i.e., those who order their hearts towards justice and truth and away from the chaos of injustice and the lie; 'for they shall see God.' 'Blessed are the peacemakers …' i.e., those who order their lives according to peace and away from violence and revenge; 'for they shall be called children of God.' Jesus calls for an order of blessing, which is the order of the divine kingdom. In the poem, the maker calls for an order of life in the world, the maker's world, upon which real blessedness or fulfilment depends.

The call is addressed to 'pale Ramon', the same Ramon to whom the question 'why?' was put, when the singing ended, and for which he had no reply. This silent Ramon is *pale*; his cheeks are bloodless. He needs to get out into the sun, away from the glassy lights and fiery poles of his own mastery, and reconnect, revisit, re-immerse himself in the living world of nature's song and nature's singer, 'striding there alone.'

In our time, even more than Stevens', pale Ramon may well encounter an angry voice, 'a *rage* to order words of the sea'. In 2007, James Lovelock wrote a book called '*The Revenge of Gaia*', by which he meant to refer to the gathering backlash of the dynamic systems of the Planet against the pressure, pollution and plundering of their bounty being applied by our consumer societies. Heat, wild weather, dwindling food and water resources, dying forests, polluted air, rising sea levels, and so on. The singing Spirit cares about her order of creation, about the harmonies of her song and the harmonies of her world. She cares about the callous disregard of these beautiful things that pale Ramon is currently displaying.[6]

---

[6] Clive Hamilton has recently expanded on this theme; see *Defiant Earth: the Fate of Humans in the Anthropocene* (Sydney: Allen & Unwin, 2017), pp. 1-35.

In the poem, the maker's passion for the world begins with the sea, but extends to other 'doorways' to her music, those 'fragrant portals, dimly starred'. The sky, the clouds, the 'sunken coral water-walled', the air. Her passion expands to include us directly. The song of the sea and the sky is intrinsically and inseparably a song 'of ourselves and of our origins'. Everything is connected. The passion of the Spirit aims to re-order *our* lives so as to bring them into better harmony with the order of our origins; 'that harmony without which we cannot live' (von Wiezsäcker).

This order in nature and in human life will find expression, says Stevens in a remarkable phrase, 'In ghostlier demarcations, keener sounds.' One can't imagine Stevens advocating that, by seriously engaging with the more-than-human-world, by attending the maker's song, we somehow become otherworldly ('spooky') in our disposition and our action. The whole drift of the poem tells against such a reading. In 1934, it was much more common than it is today to refer to the Spirit, the third person of the Trinity, as 'the Holy Ghost'. In stanza 3 Stevens asserts that in our dealings with the ocean we need to ask, and 'ask this often as she sang', 'Whose spirit is this?' That question permeates the poem, and is recalled here at its conclusion. In our reconnection with the world beyond the glassy lights of town, we face the need to have our lives ordered ('demarcated') afresh in dialogue with the spiritual (ghostly) depths that sing the world into life and form. We need to bring that demarcation to expression (as indeed this poem brilliantly does) by joining in her 'visible voice' with sharper ('keener') sounds. That is, with words and gestures of our own that bear a clearer witness to the 'blessed rage for order' that we now dimly see/hear 'beyond the genius of the sea'.

Appendix 1

Stone Circles – Medicine Wheels

Certain Native American traditions proved very helpful to us. In particular, they offer questions and gestures that can be used in developing a practice of attention to the more-than-human world in our secular, technological, consumerist society. These form part of a wider set of exercises described in a book, *Dancing with the Wheel: The Medicine Wheel Workbook*, and learned in person from Northern Cheyenne teachers.[1] They are intended for non-Indigenous people, and are carefully distinguished from traditional ceremonies, which can only be practised by those who have undergone the long rigorous training required. The 'Wheel' refers to Medicine Wheels. These stone circles are very ancient and have been found to exist all over the world.[2]

The words 'medicine' and 'wheel' are somewhat awkward in English. 'Medicine' translates a word meaning sacred power inherent in all things and 'wheel' refers to sacred circles of stones representing the Creator and all created beings. As ceremonial centres of culture, they were (and some still are) places where people came to pray, to meditate, to strengthen and deepen their connection with nature and their relationship with the Creator, to mark changes in their own lives and in the life of Earth. They also functioned as astronomical laboratories. The vision behind these practices is that 'all things and beings are related and, therefore, must be in harmony for the earth to be balanced'.[3]

The Medicine Wheel is built around a Creator stone ringed by an inner circle of stones (Mother Earth, Father Sun, Grandmother Moon, earth, water, fire and air), and then by an outer circle anchored by four stones,

---

[1] Sun Bear, Wabun Wind, Chrysalis Mulligan, *Dancing with the Wheel: The Medicine Wheel Workbook* (New York: Simon & Schuster, 1991).
[2] It is estimated that there would have been approximately 20,000 Medicine Wheels in the Americas prior to the arrival of Europeans.
[3] Bear *et al*, *Dancing with the Wheel*, back cover.

one for east, north, west and south. Each direction has a 'Spirit Keeper' who is 'responsible for teaching earth's children about the power of the direction, the times, the season the aspect of humans they represent ... to give power to work ... in a way that can bring more balance to you and the earth'.[4] The other stones of the outer circle spaced between these four stones represent the twelve moon months in the year.

'Dancing' the wheel is the journey undertaken by doing the exercises and practices offered; learning the steps.[5] A practice in this context is a way 'to connect your energy with the energy of the universe, and to thank the universe with all of its parts for the gift of life'.[6] It helps humans to learn about balance, showing where we are out of balance and how to heal our relationships with the rest of Creation. Each person has a birth position in the outer circle determined by the date of their birth, and so to a moon month, and a particular linked animal, plant, mineral and colour. Dancing the wheel, however, moves you through changing positions depending on what you next need to learn.

In Australia, Medicine Wheels are known as Bora Rings. Uncle Max describes Bora Rings as places for ceremony, for dancing. 'Dancing is about making an indentation on the land' ... 'the land, the rocks, the trees, they all hold the indentation of song and movement generated from the Bora Rings'. Energy is generated, moving under your feet, through your body, connecting to the source.[7]

---

[4] Bear *et al*, *Dancing with the Wheel*, p. 31. In asking the question 'Are you willing to communicate with me?' one waits to see in what form the Spirit Keeper will appear (as in chapter 5).
[5] Without access to a stone Medicine Wheel one can learn to visualise it. We are aware that we have learned only a small part of a beautiful, intricately interconnected and larger whole.
[6] Bear *et al*, *Dancing with the Wheel*, p. 3.
[7] Max Dulumunmun Harrison, *My People's Dreaming: an Aboriginal Elder speaks on life, land, spirit and forgiveness* (Sydney: HarperCollinsPublishers, 2013), p. 124.

Appendix 2

The Practice

This is a summary of the practice. More details can be found in the pages interleaved between the chapters.

Find a place where you feel a sense of being in the presence of nature. This may be by the ocean, on a cliff top, in the mountains, in the bush, or desert, or grasslands, by a river, a creek, a pond or wetlands. Choose somewhere you can go regularly, somewhere that calls to you, however faintly.

For city-dwellers find a place that is as near to a 'natural' wild order, as relatively intact an ecosystem, as you can find. For example, a tract of bush remaining in a large parkland, or the re-vegetated edge of a local creek or pond. It may be your own created garden, or even simply a single tree or a plant in a pot.

Our circumstances differ and change through time. The point is to find some authentic connection with the wider living world of which we are part.

We suggest you commit yourself to keeping the practice for 3 months. Like a growing plant this work is slow, organic, unfolding quietly. Half an hour each day or even once or twice a week would be a way to start. If you already have a spiritual practice; prayer, meditation, contemplation, Yoga, Tai Chi, you will already know the value of a regular commitment. Consider re-allocating some of the time you already set aside. If a practice is a new idea, you may need just to plunge in. You may already be in love with the natural world, and spend time hiking, canoeing, surfing or walking or gardening. This is a different way to attend.

The practice is done alone, but you might find a friend who would like to join you, either at the same place and time or separately. You could then agree to meet regularly to share stories and/or journals. Transformative learning is communal, and this is a deeply counter-cultural practice in our present context. Find your companions!

Do you need to take a hat, sunscreen, rain jacket, umbrella, gloves etc? Other people may walk by. Decide ahead simply to attend to the practice. They have their life (and probably dog), you have yours.

* * * * * *

Approaching

Once you have chosen a place consider how you will get there. Build in as much silence as you can. If you need to drive, turn off the radio or take some meditative music to play. Perhaps park some distance away so that you can walk in to the spot. If you do the practice in your own garden, consider a silent walk around the neighbourhood as preparation, and ensure that any other people in the house know not to disturb you (pray the baby stays asleep!).

Having arrived, decide where to stand (listen to what is calling you).

Invoking

The visible voice of the world breaks its silence only when we offer it ours.

Lightly brush yourself down with your hands—head, arms, chest, back, legs—symbolically flicking off the ordinary business of the day.

Take time to notice what you are hearing, seeing, feeling, smelling, touching, tasting.

Turn to honour each of the four directions (E, N, W, S); feel the energy of the sun pouring down, and the energy of the earth rising beneath your feet.

Dedicate the time to the flourishing of all beings and to bearing witness to their loss. If you belong within a particular faith tradition (Buddhist, Muslim, Christian, etc.) you can adjust this dedication appropriately.

Attending

Stand (or sit if needed).

Set your feet comfortably and firmly on the ground, legs slightly apart, balancing the weight of your body evenly. Push upwards gently from the top of your head.

Relax the muscles of your body, almost as if you intend to 'let the flesh fall off your bones' (as a Taoist teacher puts it!). In particular, relax the muscles of your stomach and jaw. Unlock your knees.

Place the tip of your tongue behind your front teeth.

Keep your eyes open. Soften your gaze; an angle down of about 45 degrees is comfortable to begin with.

Breathe slowly and naturally.

Empty your mind. If distracting thoughts intrude, gently let them pass by as clouds across the sky, and return to the practice.

Attending involves the use of all the senses together. Look. Listen. Smell. Taste. Touch.

Keep up the practice for 30 minutes. (At first 5 minutes may seem very long; give your body time to learn new patterns!)

Chanting and *asking questions* may at times be very helpful (For more detail see 'Learning a pratice of attention' numbers 2&3).

Taking leave

Make a simple offering of thanksgiving. You might, for example, take a hair from your head and lay it gently on the ground.

Bow to each of the 4 directions (E, N, W, S,).

Walk/drive back home in silence.

Write about your experience (e.g., half a page). Keep these pages in a folder. You will be amazed at what you find when you read them later.

* * * * * *

Sources:

Sun Bear, Wabun Wind, Chrysalis Mulligan, *Dancing with the Wheel: The Medicine Wheel Workbook* (New York: Simon & Schuster, 1991).

Lam Kam Chuen, *The Way of Energy: Mastering the Chinese Art of Internal Strength with Chi Kung Exercises* (New York: Simon & Schuster, 1991).

Max Dulumunmun Harrison, *My People's Dreaming: an Aboriginal Elder speaks on life, land, spirit and forgiveness* (Sydney: HarperCollinsPublishers, 2013).

Andrew Harvey, *The Hope: A Guide to Sacred Activism* (New York: Hay House, Inc., 2009), pp. 153-155.

Appendix 3

The Birth of Venus - Sandro Botticelli 1485

Select Bibliography

Abram, David, *The Spell of the Sensuous: Perception and Language in a More-Than-Human World*, New York: Random House, 1997.

Augustine, *Confessions*, trans. R. S. Pine-Coffin, Harmondsworth, Middlesex, England: Penguin, 1961.

Baring, Anne and Cashford, Jules, *The Myth of the Goddess: Evolution of an Image*, London: BCA by arrangement with Penguin Books Ltd, 1991.

Bradley, James, *The Penguin Book of the Ocean*, Camberwell, Victoria: Penguin Group (Australia), 2010.

Brady, Emily, "The Environmental Sublime," in Costelloe, *The Sublime: From Antiquity to the Present*, Cambridge: Cambridge University Press, 2012.

Burgess, Matt, "Case Study: The Hilborn-Worm debate on the status of global fisheries," *The Tête-à-Tête*, December 3, 2014, http//theteteatete.org/2014/12/03/case-study-the-hilborn-worm-debate-on-the-status-of-global-fisheries.

Burke, Edmund, *A Philosophical Enquiry into the Sublime and Beautiful*, (ed) James T. Boulton, London: Routledge Classics, 2008 [1756].

Chrétien, Jean-Louis, *The Ark of Speech*, trans. Andrew Brown, London: Routledge, 2004.

Chrétien, Jean-Louis, *The Call and the Response*, trans. Anne A. Davenport, New York: Fordham University Press, 2004.

Claudel, Paul, *Five Great Odes*, trans. Edward Lucie-Smith, London: Rapp and Carroll, 1967.

Costelloe, Timothy M., *The Sublime: From Antiquity to the Present*, Cambridge: Cambridge University Press, 2012.

Denny, Mark W., *Air and Water: the Biology and Physics of Life's Media*, Princeton: Princeton University Press, 1993.

Earle, Sylvia A., *Blue Hope: Exploring and Caring for Earth's Magnificent Ocean*, Washington D.C.: National Geographic Society, 2014.

Earle, Sylvia A., *Sea Change: A Message of the Oceans*, New York: Fawcett Books, 1995.

Earle, Sylvia A., *The World is Blue: How Our Fate and the Ocean's are One*, Washington, D. C., National Geographic Society, [2009] 2010.

Eliot, T. S., *Four Quartets*, London: Faber and Faber, 1986 [1944].

Hamilton, Clive, *Defiant Earth: the Fate of Humans in the Anthropocene*, Sydney: Allen & Unwin, 2017.

Harrison, Max Dulumunmun, *Mind Moon Circle*, Sydney Zen Centre, Spring 2008.

Harrison, Max Dulumunmun, *My People's Dreaming*, Sydney: HarperCollins*Publishers*, 2009.

Hart, David Bentley, *The Experience of God: Being, Consciousness, Bliss*, New Haven: Yale University Press, 2013.

Hart, Kevin, "Facing the Pacific at Night" in Bradley (ed), *The Penguin Book of the Ocean*, Camberwell, Victoria: Penguin Group (Australia), 2010.

Harvey, Andrew, *Son of Man: The Mystical Path to Christ*, New York: Jeremy P. Tarcher/Putnam, 1998.

Harvey, Andrew, *The Hope: a Guide to Sacred Activism*, New York: Hay House, Inc., 2009.

Harvey, Andrew, *The Return of the Mother*, New York: Jeremy P. Tarcher/Putnam, 1995.

Harvey, Graham, *Animism: Respecting the Living World*, London: Hurst & Company, 2005.

Hepburn, Ronald, "Contemporary aesthetics and the neglect of natural beauty," in Bernard Williams and Alan Montefiore (eds), *British Analytical Philosophy*, London: Routledge and Kegan Paul, 1966.

Hepburn, Ronald, "Landscape and Metaphysical Imagination," *Environmental Values* 5 (1996), in Costelloe, *The Sublime: From Antiquity to the Present*.

Hepburn, Ronald, "Nature Humanised: Nature Respected," *Environmental Values* 7, 1998.

Hilborn, Ray, "Faith-based Fisheries," *Fisheries*, Vol. 31, No. 11, November 2006.

Hume, David, *A Natural History of Religion*, 1757 §3, quoted in Graham Harvey, *Animism: Respecting the Living World*, London: Hurst & Company, 2005.

Husserl, E., *Cartesian Meditations: An Introduction to Phenomenology*, trans. Dorion Cairns, The Hague: Martinus Nijhoff, 1960 [1929].

IUCN Red List Version 2015-4, www.iucnredlist.org

Junger, Sebastian, "The Perfect Storm," in Bradley, *The Penguin Book of the Ocean*, Camberwell, Victoria: Penguin, Hamish Hamilton, 2010.

Kant, Immanuel, "Religion in the Boundaries of Mere Reason," in *Religion and Rational Theology*, Allen W. Wood and George di Giovanni (eds). Cambridge: Cambridge University Press, 1996.

Kant, Immanuel, *The Critique of Judgement*, trans. James Creed Meredith, Oxford: Oxford University Press, 1911 [1790].

Kierkegaard, Søren, *Christian Discourses and The Lilies of the Field and the Birds of the Air and Three Discourses at the Communion of Fridays*, trans. Walter Lowrie, London: Oxford University Press, 1952 [1848-49].

Klein, Naomi, *This Changes Everything: Capitalism vs. The Climate*, London: Penguin Random House UK, 2015.

Lam Kam Chuen, *The Way of Energy: Mastering the Chinese Art of Internal Strength with Chi Kung Exercises*, New York: Simon & Schuster, 1991.

Lavers, Jennifer L. et al, "Plastic Ingestion by fish in the Southern Hemisphere: A baseline study and review of methods," *Marine Pollution Bulletin*, 2016, available at www.elsevier.com/locate/marpolbul,

Lavers, Jennifer L. et al, "Plastic ingestion by Flesh-footed Shearwaters (*Puffinus carneipes*): Implications for fledgling body condition and the accumulation of plastic-derived chemicals," *Environmental Pollution* 187, 2014.

Lavers, Jennifer L., "Seabirds as sentinels of marine health," www.

jenniferlavers.org/research/.

Le Guin, Ursula K., *The Compass Rose*, London: Panther Books, 1983.

Luther, Martin, *Luther: Lectures on Romans*, trans. Wilhelm Pauck, The Library of Christian Classics, Vol. XV, London: SCM Press, 1961.

Marshall, George, *Don't Even Think About It: Why our brains are wired to ignore climate change*, New York: Bloomsbury, 2014.

Mathews, Freya, "On Desiring Nature," *Indian Journal of Ecocriticism*, 3, 2010.

McGilchrist, Ian, *The Master and His Emissary: The Divided Brain and the Making of the Western World*, New Haven: Yale University Press, 2009.

McGlade, Christophe & Ekins, Paul, "The geographical distribution of fossil fuels unused when limiting global warming to 2°C," *Nature* 517, Jan 2015.

McKibben, Bill, "This is not ideology," *The Monthly*, Issue 119, February 2016.

Merleau-Ponty, Maurice, *Le Visible et l'invisible*, Paris: Gallimard, 1964.

Merleau-Ponty, Maurice, *Phenomenology of Perception*, trans. Colin Smith, London: Routledge & Kegan Paul, 1962.

Mitchell, Alanna, *Sea Sick: The Global Ocean in Crisis*, Millers Point, NSW: Murdoch Books Australia, 2010.

Myers, Ransom A. and Worm, Boris, "Rapid worldwide depletion of predatory fish communities," *Nature*, May 15, 2003.

Nancy, Jean-Luc, *Adoration: the Deconstruction of Christianity II*, trans. John McKeane, New York: Fordham University Press, 2013.

O'Donohue, John, *The Invisible Embrace of Beauty: Rediscovering the True Sources of Compassion, Serenity, and Hope*, New York: Harper Perennial, 2004.

Otto, Rudolf, *The Idea of the Holy*, trans. John W. Harvey, Harmondsworth, Middlesex: Penguin, 1959.

Papal Encyclical, *Laudato Si': On Care for Our Common Home*, 2016.

Prechtel, Martín, *The Smell of Rain on Dust: Grief and Praise*, Berkeley,

California: North Atlantic Books, 2015.

Rich, Nathaniel, "Bellow: The "Defiant, Irascible Mind"," *The New York Review of Books*, June 4, 2015.

Rilke, Rainer Maria, *Der Schauende*.

Rittell, Horst W. J. & Webber, Melvyn M., "Dilemmas in a General Theory of Planning," *Policy Sciences* 4, 1973.

Rose, Deborah Bird et al, *Country of the Heart: An Indigenous Australian Homeland*, Canberra: Aboriginal Studies Press, 2002.

Rose, Deborah Bird, *Wild Dog Dreaming: Love and Extinction*, London: University of Virginia Press, 2011.

Rumi, Jelaluddin, *The Illuminated Rumi*, trans. Coleman Barks, illuminations by Michael Green, New York: Broadway Books, 1997.

San Roque, Craig, "On *Tjukurrpa*, Painting Up, and Building Thought," *Social Analysis*, Volume 50, Issue 2, Summer 2006.

Scheler, Max, *On the Eternal in Man*, trans. Bernard Noble, Connecticut: Archon Books & SCM Press, 1960.

Steiner, George, *Martin Heidegger*, New York: Viking, 1978.

Stevens, Wallace, *The Collected Poems of Wallace Stevens*, New York: Vintage Books, 1982.

Sun Bear et al, *Dancing with the Wheel: The Medicine Wheel Workbook*, New York: Simon & Schuster, 1991.

Suzuki, David, *The Sacred Balance: Rediscovering our Place in Nature*, New York: Prometheus Books, 1998.

United Nations Environmental Programme, *Marine Litter: A Global Challenge*, 2009 at www.unep.org/Regionalseas/marinelitter/publications/docs/Marine_Litter_A_Global_Challenge.

United Nations Environmental Programme, *Marine Litter: an analytical overview*, 2005 at www.unep.org/regionalseas/marinelitter/publications/docs/overview.

United Nations Food and Agriculture Organization (FOA), FOA 2016. *The State of World Fisheries and Acquaculture. Contributing to food security and nutrition for all*. Rome, 2016.

von Weizsäcker, Carl Friedrich, *Aufbau der Physik*, München: Carl Hanser Verlag, 1985.

von Weizsäcker, Carl Friedrich, *Der Garten des Menschlichen: Beiträge zur geschichtlichen Anthropologie*, München: Carl Hanser Verlag, 1977.

von Weizsäcker, Carl Friedrich, *Zeit und Wissen*, München: Carl Hanser Verlag, 1992.

White, Mary E., *Earth Alive!: from Microbes to a Living Planet*, Dural, NSW: Rosenberg Publishing, 2003.

Williams, Rowan, *Faith in the Public Square*, London: Bloomsbury, 2012.

Williams, Rowan, *The Edge of Words: God and the Habits of Language*, London: Bloomsbury, 2014.

World Economic Forum, *The New Plastics Economy: Rethinking the future of plastics*, 2016 at www3.weforum.org/docs/WEF_The_New_Plastics_Economy.

Worm, Boris *et al*, "Impacts of Biodiversity Loss on Ocean Ecosystem Services," *Science*, New Series, Vol. 314, No. 5800, Nov. 3, 2006.

Worm, Boris, Hilborn, Ray *et al*, "Rebuilding Global Fisheries," *Science*, 31 July 2009, Vol. 325, Issue 5940.